D1079492

the practice of
PROJECT
MANAGEMENT

a guide to the business-focused approach

room use only

Enzo Frigenti • Dennis Comninos

KOGAN
PAGE

London and Philadelphia

First published in 2002
Paperback edition 2006
Reprinted 2006

Kogan Page
120 Pentonville Road
London N1 9JN
UK

Kogan Page US
525 South 4th Street, #241
Philadelphia PA 19147
USA

British Library Cataloguing in Publication Data

A CIP record for this book is available from the British Library

ISBN 0 7494 4536 X

Typeset by Jean Cussons Typesetting, Diss, Norfolk
Printed and bound in Great Britain by Antony Rowe, Chippenham and Eastbourne

Contents

iv ▮ Contents

List of acronyms

ACWP	Actual cost of work performed
AF	Actual finish date
AIPM	Australian Institute of Project Management
APM	Association of Project Managers
AV	Accounting variance
BAC	Budget at completion
BCAC	Budgeted cost at completion
BCSP	Budgeted cost at scheduled performance
BCWP	Budgeted cost of work performed
BCWS	Budgeted cost of work scheduled
BFPM™	Business Focused Project Management
BTAC	Budgeted time at completion
CBS	Cost breakdown structure
CDP	Critical decision point
CPA	Critical path analysis
CPFF	Cost plus fixed fee (contract)
CPI	Cost performance index
CPIF	Cost plus incentive fee (contract)
CPM	Critical path method
CV	Cost variance
DBS	Deliverables breakdown structure
EAC	Estimate at completion
ECAC	Estimated cost at completion
ECTC	Estimated cost to complete

EF	Early finish time
ES	Early start time
ETAC	Estimated time at completion
ETC	Estimate to complete
ETTC	Estimated time to complete
EV	Earned value
F	Float
FF	Finish-to-finish
FFP	Firm fixed price (contract)
FPIF	Fixed price incentive fee (contract)
FS	Finish-to-start
IPMA	International Project Management Association
KPI	Key performance indicator
KRA	Key result area
LF	Late finish time
LS	Late start time
MOC	Milestone objective chart
MRM	Milestone responsibility matrix
NPV	Net present value
OBS	Organizational breakdown structure
ODPM™	Objective Directed Project Management
OME	Order of magnitude estimate
PC	Percent complete
PDR	Project definition report
PDW	Project definition workshop
PERT	Programme evaluation and review technique
PIR	Post implementation review
PM	Project management
PMBOK™	Project Management Body of Knowledge
PMI	Project Management Institute
PMIS	Project management information system
PMT	Project management team
QA	Quality assurance
QC	Quality control
RAM	Responsibility assignment matrix
RFI	Request for information
RFP	Request for proposal
RFQ	Request for quotation
SD	Status date
SF	Start-to-finish
SOW	Statement of work
SPI	Schedule performance index
SS	Start-to-start
STEEPOL	Social, technology, economic, environment, political, organizational, legal

SV   Schedule variance
TQM   Total quality management
TV   Time variance
WBS   Work breakdown structure

Preface

Te ohonga ake i täku moemoea, ko te puawaitanga i ngä whakaaro – I awoke from my dreams to the blossoming of my thought; dreams require action to become reality.
Whakatauaki by Princess Te Puea Herangi from Waikato, New Zealand

We have always had a dream to write a book that reflected our understanding of, and personal views on, project management. Over the years, we have always believed there was a need for a book that was based on practice, linked to the business of organizations, and underpinned by a process. We believe this book is unique in that it not only provides the building blocks of project management, but also links them through a detailed process based on the concepts of managing by strategic, business and project results and objectives – Business Focused Project Management (BFPM™) and Objective Directed Project Management (ODPM™).

We firmly believe that project management needs to demonstrate that it adds value at the top end of an organization. Projects must contribute to the organization's bottom line or to service delivery, and this must be clearly demonstrated and communicated to upper management and important stakeholders. We believe that this book contributes to the knowledge and understanding of this important direction in which project management is heading.

Finally, this book brings to light our experiences over many years with various professions and industries we have been fortunate enough to be associated with and learn from in South Africa, New Zealand, Australia, France, the UK and the United States. It also answers the expressed wish of countless students of ours over the years that have urged us to 'put it in a book'.

AUDIENCE

The book was written primarily with the following audience in mind:

- senior managers responsible for converting organizational strategies into business outcomes;
- project portfolio managers overseeing a business-focused group of initiatives;
- project managers and project team members responsible for the delivery of results that enable business outcomes to be achieved;
- programme and project sponsors responsible for delivering the initiatives that enable business outcomes to be achieved;
- students of project management requiring a practical and business approach to the subject.

We believe that the contents of this book will:

- be of value to both the new project manager and the experienced professional seeking better integration of the customer's business and projects;
- increase the understanding of project portfolio management by dealing with the essential building blocks, focusing projects on the business, and using a unique approach – Objective Directed Project Management (ODPM™);
- assist senior managers in prioritizing and selecting a portfolio of projects that will contribute to achieving organizational strategies;
- help readers develop value-adding project management strategies and processes, and build stakeholder confidence;
- assist those tasked with formulating project management policies, processes and standards in organizations.

Acknowledgements

In 1999, the Institute of Chartered Accountants of New Zealand (ICANZ) gave us the opportunity to write this book and published our initial work. It proved to be successful in New Zealand, Australia and South Africa and is used as a prescribed textbook by a number of tertiary education institutions in those countries. In 2001, we decided to enhance the book and make it available to a larger international audience. With ICANZ's blessing, Kogan Page was approached to publish this version of the book. We are privileged to have them as our new publishers and we thank them for their patience and support during the creation of this edition. Special thanks here must go to Emily Steel for graciously granting us the extra time to complete the manuscript while travelling the world.

It is not possible to write a book of this nature without the assistance and support of many individuals and organizations and we wish to express our deep appreciation to all who have contributed in whatever manner to this book. Students who have attended our classes and seminars, organizations for whom we have worked, and colleagues, family and friends all in some manner or other have contributed wittingly and unwittingly to the contents of this book.

Special thanks must go to Chris Mundy, our editor, Andrea Horton who did the artwork, and Nicola Sutich who assisted with the proofreading. Special thanks must also go to Gillian Christie, the editor of the ICANZ edition who originally untangled our writing and gave us a manuscript on which to build this edition.

To all our colleagues and friends in the Royal New Zealand Police Services, rbz, Quanto Strategies and MST – thank you for your contributions, suggestions and, above all, your support. You were always there for us when we needed support, time and someone to bounce our ideas and thoughts off.

Authors of many project management books, articles and other materials have contributed to our understanding of the complex subject of project management. In particular we would like to thank Erling S Andersen, Kristoffer V Grude and Tor Haug, the authors of *Goal Directed Project Management* [2]. Their work has had a profound influence on our approach to project management over the past years.

We have made many notes while researching project management over the years. This, together with our years of teaching the subject, has blurred the distinction of what is ours and what initially came from others. We have attempted to attribute as much as we could to the original authors. If we have perhaps used material without acknowledgement, it was not intentional and we apologize.

Both of us are gifted with wives and children who have always understood our passion and dedication to the subject of project management and have given us the space and support to achieve our dreams. Des and Koka, Helen, John, Dianna, Nic, Vanessa, Gianni, Paolo and Gabriella, you are as much part of this book as we are.

Finally, the two of us are truly partners. Whatever is contained within the covers of this book was created jointly between us and therefore we take equal accountability for the ideas, concepts and contents irrespective of who wrote what. Our partnership is one that has endured the test of time, distance and crises – long may it continue.

We are living our dreams...

Introduction

You see things; and you say 'why?' But I dream things that never were; and I say 'why not?'

George Bernard Shaw (1856–1950), Anglo-Irish playwright, critic

THE BUSINESS OF PROJECT MANAGEMENT

In today's highly competitive and fast-paced environment, the rapid creation and delivery of high quality products and services is critical to business survival. Organizations are having to focus their energies on being highly innovative – delivering products and services involving greater technical complexity and requiring a greater diversity of skills. And this must be done with leaner organizations and tighter budgets while maintaining the highest quality standards.

To meet these demands, modern businesses need to operate at high performance levels, harnessing the full power of their resources to focus on strategic and business objectives. In this environment, general management approaches alone no longer suffice. The management processes used in the past to enable the delivery of new products and services are no longer effective.

Chapter 1 of this book defines a project as being a 'temporary endeavour undertaken to create a unique product or service' and identifies the process of achieving a successful project as project management. The need to deliver new and unique products and services (projects) usually arises from organization strategy and business plans. Therefore, to achieve superior delivery performance, the management approach must build on organization strategy, integrate with business imperatives, and focus on the objectives (the projects).

Traditional project management tended to focus primarily on the processes of managing projects to successful completion. To manage projects from their inception through to actual delivery of the business-enabling objectives, a different project management approach is needed. Project management needs to become part of the business and, in order to achieve that, organizations need to come to terms with the business of project management.

The struggle of many organizations to implement and apply project management has demonstrated that the classical, highly structured, engineering/construction approach does not meet the project management needs of business projects. Projects in the field of social and culture change, business redesign and service improvement create management challenges that require a more flexible and organic approach.

As organizations need to convert their strategies into reality through programmes and projects, they have to ensure that projects are efficiently delivered and effectively integrated into the business. A sound understanding of how an organization's portfolio of business programmes and projects is managed through prioritization and selection is required, but there must also be an understanding of the more detailed aspects of project implementation.

A business project management approach can bridge this gap between strategy and detailed action plans. Project management must be equally at home in the boardroom, where projects are often initiated to deliver strategy, as it is at the coal face, where the work is done to realize strategic and business objectives.

This book addresses the concepts and issues of business project management. It aims to assist organizations in making the shift from a narrow, strong, technical focus on project management to a broader, more business-oriented focus. The authors introduce the reader to three important concepts and components that underpin the philosophy of the business of project management. These components are briefly introduced in the following sections and developed throughout the book. They combine to form an approach that allows projects to make things happen, and to be the 'engines of growth' for organizations.

BUSINESS FOCUSED PROJECT MANAGEMENT

> This is a very simple business. When we complicate it, we really mess things up.
>
> Roberto Goizueta, Chairman, The Coca-Cola Company

The first of the components, Business Focused Project Management (BFPM™), is an overall approach developed in response to the need for managing business projects. BFPM takes an organization-wide view of project management by focusing on the needs of project owners, while integrating closely with the requirements of executives, upper managers and the project management environment.

BFPM is based around the two other components, the Wrappers™ model and Objective Directed Project Management (ODPM™). These two components fit together to provide the philosophies, processes, concepts and tools used to enable BFPM.

THE WRAPPERS MODEL

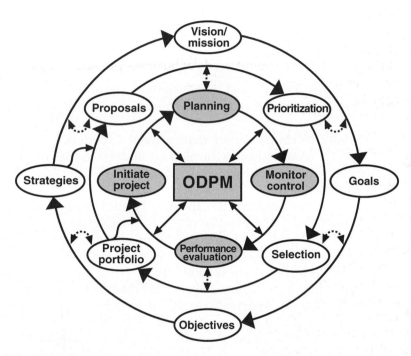

Figure 0.1   The Wrappers™ model

The Wrappers model shown in Figure 0.1 is a model that integrates the organization's strategic, business and project management levels. At the core of the model is the ODPM process. This core is then 'wrapped' with a series of interrelated layers, each adding functionality to the next until the overall functionality of BFPM is provided.

OBJECTIVE DIRECTED PROJECT MANAGEMENT

The authors developed the Objective Directed Project Management (ODPM) process to provide a process for initiating, defining, planning, executing and closing out a project. ODPM was specifically designed to provide effective planning tools in the early phases of a project, and to allow a better management focus on the business outcomes that projects deliver.

ODPM consists of a series of interrelated steps, tools and techniques sequenced in a systematic and logical manner. It forms the core of the BFPM approach and the heart of the Wrappers model.

GETTING THE MOST FROM THIS BOOK

This book describes the concepts and philosophies of Business Focused Project Management (BFPM). It is intended for everyone involved in projects and project management, including executives, upper management, project sponsors, project managers, functional managers and project team members. It is not industry-specific, and therefore does not cover industry-specific project management tools and techniques. As such, it will appeal to readers from a broad spectrum of businesses – both profit and non-profit sectors.

Readers with varying levels of project management experience will find the book useful – from the novice who wishes to develop an understanding of project management from a wider perspective, to the experienced project manager who wishes to better integrate projects with business.

Although it discusses the fundamental theories behind project management, this book lives out its title of being 'the practice of project management'. The practices and processes described in the book are based on the project management practice, consulting and teaching experiences of the authors over more than 25 years.

The book is divided into four main sections (three parts and a set of appendices), which are introduced below. The authors suggest that readers will gain the most benefit by reading the text in sequence, particularly the three parts as full blocks, and referencing the appendices as required. However, the overview below will help more experienced readers who wish to focus on a particular topic. Cross-references within the chapters are aimed at assisting the reader in developing a fuller understanding of the subject matter.

Interspersed throughout the book are 'In practice...' cases, which describe real-life situations relating to important concepts and subject areas. Each concludes with 'Important lessons…' from the case. The four sections of the book are as follows.

Part I – The Essential Building Blocks

The focus of Part I is on the building blocks required to understand the context of projects and project management. It is divided into two chapters covering the following topics:

● **Chapter 1** describes the essential building blocks needed to gain an understanding of projects and their context in business. It discusses project types, project participants, stakeholders, project structures, and project phases and the project life cycle.

- **Chapter 2** discusses the concepts of project management. It develops an understanding of the management roles; project management knowledge areas; the trade-off between scope, time, cost and quality; management power flows; project management methodologies; and an integrated view of projects.

Part II – Focusing Projects on the Business

Part II focuses on bringing the business of projects and operations closer together by using processes that are owned and executed by the organization. Part II builds on the foundations laid down in Part I. The three chapters in Part II cover the following topics:

- **Chapter 3** develops the concepts of BFPM and discusses the importance of linkages between strategy and projects. It contains a unique set of project paradoxes that assist the reader in developing a wider understanding of projects, and the tensions that exist in delivering project work in a traditional functional organization.
- **Chapter 4** builds the concepts of BFPM further through the presentation and explanation of the Wrappers model, as illustrated in Figure 0.1. This model assists the reader in developing an integrated view of projects and business within the context of organizational strategy.
- **Chapter 5** explains the organizational implementation of BFPM. It provides a layered model for the introduction of project management in an organization and describes how it can be built on step by step to obtain the full benefits of BFPM. It further focuses on the prioritization and selection process and concludes with an explanation of the special requirements for effectively managing multiple projects as a programme.

Part III – Objective Directed Project Management (ODPM™)

Part III contains the ODPM process that is at the core of Business Focused Project Management. Because of its strong focus on results or objectives, ODPM is often used to plan and manage 'fuzzy' projects that do not respond well to the more scientific project management tools, techniques and processes. Such 'fuzziness' commonly occurs in business, information technology, human resources, and culture change or transformation projects. Part III comprises six chapters, which cover the following topics:

- **Chapter 6** introduces the ODPM process, and discusses the characteristics and details of the process in a project life-cycle format. It contains a table summarizing the full process.
- **Chapter 7** describes the project initiation phase in terms of the essential process steps required to initiate a project and to produce a project charter.
- **Chapter 8** focuses on the definition phase of a project, exploring it in detail as the most important stage of project development. The result of the definition phase is a project definition report that enables the project team to develop a detailed project plan.

- **Chapter 9** describes the detailed project planning phase that focuses on detailed scope, time, cost, resource, quality, risk, human resources, communications, and procurement plans. The result of this stage is an integrated project plan baseline, against which progress and performance are measured.
- **Chapter 10** addresses the project execution phase, including the monitoring and control systems and infrastructure, project management information systems, and progress monitoring tools and techniques. Performance evaluation approaches, including the earned value concept and progress reports, are also discussed.
- **Chapter 11**, the final chapter, discusses the steps required to ensure effective close-out of a project. The emotional issues of project close-out are highlighted, as is the value of the close-out as a learning experience for an organization.

Appendices

- **Appendix A** provides a worked example of the application of the ODPM process to a project. Forms and templates are used to support the process, and these are provided to present the example. Reference to this case study is made throughout Part III.
- **Appendix B** contains detailed discussions of selected basic concepts, tools and techniques of project management for readers to refer to as needed.
- **Appendix C** examines certain issues, and provides suggestions and recommendations for addressing them. In particular, it considers the reasons for project failure and provides guidelines for success. A discussion on the perception of failure and success gives the reader an understanding of the complexity involved in the phenomena of success and failure. Business performance criteria versus project process criteria are discussed, and a set of guidelines to enhance success is provided.
- **The Glossary** defines project management terms.
- **The Bibliography** lists the sources of references and works researched.

> To business that we love we rise betime,
> And go to't with delight.
>
> William Shakespeare, *Antony and Cleopatra*, Act IV, Scene 4

Part I

The Essential Building Blocks

1

Projects and project management

A project is different from usual work. It has a single focus. It is a child in the midst of a family of adolescent and adult tasks.
Bennet Lientz and Kathryn Rea, *Project Management for the 20th Century*

DEFINING A PROJECT

Projects exist in every sphere of business, markets, segments and industry. They come in a myriad of types, sizes and complexity – from small initiatives such as weddings, parties, fundraising drives; to medium-size initiatives such as advertising campaigns, capital acquisitions, business re-engineering, restructuring, information systems; through to mega-projects such as the Channel Tunnel, NASA space station, hydro-electric dams and military campaigns.

Finding a definition that encompasses all kinds of projects has occupied the minds of many academics and practitioners for some time. Rather than replicate a long list of definitions developed by various writers, the authors find the simplicity and completeness of the Project Management Institute's definition most appropriate.

The Project Management Body of Knowledge (*A Guide to the Project Management Body of Knowledge*[73]) defines a project in terms of its distinctive characteristics: 'A project is a temporary endeavour undertaken to create a unique product or service'. The Project Management Institute intends to amend the definition to refer to the creation of '... a unique outcome or result' (*PM Network*, December 1998: 19). This is a more useful definition, as outcome or result has a wider business connotation and covers products and services.

In the context of the business focus of this book, it is important to differentiate between business outcomes or results and project results. Projects deliver results that assist the organization to achieve its business outcomes. Integrating the project results as soon as possible into the business and transferring ownership will contribute to the organization's business outcomes. Although projects are critical components in the achievement of an organization's business strategy, they can rarely ensure business outcomes. Rather, they are vehicles through which the organization achieves its changes.

Andersen, Grude and Haug's pioneering work *Goal Directed Project Management*[2] contains a definition of change management that deserves special mention:

Change Management is:
The process of aligning an organization's people and culture with changes in business strategy, organizational structure, systems and processes which results in:

- Ownership of and commitment to change;
- Sustained and measurable improvement;
- Improved capability to manage future change.

This definition highlights firstly the need for organizational ownership and commitment to the changes created by the project. The project manager has the challenge of developing a project in close harmony with the owners of the business functions, thus building commitment, while always carefully guarding against alienation of the project team. Placing the ownership where it belongs as early as possible will reduce the chances of project failure.

Secondly, sustained and measurable improvement is the outcome from integrating project deliverables and results into business operations. Part II, Focusing Projects on the Business, expands on this concept.

Thirdly, the definition identifies that the organization learns from project implementation. As ownership and commitment have to be extensive to achieve sustainable change, the project team and stakeholders will share knowledge and participate in workshops and like forums. Capturing the learning in a system that is accessible organization-wide establishes the institutional memory necessary for 'improved capability to manage future change'.

Most definitions of projects attempt to define every aspect of what a project comprises, and they tend to be long or complex. Several common threads are found in these definitions:

- complex endeavours to do work that creates change;
- involvement of people working outside their usual functional areas;
- constraints brought about by scope, cost, time and quality;
- a temporary nature (not infinite or continuous);
- uniqueness;
- progressive elaboration.

Consideration of these factors, however, leads us quickly to a realization that three factors differentiate projects from routine operations:

- uniqueness;
- a temporary nature;
- progressive elaboration.

Uniqueness

Projects involve doing something that has not been done before. Uniqueness derives either from activities that have not been done before, or from some product or service feature that distinguishes it from all other products or services the organization has produced before.

How unique is unique? Consider the following:

- **Building a series of similar houses** – Plans may be identical, but each is an individual project. The uniqueness is in the geographic location, local building by-laws, the house owner and the building crew.
- **Performing annual audits** – Each audit may follow the same pattern and sequence of events, but each audit is unique because of the client involved, the audit team and the organization structure.
- **Rollout of an information system in an organization** – The installation of the system in each department of an organization may be similar, but each rollout is made unique by the department involved, the requirements of the department and the users.

Identifying and focusing on uniqueness is important to project management. It helps identify new organization risk areas, enabling management to develop and implement timely risk management strategies.

A temporary nature

Temporary implies that projects are of a transient nature, with a defined beginning and end. The end is reached when the project's objectives have been achieved and effectively handed over to the business. A project may also be terminated when it becomes clear that it cannot achieve the stated objectives, or when the business outcomes are no longer feasible for the owner. Temporary does not mean short in duration, nor does it mean that the results are temporary in nature, as these are integrated into the business and become part of the ongoing improvement.

Once projects have achieved their objectives, they no longer exist in the organization, and they should be closed down. In certain situations the project itself is a one-off event and not integrated into an organization, for example a rock concert, an election, or the Olympic Games. Change is still created by these initiatives, in terms of stakeholders' benefits and spin-offs to the communities involved.

Where the project involves the creation of a new business service or product, essential team members are chosen because of knowledge they possess about the current business and service. At completion of the project they often become part of the department operating the new service.

Progressive elaboration

Due to the uniqueness of project results, the precise details in terms of the deliverables contributing to the results are not known from the outset. Because of this, the deliverables' characteristics, and in fact the project parameters, will need to be **progressively elaborated**. The two words are defined as follows: 1) **progressively** – proceeding in steps; continuing steadily by increments; 2) **elaborated** – worked out with care; developed thoroughly.

At the start of a project, the characteristics of its deliverables and the project parameters of scope, time, cost and performance will be broadly defined. During the development of the project plans, and as the early stages of the project progress, a better understanding of the project will be obtained – it will be **progressively elaborated**.

The 'amount' of elaboration needed to obtain a detailed definition of a project will depend on the level of knowledge about the project. We can differentiate projects between two extremes: **fuzzy** and **clear**. Projects occur between the two extremes, placed according to the level of knowledge. If the project's deliverables are well defined, it will be closer to the **clear** end of the spectrum, and less elaboration will be required. The more **fuzzy** the project's deliverables are, the more elaboration will be required. This concept is illustrated in Figure 1.1.

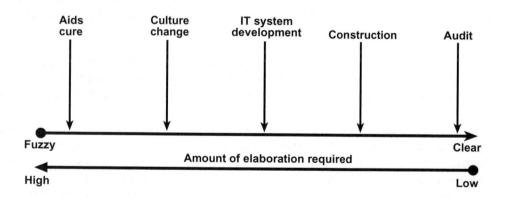

Figure 1.1   Progressive elaboration

Note: The positions of the types of project along the continuum are for illustration only, and are not to scale.

Progressive elaboration of projects must interface closely with proper definition of the project's deliverables, which is also known as scope definition. Scope is the sum of the deliverables (often described as products and services) to be developed through the project process. Tensions result from the pressures of early scope fixing versus the progressive elaboration of the project deliverables. Scope growth (also known as scope creep) can easily result from progressive elaboration. This is one of the more difficult paradoxes to manage, as organizations frequently demand an early fixing of time, cost and performance when the project scope is not clear. Part II, Chapter 3 discusses this as one of the paradox principles relating to project management.

PROJECT TYPES

Obeng[68] identifies the four corresponding types of projects as Fog, Movie, Quest and Painting by Numbers:

- **Fog**-type projects can be described as walking in thick but uneven fog. On these projects, the project participants and stakeholders are not sure what is to be achieved or how it is to be carried out.
- **Movie**-type projects are projects where participants and stakeholders have a high degree of certainty of how the project is to be carried out, but not what is to be delivered.
- **Quest**-type projects are also known as semi-closed projects. On Quest projects, the project participants and stakeholders have a high degree of certainty of what should be done, but they are not sure of how to achieve it.
- **Painting by Numbers** projects are known as closed projects. The project participants and most of the stakeholders have a high degree of certainty about what is to be done and how to achieve it.

Figure 1.2 sets out the four project types in terms of objective clarity, and project management process and tools development. Table 1.1 analyses the four project types in terms of general description, project processes and tools, and a suggested management approach.

Projects can generally be classified as being of a Fog, Quest, Movie or Painting by Numbers type. As a project elaborates it can move from one state to another; for example, the early stages of a business improvement project could be described as 'fog' as the organization knows it needs to improve performance but is not sure exactly where to focus. As clarity emerges, targets for improvement are set, moving the project into a 'quest' state, but the best approach to achieve the project is not yet clear. As the project further elaborates, the design and implementation details emerge which, when sufficiently clear, lead to the 'painting by numbers' state. During the implementation the project is predominantly in the 'painting by numbers' state, although it may at times need to revert back to 'quest' or 'fog' if unforeseen factors arise, requiring further elaboration.

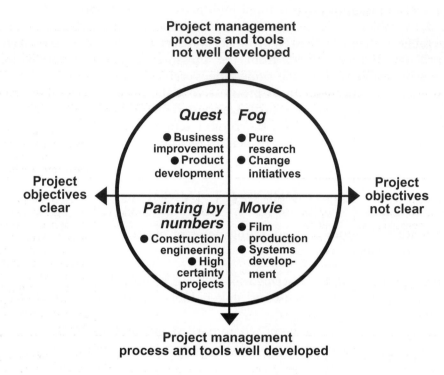

Figure 1.2 Project types

The management approach described in Table 1.1 is useful when undertaking project planning. Adopting a detailed planning approach when in 'fog' or 'quest' is not useful as it creates expectations that appear certain when in reality they will be elaborated downstream. In most cases planning software implicitly assumes that the planner has sufficient details to develop a complete plan as if the project is in the 'painting by numbers' state, whereas it may be in the 'fog' or 'quest' state, leading to expectations that often cannot be achieved downstream.

PROJECT PARTICIPANTS

In the context of this book, the following terminology applies to projects undertaken in service delivery or production organizations. These are referred to as organizational projects.

The term 'project participants' includes everyone who has a role to play on the project. Some of the more important project participants are explained below.

Table 1.1 Project classification

Project type (description by Obeng)	General description	Project		Management approach
		Process	Tools	
Fog ● Pure research ● Change initiatives ● First-time projects	● We are not sure where we are going ● We are also not sure how to get there	Not well understood	Not well developed	Proceed with caution one step at a time. Focus on the next beacon and carefully move towards it. Having reached a beacon, the path to the next beacon becomes clear through the fog.
Movie ● Film production ● Systems development ● Prototype development	● We are not sure what our final destination will be ● Once we have some idea we will know how to get there	Well understood	Well developed	Because the project management and production processes are well known, avoid spending too much time on definition and planning. It is better to concentrate on finding a good product (script), and the project process will be easily managed.
Quest ● Business improvement ● Product development	● We know what our destination is, but we are not entirely sure how to get there	Not well understood	Not necessarily well developed	These projects require considerable research in the project initiation and definition phases, so a picture can be built up of a means and approach required to achieve the final outcome. Care should be taken not to get into too much detailed planning and design, but rather progressively elaborate the project. This project type usually requires considerable buy-in from the performing organization as well as important stakeholders.
Painting by Numbers ● Construction and engineering ● Similar projects done in the past	● We know what our destination is ● We are confident of getting there	Very well understood	Very well developed	Painting by Numbers projects are complex, and tend to be large and involve many parties. As time and costs are predictable, the challenge is to deliver within tight financial, time and specification constraints. Diligent application of process and workflow is critical to success.

See notes overleaf.

Notes to Table 1.1

In the context of Table 1.1, 'Process' refers to the extent of understanding of project management processes and procedures.

'Tools' refers to the degree of development of planning and control tools and techniques, as discussed in Part III – ODPM and Appendix B – Basic concepts, tools and techniques.

The information in Table 1.1 draws on Eddie Obeng's[68] description of Fog, Quest, Movie and Painting by Numbers project types.

Owner or client

The **owner** and **client** are considered to be the same group of participants. The owner is the person or group who will own and operate the project deliverables. The client is the internal or external person or group that purchases the project deliverables. Benefits resulting from the integration of the project deliverables accrue to the owner.

In the case of a new cure for AIDS, the organization that has the right to manufacture the products required for the cure is the owner. The clients are the purchasers and users of the products.

There may be multiple layers of clients and multiple interactions between the owner and clients. For example, the clients of a new cure for AIDS may include the doctors who prescribe it, the patient who takes it and the insurers who pay for it.

Performing organization

The performing organization is described in the PMBOK® Guide[73] as: 'The enterprise whose employees are most directly involved in doing the work of the project'.

The performing organization can be an internal group or an external organization undertaking the project work. If an external organization is delivering the project, it must do so within the project management purview of the client/owner.

Upper management

Upper management includes the executive and senior management of the performing organization. In organizational projects, upper management own the business and sponsor the project.

Upper management must be willing to commit resources and provide the necessary administrative support so project deliverables can integrate seamlessly into ongoing operations.

Upper management influences project success through setting strategic direction for the project. Although this strategic direction is essential, it may be insufficient if upper managers demonstrate outdated behaviour, such as rewarding functional performance while paying lip service to project performance. To improve the chances of satisfactory project results, upper management must not only give initial project direction, they must consistently demonstrate support for the project and project participants. Part II Chapter 4, The Wrappers model, elaborates on upper management's role in projects.

The project sponsor is the executive-appointed upper manager who champions the project.

Project sponsor

The project **sponsor** and project **champion** are considered to be the same role. Distinction is often made in that a sponsor makes resources available to 'buy' the project's deliverables, while satisfying the owner's business improvement objectives. A champion is a person who seeks and convinces a sponsor that a project should be supported and has priority in the organization. Often the champion is best placed to act as sponsor if they are upper management level.

The sponsor is accountable for the success of the changes resulting from the project and the effective integration of these changes into the business. In organization improvement projects, those who own and operate the products from the project should act as sponsor.

From a project perspective a sponsor should:

- champion the project; obtain and retain strong support for the project;
- appoint the project manager;
- provide a clearly defined high-level decision-making process;
- actively manage issues that cannot be resolved at project level;
- resolve high-level conflicts;
- facilitate interfacing with functional departments who resource the project;
- ensure adequate resourcing for the project work;
- monitor and maintain alignment with organization strategy;
- protect the project manager and team from political infighting;
- define what constitutes project success, and agree the associated performance measures with upper management and the project manager and team;
- communicate with and provide reports to the executive;
- give feedback to the project manager on their performance;
- provide the opportunity for the project manager's professional growth.

Implicit in the sponsor role is the mentoring of the project manager. The authors have observed in many cases the lack of direction and mentoring expected from a sponsor. Contributing to this problem are upper managers' limited personal project management experience and their lack of competency to act as sponsors. In many cases sponsorship skills required to lead projects are not specifically developed, and the assumption made is that being a senior manager automatically equates to competency in project delivery. Another factor that sponsors often raise is the limited time they have to play the sponsor role, which is of concern as managers manage change through projects.

Project manager

The project manager is responsible for the efficient management of the project management process, and the effective delivery of the project objectives.

Upper management, and specifically the sponsor, expect the project manager to:

- be accountable for the achievement of the project objectives;
- efficiently manage the project process by planning, leading, organizing, coordinating and controlling the project;
- manage the project in a cross-functional manner, ensuring integration with the functions of the organization;
- appoint the team members (jointly with the sponsor and functional managers);
- build the project team;
- establish an appropriate office environment;
- support, guide and facilitate the project team through the process;
- act as a change agent for the project team and other project participants;
- effectively resolve issues and manage risks;
- minimize organizational disruption during the execution of a project;
- have the capacity to handle most interpersonal issues;
- communicate progress to upper management and other project participants;
- interface and communicate with internal and external stakeholders.

Kimmons and Loweree[48] have this to say about the performance of a project manager: 'The performance of a project manager results from the development of a range of management skills, not innate skills but skills acquired through hard work. Leadership is the resultant of performance. Authority is a resultant of leadership. The road to excellence – management skills, performance, leadership, authority – is a long road with many detours, but achievable for those with a commitment to excellence.'

Project manager is a role, not just a title. Projects are temporary, and while an organization may have a pool of managers competent in project management, they are not always working on projects. The exceptions are project management in a consultancy environment, and purely project-driven organizations.

Profile of a project manager

The Association of Project Managers (APM) in its *Body of Knowledge*[4] considers the profile of a project manager in two areas: experience and personality. In terms of experience, the APM considers the type of project a project manager manages at four levels (quoted below):

Level One
A Project Manager working at level one would be managing an 'in-house' project with no responsibility (or very little) for external contractors or suppliers. The predominant management activity at this level would be the application of management tools and techniques to enable work to be managed more effectively.

Level Two
The Project Manager at this level may be involved in managing a number of disciplines within a single company, again with limited involvement with external contractors or suppliers with the possible exception of procurement. The Project Manager's activities would be associated mainly with the tools and techniques, limited people and organization skills and some appreciation of wider project management issues.

Level Three
A Project Manager working at this level would be either a) managing a multi-disciplinary team from a number of independent companies, where the team has been established for the purpose of the project, or b) responsible for a team of people undertaking a set of projects. At this level a detailed understanding of the application of the appropriate tools and techniques, experience in managing people and an understanding of organizations, and a full understanding of project management issues in the widest sense, would be necessary.

Level Four
A level four project would involve a multi-disciplinary team from a variety of companies and working in a number of different countries. Projects at this level are the exception rather than the rule.

A person with responsibility for managing a level three project would certainly have the experience to become a Certified Project Manager. It is accepted that many people managing level two projects could also have the appropriate knowledge and experience which should allow them to attain the status of a Certified Project Manager. Someone managing a level one project is unlikely to have the wider understanding necessary to gain Certification status.

The APM goes on further to define the principal personality characteristics of a project manager to include the following:

Attitude – an open, positive 'can do' attitude which encourages communication and motivation, and fosters co-operation.

Common sense – a strong ability to spot sensible, effective, straight forward, least risky, least complex solutions i.e. 90% right on time is better than 100% far too late!

Open mindedness – an approach where one is always open to new ideas, practices and methods, and in particular gives equal weight to the various professional disciplines involved on the project.

Adaptability – a propensity to be flexible where necessary and avoid rigid patterns of thinking or behaviour, to adapt to the requirements of the project, the needs of the sponsors, its environment and people working on it and for it to ensure a successful outcome.

Inventiveness – an ability to discover innovative strategies and solutions either from within oneself or by encouragement with other members of the project team and to identify ways of working with disparate resources to achieve the project objectives.

Prudent risk taker – a willingness and ability to identify and understand risks but not to take a risky approach in an unwise or reckless fashion.

Fairness – a fair and open attitude which represents all human values.

Commitment – a very strong overriding commitment to the project's success, user satisfaction and team working. A strong orientation towards goal achievement.

The APM's well-developed profile of a project manager strongly reflects the authors' own views on the subject.

What then characterizes a competent project manager? The capability or ability to manage projects – proved by five attributes: knowledge, skill, aptitude, attitude and experience. All five attributes must be present to a greater or lesser extent to ensure competency. The level of competency then can be defined as how knowledgeable, skilled and experienced a project manager is. The other two attributes of aptitude and attitude are, to a certain extent, innate traits linked to behaviour and personality that must be present in a competent project manager.

How is competency attained? To answer that question, the five attributes need to be addressed:

- **Knowledge** is acquired through formal study and reading.
- **Skills** are obtained through study and practice. Knowledge and skill acquisition is wasted on a person who does not have an aptitude for project management.
- Certain **personality** characteristics were discussed above in the descriptions of attitude, common sense, open mindedness, adaptability, inventiveness, prudent risk taking, fairness and commitment.
- The right **attitude** is vital – both towards others and the job of project management. Attitude can be modified through training in the 'softer' skills of people management, as well as training in personal development areas such as stress management and assertiveness.
- **Experience** cannot be gained overnight, nor can the gaining of experience be speeded up or compressed. The level and length of experience in reality has a large bearing on a project manager's competence.

In practice...

The reluctant sponsor

During the tea-break of a three-day training course, Sacha approached Mark, the consultant trainer, and asked for advice on how to deal with a difficult situation on her project. From the look of desperation on her face, Mark felt compelled to listen.

It had all started about six months ago. Sacha, a qualified theatre sister, had a desire to further her career in health management. Project management was seen as a challenging and interesting avenue, and one that could enhance her career growth. When the project to reduce staff waiting lists by 50 per cent over a nine-month period was announced by the

Health Board, Sacha jumped at the opportunity to manage it. She could make a difference, assist the organization, and demonstrate her value to senior management.

The Health Board made it clear from the beginning that this project had a high priority, and a wide range of stakeholders from the individual patients to the Minister of Health. Failure would not be viewed favourably. Project funding would be made available, but not for additional staffing, as the Health budget was already tight and overruns were projected for most health boards.

Project sponsorship was given to the head of medical and surgical services, which reflected the priority of the project. Sacha had successfully managed a few smaller projects, and in view of this, and together with her desire to manage a project of this nature, she was appointed as project manager.

The project had hardly started when it became obvious that the sponsor was not completely supportive when he missed key planning workshops, and delayed sign-off for project initiation documents. At first she thought that the behaviour was due to the traditional surgeon/nursing relationship which existed in the health sector, and believed that things would settle down once the new roles were understood and the sponsor felt comfortable with Sacha's position. After all, projects require authorities and management approaches that cut across functional boundaries, which is not the traditional way of doing business in hospitals. Arranging time to meet with him was virtually impossible, and when they met he appeared irritated that she was not progressing the project.

As the project unfolded it became clear to Sacha that the project touched every department in the organization, from administration to support services to medical services. This was a highly integrated project that required considerable support and leadership from the sponsor that was not forthcoming. She was starting to feel isolated, as her colleagues soon realized that the sponsor was not actively championing the initiative, and consequently they perceived the project as having a low priority. The 'grapevine' message was that the sponsor did not support the reduction of patient waiting lists in the absence of additional permanent staff and resource funding. Medical standards would not be compromised, and surgeons were not to place themselves and the hospital at risk.

The situation was getting worse. The Health Board was unimpressed with the progress reports, and stated in no uncertain terms that performance and action were urgent and a top priority. The hospital CEO conveyed to the sponsor the Board response and suggested that the project be managed more vigorously. Sacha was summoned to the sponsor and his displeasure with progress strongly expressed. As head of medical services, he did not have time to hold her hand and suggested that if she had problems in managing her project, perhaps she should attend some project management training and purchase some planning software or he would get someone competent to manage the project.

Mark could not help but feel sorry for her as the story unfolded. What could she do? Her sponsor was supportive of neither her nor the project objectives. Senior management and the Board wanted results, team members were giving the initiative a low priority and users were not fully committing to workshops. Her performance review was due in two weeks and she was dreading the appraisal meeting with the sponsor. Her department manager, head of nursing services, offered little support as she saw Sacha as a 'tall poppy' trying to make a name for herself. Sacha had transformed from being a confident and respected theatre sister to a nervous wreck by taking on the challenge of managing this project. She seemed to recall reading somewhere that managing projects was supposed to be challenging, fun and satisfying.

Mark and Sacha spent some time discussing options on how one engages a reluctant sponsor and ensuring that they take on their responsibilities. A member of senior management in charge of support services was brought in to support Sacha and assist the sponsor in understanding his sponsorship role. At first the meetings were strained and Sacha felt uncomfortable, as the sponsor largely ignored her. Little progress was made until the CEO took charge and stipulated that the project was now critical and that project performance would cover not only deliverables, but also the performance of all key participants, including sponsor leadership and support. As CEO, he would look both to the sponsor and the project manager for project delivery and specifically to the sponsor for the business improvement resulting from the project. Now that the situation was out in the open and other members of the senior management team were aware of the issues, the project picked up direction and momentum. The CEO communicated organization-wide the priority of the project, and demanded that staff support the objectives.

Mark bumped into Sacha three months later. She was beaming and excitedly as she explained how the project had turned around, and was back on track to deliver the expected benefits. The sponsor had slowly changed his attitude towards her and was playing the sponsor role actively. The first key deliverables were in place and celebrated. She was actually having some fun on the project!

Important lessons…

1. Before taking on a project as a manager, establish sponsor support for the objectives. This can be tested by drawing up early project planning documentation reflecting objectives and measures, purpose, key roles and responsibilities, and rationale for delivering project benefits to the business.
2. Submit regular reports to the sponsor, requesting resolution of high-level issues, and responses to risks. Also ask for verification that the direction the project is taking is the correct one.
3. Build in specific sponsor approval milestones, and highlight in a professional manner the consequence of slow approvals in the report. This is usually done in a manner that demonstrates the impact on the business if approval is late. Acting in the best interest of the organization is a positive way to engage sponsors.

Project team members

> There are many objects of great value to man which cannot be attained by unconnected individuals, but must be attained if at all by association.
> Daniel Webster (1782–1852), US politician

The PMBOK® Guide[73] defines project team members as 'the people who report either directly or indirectly to the project manager'.

Although upper management support and influence are essential for success, it is the project teams who deliver successful projects.

A project **core team** consists of individuals from the key contributing functional areas, who remain on the project from the project definition phase through to project completion. The project core team members represent their department and they direct the work of the people in that department on the project. Others from various departments may come and go as needed, but the project core team is the stable group (Graham and Englund[34]).

Contrary to upper management belief that team members' time on a project should be minimized so they can contribute to other projects, experience has shown that early removal of core project team members has a negative effect on timely delivery. The impact of late delivery on an organization's credibility and finances is far greater than the potential marginal cost overrun of keeping a core team on for the duration of the project.

Kimmons and Loweree[48], discussing the future challenges of project management, state: 'Project teams, and certainly the project manager, will have to be business oriented, with a high comfort factor in areas such as financial controls, personnel motivation, productivity, and general business management. The vitality and willingness to adjust to changing times, the ability to contribute to positive team attitudes, the skills to deal constructively with internal political issues, the handling of uncertainty, the nurturing of client and partner relationships, and the ease of movement in international circles. All of these will be the hallmark of the members of the future project staff.'

Steering committees

A quotation from Nietzsche best introduces the topic of steering committees.

> Madness is the exception in individuals but the rule in groups.
> Friedrich Nietzsche 1844–1900

The *Collins English Dictionary and Thesaurus* (1998) describes a steering committee as: 'A committee set up to prepare and arrange topics to be discussed, the order of business, etc, for a legislative assembly or other body'. The role as described adds little value to projects.

In project organizations steering committees have come to play a different role, often to the detriment of the project and its management. Power politics and control have become the norm rather than the exception of these committees. They have moved from a supporting and guiding role to a directive and controlling mode. This view is shared by Andersen, Grude and Haug[2] , who state: 'There is always a tendency for a project steering committee to become a project decision group and make decisions which it does not have the qualifications or the right to make. We strongly reject the idea that such a group function as decision-makers concerning professional questions. A project must not deprive the base organization of its responsibility for making professionally-related decisions.'

The sponsor has a key role in ensuring support for the project and integration of the project results into the business. Organization-wide projects often establish a group to provide guidance to the sponsor and project manager, and take ownership of the project deliverables. People forming the group represent the functions and operations of the organization at upper management level.

The authors suggest a **Project Council** that provides support and guidance to the sponsor, and contributes to the business focus of the project. Further, the Council encourages ownership of the deliverables resulting from the project, and their effective integration into the performing organization.

The Project Council has representation from the functions contributing resources, as well as upper managers from operations who will own and operate the deliverables, including the sponsor. Graham and Englund[34] refer to an upper management team that bears some resemblance to the Project Council concept.

STAKEHOLDERS

> To the perceiver, perception is reality.
>
> Dennis Comninos and Enzo Frigenti

The PMBOK® Guide[73] describe stakeholders as 'Project stakeholders are individuals and organizations who are actively involved in the project, or whose interest may be positively or negatively affected as a result of project execution'.

Obeng states in *The Project Leader's Secret Handbook – All Change!*[68] that 'Project success **is** and **can only** be defined by the stakeholders.' Project stakeholders are individuals and organizations who are actively involved in the project, or whose interest may be positively or negatively affected as a result of project execution or successful project completion. The project management team must identify the stakeholders, determine what their needs are, and then manage and influence those expectations to ensure a successful project (PMBOK® Guide[73]).

Stakeholder identification is often challenging as stakeholders span a wide spectrum of interested parties. In order to analyse stakeholders and develop an appropriate stakeholder management strategy, it is useful to identify important players. Key stakeholders on every project are listed above under the heading of project participants.

In addition to those, there are many different categories of stakeholders, both internal and external – owners and funders, suppliers and contractors, team members and their families, government agencies and media outlets, individual citizens, temporary or permanent lobbying organizations, and society at large. The naming or grouping of stakeholders is primarily an aid to identifying which individuals and organizations view themselves as stakeholders, and assists in developing stakeholder strategies.

Influencing stakeholders

A further important characteristic of a competent project manager is the ability to influence others in the organization to act for the project. The concept of influence is appropriate as the project manager does not generally have the formal organizational authority residing in the functional departments. In project management, lack of direct authority over project team members and other stakeholders is the norm.

Graham and Englund[34] expound the view: 'Consensus on action is reached not by positional power but by influence – the ability to persuade rather than to command. The ability to persuade is based on knowledge of the issues, commitment to shared goals, and proven effectiveness. Each person in the group understands how his or her performance affects the overall strategy.'

Some of the most important stakeholders are shown in Figure 1.3. This illustrates that both the project manager and sponsor have responsibility for influencing upper management and the Project Council, and for a high-level interface with external stakeholders. Sponsor focus will be on upper management, Project Council, and executives of external organizations.

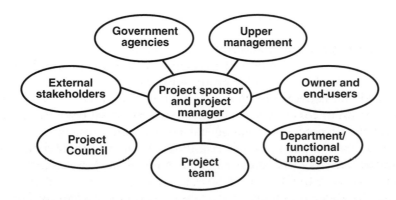

Figure 1.3   Project stakeholders

Graham and Gabriel, quoted in *The Project Manager* as *Change Agent* by Turner, Grude and Thurloway[90], discuss the need for a stakeholder influence strategy for stakeholder groups as well as for team members. This strategy is a living document that needs to be continuously elaborated and converted into tactical actions by the project core team.

Stakeholder identification must be as comprehensive as possible. Essential to the process is the identification of both internal and external stakeholders to determine the degree to which they are able to influence the project.

After developing the list of stakeholders, the next important step is to consider why these individuals support the project by asking how they will benefit from a successful project.

Further, it is important to know how to maintain stakeholder support throughout the project, as focusing on the end benefits, which are too far in the future, results in a loss of stakeholder focus. Stakeholder support requires nurturing through regular, well-directed communications, from initiation to close-out and sometimes even beyond project completion.

Experienced project managers know who the supporters or beneficiaries of the project are. They also know who is likely to resist the project, as these resistors do not see the benefits or may feel their position is threatened by the project. People resist changes when they cannot see the benefits to either the organization or themselves. If the resistors have strong influence over the project process or outcome, their resistance must be overcome, or the project could proceed in fits and starts and possibly derail along the way.

Influence strategy through benefit and risk

The key to influencing stakeholders is to demonstrate that the benefits of undertaking the change are greater than the associated risks. If people value the benefits of being associated with the project and perceive the risks to be acceptable, they will support it. Some of the perceptions of benefits and risks are discussed below:

- **Benefits (perception of value).** Projects have value for the participating organizations, external groups, and project participants. The project team must carefully communicate to each stakeholder group why the project is being undertaken and what the potential benefits are.
- **Risk (perception of loss).** Projects always have potential risks for the organization and project participants. As change creates fear and resistance, the individuals facing change have a perception of risk that is related to their own risk profile. To understand these risks, the project manager must have answers to the following questions:
  - What could the participating organizations, groups and individuals potentially lose if they participate in this project?
  - What will be the consequence of the perceived loss to organizations, groups and individuals?

Unless the project core team has answers to these questions, their ability to influence stakeholders will be limited.

ORGANIZATION STRUCTURE WITH A PROJECT FOCUS

Project structures are influenced by the organization or organizations that set them up. Typically, projects are a temporary part of an organization larger than the project, also known as the performing organization. The structure of the performing organization influences the availability of resources. Resources are usually allocated to projects by functional managers (sometimes called resource managers).

Organizational structures can be classified in a wide range, from functional at the one end of the spectrum to pure project at the other. Work is integrated horizontally through matrix management. Organizations that operate in established hierarchies will tend to manage projects through a weak matrix, where the project manager's authority to coordinate horizontally is limited. Organizations that strongly manage work horizontally have project managers with considerable authority to integrate across the various functions.

Matrix structures

In reality, very few organizations operate as either a pure functional or a pure project structure. Most operate some form of matrix – weak, balanced or strong. The choice of structure reflects the organization's approach and maturity to the management of projects. Organizations new to project management will tend towards a weak matrix, as the cultural shift required to adopt a strong matrix is considered too great a risk. The stronger the matrix, the more authority and accountability are delegated to the project manager and participants. Functional managers may perceive this as undermining their authority, and become less cooperative in resourcing and supporting the project.

A major feature of the matrix organization is the conflict it induces, which if managed correctly can assist project delivery. This feature is more prominent in the strong matrix than the weak matrix.

Figures 1.4, 1.5 and 1.6 illustrate the weak, balanced and strong matrix organization structures. In the figures, the black boxes represent staff engaged in project activities.

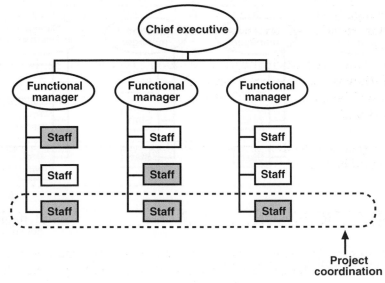

Figure 1.4   Weak matrix organization

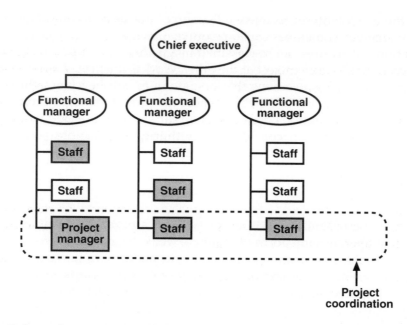

Figure 1.5   Balanced matrix organization

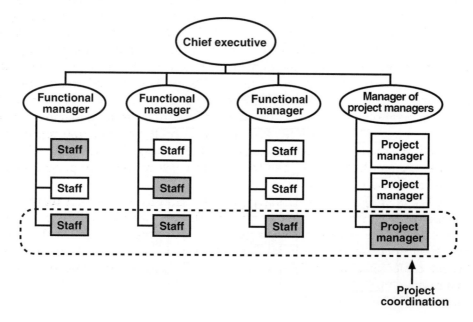

Figure 1.6   Strong matrix organization

The role of project manager can be played in any of the weak, balanced or strong matrix structures. The title of the person undertaking the role in a weak matrix is usually that of coordinator. This person does not have sufficient authority to act as a project manager. In both the balanced and strong matrices, the role carries the title of project manager. In the balanced matrix, the role of project manager is played by a functional staff member with demonstrated competencies for the role. In a strong matrix, the role is taken by a project person from the project management department. The strong matrix structure is more prevalent in organizations whose business is mainly that of delivering projects.

Projectized organizations

A projectized organization is defined as 'any organizational structure in which the project manager has full authority to assign priorities and to direct the work of individuals assigned to the project' (PMBOK® Guide[73]).

Projectized organizations can operate in a balanced or strong matrix, provided the project manager has the appropriate authority and responsibility.

Project versus function conflicts

The matrix approach has been used for many years by organizations in an attempt to integrate projects across functions. Functional managers control organization departments while project managers coordinate and integrate work across functions. This causes conflicts in that project team members usually have to serve two managers: the manager of the functional department to which they belong and the project manager. When project demands conflict with the needs of the functional managers, problems arise. Trapped in the middle are the team members trying to meet the expectations of both. As the project manager rarely controls the team members' remuneration and promotion, the team members' loyalty will usually be strongest towards their functional manager. Organizations that are serious about project management ensure that project managers evaluate the team members' performance on the project, and report these to both the functional manager of each team member and the project sponsor. Additionally, project managers should be authorized to make rewards available to project teams that perform well and deliver the results.

Functional and project managers have an obligation to ensure that team members caught in the middle of the project/function conflict are not stressed by trying to meet the needs of both. If a project manager cannot resolve conflicts with functional managers, they may need to call in the project sponsor to do so. This should be a last resort, as the project manager will be seen as being unable to negotiate and work with functional managers.

Graham and Englund[34] state:

The major fault was that it was a marginal change – a mere modification to the old hierarchical organization. This meant that many of upper management's assumptions were based on the functional organization or mechanistic model. As a result, many of the behaviors that were rewarded by upper management were actually counter-productive to successful projects. Project team members felt that organizational rewards favored departmental work, and that working on projects was actually bad for their careers. Many people working in the matrix complained of being 'caught in a web' of conflicting orders, conflicting priorities, and reward systems that did not match the stated organizational goals. Effective behavioral change requires a change in the reward system, and this did not occur in many matrix organizations.

In the case quoted above, although team members were told that working on projects was beneficial to their careers, experience proved that project work decreased their chances of departmental promotion. Consequently, people did not see project work aligned with their own interests, and the project work suffered.

Changes in the business environment in recent years has resulted in team members perceiving personal value in project work, as organizations are including project experience and project management competency in job descriptions. Coupled with performance and reward systems that recognize project work, some of the problems of the matrix structure are being overcome.

The balanced matrix structure attempts to harmonize the powers of the project manager and the functional manager. The project manager is responsible for all project managerial aspects, while the functional manager is responsible for all technical aspects. Joint accountability has now been created as the project manager determines:

- what is to be done (the project);
- how the project will be approached;
- when the project will be done;
- how much money is available to do the project.

In turn, the functional manager determines:

- how the work will be done;
- where the work will be done;
- whether the work done is quality work;
- who will do the work.

The evaluation norm for the project manager is – 'How well has the total project been managed and executed?' and for the functional manager it is – 'How well has the functional input been integrated in the project?'

PROJECT PHASES AND PROJECT LIFE CYCLE

Project life cycle

Due to their uniqueness, projects involve a high degree of uncertainty. Organizations performing projects usually divide a project into phases to better provide management planning and control, and identify appropriate links to the organization's ongoing operations. Collectively, the project phases are known as the project life cycle.

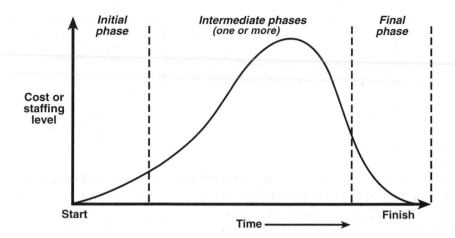

Figure 1.7   Generic project life cycle

Generally an initial phase and final phase are identified, with a number of intermediate phases in between.

The authors distinguish between two life cycles and a project management process, as follows:

- product or service life cycle;
- project life cycle;
- project management process across a project life cycle.

Product/service and project life cycles

Organizations undertake projects to create new services or products or improve existing ones. A project life cycle is thus part of a product or service life cycle, as shown in Figure 1.8.

A business product usually has a limited life span of years or months. Often products or services are enhanced through a project to extend the useful life, when the benefits to be derived from the additional investment are greater than the cost of redeveloping the product or service. Therefore, a product or service life cycle can include multiple project life cycles.

Project management process

A project management process is a generic description of a process that applies to all projects. It forms the basis for a methodology that can be described in terms of project

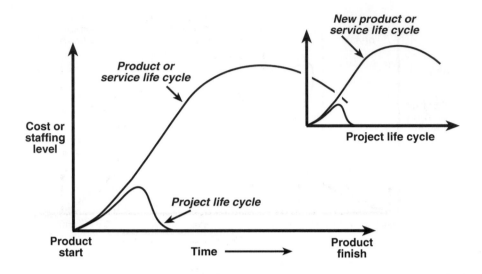

Figure 1.8   Product and project life cycles

management practice and a set of supporting tools and techniques. Applying a project management process across the project life cycle is the challenge facing the project manager and team.

Project management is most effective when applied in a consistent repetitive manner in the form of a process. A typical project management process contains four phases: initiation, planning, execution and close-out. The Objective Directed Project Management (ODPM) process described in Part III contains five phases: initiation, definition, planning, execution and close-out, as reflected in Figure 1.9.

Although the process is shown to apply across a complete project, it equally applies to every phase of a project. Therefore, each phase has its own five phases or 'sub-phases' in terms of the project management process. Project managers implement and rely on the process to effectively manage the project, as it provides both focus and consistency to project management.

Each project phase is named or defined in terms of the major deliverable produced in that phase. A deliverable is a tangible, verifiable work product such as a feasibility study, user requirements specification, functional requirements specification, system requirements specification, detailed design, implementation plan, or system development. The deliverables, and hence the phases, are part of a generally sequential logic designed to ensure proper definition of the project's product. Each project phase normally includes a set of defined work products. The majority of these products are related to the major phase deliverable.

The completion of a project phase is generally identified by a review of both key deliverables and project performance in order to:

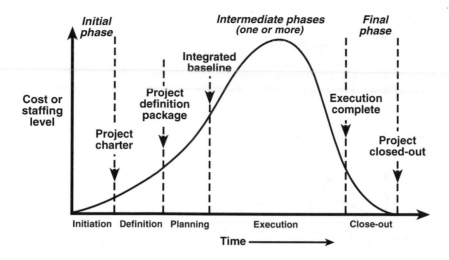

Figure 1.9 Project management process (ODPM)

- determine if the project should continue into the next phase;
- detect and correct errors in a cost-effective manner;
- review performance of the project team.

These phase-end or close-out reviews are often called phase exits, stage gates or termination points.

Example of a project life cycle

A typical organizational transformation (restructuring) project life cycle for a nationwide organization is indicated in Figure 1.10. The three phases identified derive their names from the key products delivered in each phase.

In the initial phase, the focus is on consultation, analysis and initial design, resulting in a high-level organization-wide specific implementation plan. After the approval of the plan, the project is handed over to the districts to develop their own district implementation plans. Transition implementation becomes the responsibility of the district. The product that results from the transition implementation is a structure where all positions have been filled. The final phase is where the organization settles down and implements the new processes in the transformed organization, and ownership has been passed on to operational managers for continuous improvement.

The project life-cycle phases will also determine which transitional actions at the end of the project are included, and which are not. This is not only applicable to the complete project life cycle but also to each phase, as certain deliverables can be released and integrated with the business as early as possible. In this manner, the project life cycle is used to link the project to the ongoing operations of the performing organization.

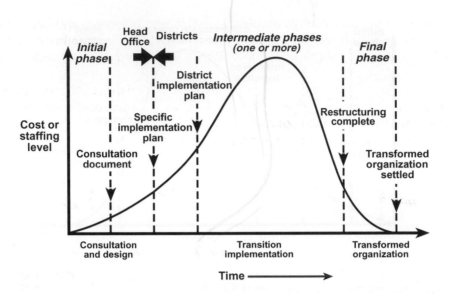

Figure 1.10　Restructuring project life cycle for organization ABC

The phase sequence defined by most project life cycles involves some form of responsibility transfer or technology handover, such as requirements to design, design to construction, or design to manufacturing. Deliverables from the preceding phase are usually approved before work commences on the next phase. Subsequent phases can sometimes begin before approval of the previous phase deliverables when risks are deemed to be acceptable. This practice of phase overlapping is called **fast tracking**.

Project life cycles generally define:

● what technical work should be done in every phase to produce the phase deliverables;
● who should be involved in each phase to produce the deliverables;
● the major management responsibility for each phase (sponsor drives the initiation, project manager drives the definition, project manager and core team drive planning, operations managers could drive the execution and close-out phases);
● key go/no-go points, for example where the feasibility of continuing is reviewed. These points are also described as critical decision points and are further discussed in Chapter 8.

Project life-cycle descriptions may be general or detailed. Highly detailed descriptions may have numerous forms, charts and checklists to provide structure and consistency. Such detailed approaches are often called project management methodologies.

Most project life cycle descriptions share a number of common characteristics:

● The probability of successfully completing the project is lowest, and hence the risk and uncertainty are highest, at the start of the project. The probability of successful completion generally gets progressively higher as the project continues, while the risk diminishes.

● The ability of stakeholders to influence the final characteristics of the project product and the final cost of the project is highest at the start, and gets progressively lower as the project continues. A major contributor to this is that the cost of changes and error correction generally increases as the project continues.

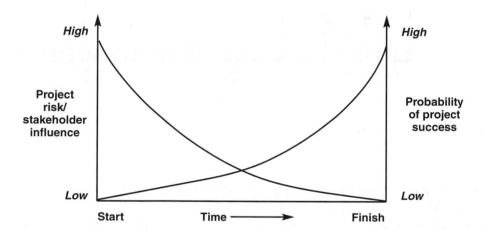

Figure 1.11   Project risk and success profile

2

The context of project management

THE MANAGEMENT ROLE

The role of management is to integrate resources and tasks to achieve organizational goals. All managers, including project managers, have this role in addition to their specific responsibilities.

Management functions

The classic functions of a manager were identified as far back as 1908 by Henri Fayol[26]. A manager's functions are to:

- **Plan**
- Lead
- Organize
- Coordinate (staffing)
- Control.

These are defined as follows:

- **Plan** – Thinking ahead on how to achieve selected goals; creating a measurement standard (baseline) and communicating it to others.
- **Lead** – Influencing people so they will contribute to goals.
- **Organize** – Establishing an intentional structure of roles for people to fill, in an organization.

- **Coordinate** (staffing) – Staffing the roles and ensuring that the selected people remain motivated and communicate with each other.
- **Control** – Measuring and correcting the performance to ensure that events conform to plans.

Management's role is to carry out these five functions in an integrated manner across the organization. Similar to classic general manager functions, project managers have to plan, lead, organize, coordinate and control their projects.

Relationship between different management disciplines

The knowledge required to manage projects brings a degree of uniqueness to the discipline of project management. This knowledge, however, does overlap with other management disciplines such as general management and application area or technical management. This relationship is shown in Figure 2.1. (Courtesy PMBOK® Guide[73]).

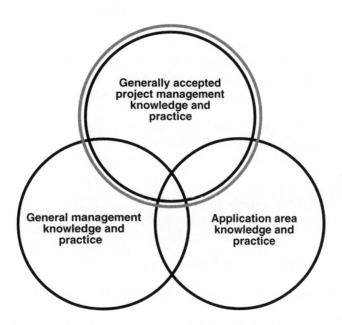

Figure 2.1 Relationship between knowledge areas and practice

Note: This figure is a conceptual view of these relationships. The overlaps shown are not proportional to the importance of the component.

...e and practice encompasses the sum of the knowledge ... st projects most of the time, and there is widespread ... sefulness. 'Generally accepted' does not imply that all of ... should be applied to all projects all the time; the extent of a... plica... determined by the project manager.

General management encompasses knowledge and functions such as planning, organizing, staffing, executing and controlling operations. It also encompasses law, statistics, logistics, sales and marketing.

Application area or technical management contains those areas specific to the type of industry in which the organization or project exists. Examples are systems development, financial, construction, government, automotive and engineering.

For an individual project manager, the extent of overlap between the three knowledge areas and practice derives from that manager's education, training and professional experience.

WHAT IS PROJECT MANAGEMENT?

The direct answer to this question is that project management is the process by which a project achieves its stated objectives. This statement is a high-level definition that requires some elaboration in order to understand it.

The PMBOK® Guide[73] describes project management as:

> ... the application of knowledge, skills, tools, and techniques to project activities in order to meet or exceed stakeholders' needs and expectations from a project. Meeting or exceeding stakeholder needs and expectations invariably involves balancing competing demands among:
>
> - Scope, time, cost, and quality.
> - Stakeholders with differing needs and expectations.
> - Identified requirements (needs) and unidentified requirements (expectations).

Project management knowledge areas

Modern project management recognizes nine knowledge areas, as described below:

1. **Project integration management** relates to the processes required to ensure that the various elements of a project are properly coordinated. It includes plan development, execution and overall change control.
2. **Project scope management** means ensuring that the project includes all the work required, and only the work required, to complete the project successfully. It covers scope initiation, planning, definition, verification and change control.
3. **Project time management** includes the decisions and actions required to ensure timely completion of the project, such as activity definition, sequencing, duration estimating, schedule development and control.

4. **Project cost management** refers to the processes required to ensure that the project is completed within the approved budget – resource planning, cost estimating, cost budgeting and control.
5. **Project quality management** means the processes required to ensure that the project will satisfy the needs for which it was undertaken. It covers quality planning, assurance and control.
6. **Project human resource management** is making the most effective use of the people involved with the project. It includes organizational planning, staff acquisition and team development.
7. **Project communication management** refers to the processes required to ensure timely and appropriate generation, collection, dissemination, storage and ultimate disposition of project information. It entails communications planning, information distribution, performance reporting and administrative closure.
8. **Project risk management** means identifying, analysing and responding to project risk. It includes risk identification, risk quantification, risk response development and risk response control.
9. **Project procurement management** covers the processes required to acquire goods and services from outside the performing organization – procurement planning, solicitation planning, solicitation, source selection, contract administration and contract close-out.

The knowledge areas are extensively described in the PMBOK® Guide[73].

The project management knowledge areas can also be referred to as dimensions of project management. The five core project dimensions are scope, time, cost, performance and human resources. The facilitating dimensions are risk, communication, procurement and integration. The relationship between the dimensions is reflected in Figure 2.2.

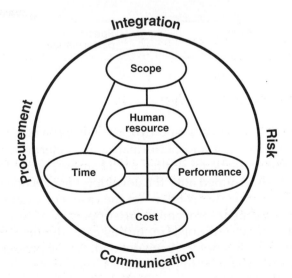

Figure 2.2 Project management knowledge areas/dimensions

Figure 2.2 places the five core dimensions in relationship with one another, while the four facilitating dimensions surround them. These dimensions need to be integrated to achieve efficient and effective project results. This integration is a key responsibility of a project manager and is achieved by planning, monitoring and controlling the work of the project over its life cycle, across functions and organizations, and effectively engaging stakeholders.

Scope constraints

The project purpose, in support of the business change and benefits, drives its scope. Project staffing requirements are a result of scope, time, cost and performance analysis.

Four of the five core dimensions – scope, time, cost and performance – relate in a unique manner, as reflected in Figure 2.3. Time is the time schedule, cost is the project budget, performance encompasses the specifications of the project deliverables, and scope is the sum of the deliverables (products and services) to be developed through the project process.

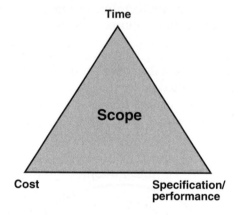

Figure 2.3   The trade-off triangle

As indicated in Figure 2.3, scope is bound by the constraints of time, cost and performance. Often a project's time, cost and performance are determined before the scope is defined, resulting in the scope being limited to the surface area of the triangle. Ideally, time and cost should be determined after the development of scope to meet the performance requirements. In practice, this is often not the case. For example, a chief executive may state that a 20 per cent improvement in support service is required within 12 months, and within a budget limit of $1m. In this case, the boundaries of the triangle have been set, but the scope has not yet been defined. As the project team scopes out the redesign to achieve the 20 per cent improvement target, the time and cost dimensions are continually constraining the team's work. There are rare occasions when the stated time and cost dimensions exceed the scope and performance requirements.

Unless initial dimensions of time, cost and performance are generous, fixing these three dimensions, and effectively the sides of the triangle, before scope is defined, is poor management and must be avoided. At least one and preferably two sides of the triangle should remain flexible so that the scope can be effectively defined to fit the triangle. Alternatively, if scope can reduce, the project team could possibly fit it into a fixed triangle. The trade-off between time, cost, performance and scope is an iterative process that must be understood by the project team, project manager and upper management if a realistic project result is to be achieved.

Competent project managers make it their business to know which of the four dimensions are negotiable. A sponsor should support a project manager who is pressured by upper management or an external client to accept fixed time, cost and performance dimensions of the triangle. This will lead to unrealistic stakeholder expectations and the perception of project failure when in fact the project could not have been delivered successfully in the first place. Unfortunately, the three 'facts' stakeholders always remember are the initial 'promises' of what the project would deliver, what it would cost and when it was going to be delivered, although these promises are often made with limited knowledge on scope. The assumptions made and qualifications stated around these 'facts' are soon forgotten. Competent project managers are reluctant to communicate promises that they are not confident of delivering.

It is the sponsor's responsibility to state clearly which of the dimensions are not negotiable, as well as the negotiability of the remaining ones. The trade-off amongst these dimensions is present from project start to end, and project participants will experience the trade-offs with every important change or important decision as the project unfolds. One dimension cannot be traded off without impact on the others. Ranking the priorities of the four dimensions usually engenders lively debate among project participants and stakeholders.

A point of balance between the four dimensions will exist at various times during the project process, for example at the completion of project definition, detail planning and, of course, at project completion. These points of balance are when the best scope, the most optimistic time and the most probable cost for a specific project performance are achieved. Thus the three sides of the triangle comprehensively contain the scope. During the project's life cycle the triangle is dynamic with the surface (scope) changing and the sides adjusting to accommodate scope changes.

In practice...

The Gantt chart guru

A Gantt chart guru is someone who is inexperienced in project management, and who locks onto one of the most visible results from planning, the Gantt or bar chart, and uses it to plan and manage projects exclusively. The following incident demonstrates the project management culture that can arise when the Gantt chart is used extensively and as virtually the only planning tool.

In a large organization, a senior executive paid the newly formed project support office (PSO) a visit. After introducing himself to Helen, the PSO manager, the executive asked, 'So tell me, Helen, what is the function of a project support office?'

Helen replied, 'We supply project management related services such as project administration, planning and monitoring of projects, training, and consulting in project management.'

A perplexed look came over the executive's face. He walked round the office, closely examining the many charts stuck on the walls. He came to a halt in front of a large colourful Gantt chart and his eyes lit up in recognition. 'I know this type of chart. We call them bar charts. What do you project people call them?'

'We call them Gantt charts, but they can be called bar charts', replied Helen.

The executive smiled, 'OK! I now understand what you people do. We always draw up Gantt charts for our projects at head office. Yep! We sure have been using project management for years. All proposals have a Gantt chart attached to them to show how the project will be achieved. It just goes to show, there is nothing really new under the sun.'

With that, the executive wished Helen well with the PSO and departed with a satisfied look on his face. Helen smiled, leaned back in her chair, sipped her coffee and reflected on the understanding of project management at upper management level.

Important lessons...

1. While it is true that a Gantt chart is an effective reporting tool, it represents only a small slice of the complete project management planning approach. Typically, people new to project management see a Gantt chart as being a major project management tool. Project management software is partly to blame for this view. The typical sales pitch is 'This software will solve all your project management problems.' Many project planning software packages are purchased as a Gantt chart printing tool rather than as planning packages.
2. The novice stage in project management is typified by some Gantt chart development. Very little attention is given to project initiation and the progressive elaboration approach.

MANAGEMENT POWER FLOWS

There are three areas of management responsibility: authority, responsibility and accountability. These are defined as follows:

● **Authority** is the power to make final decisions that others are compelled to follow. With authority go accountability and responsibility.
● **Responsibility** is an obligation that results from a person's formal role in an organization to perform assigned tasks effectively.

- **Accountability** means being answerable for the satisfactory completion of specified objectives.

Delegation and abdication

Management usually starts with a task and a delegation of authority. With it generally goes the authority to get a job done. This authority must be clear. Personal accountability, however, cannot be delegated. For example, the managing director of a company is responsible for the entire direction of the organization and is accountable to the Board of Directors for the efficient discharge of this responsibility. The MD can delegate the direction of day-to-day company operations to a company general manager, and can even direct that the authority for expanding or contracting the workforce or expending funds be given to a general manager. The MD can then hold the general manager responsible for these tasks, but cannot delegate overall accountability for company profits.

Accountability and responsibility, however, expand with delegation. The general manager is responsible or accountable to the MD, who in turn is responsible and accountable to the Board of Directors, who are accountable to the shareholders. Any attempt to delegate complete responsibility results in management's abdication and not delegation.

Theoretically then, authority and responsibility are coupled in their initial travel downward. On the other hand, accountability usually travels upwards only. In practice, this theoretical flow rarely occurs. Individuals and organizations influence the flow in accordance with their own ideas and intentions. Successful managers recognize this and learn to manage within the power relationships that result when exercising authority.

Figure 2.4 shows the ideal flow of power between levels.

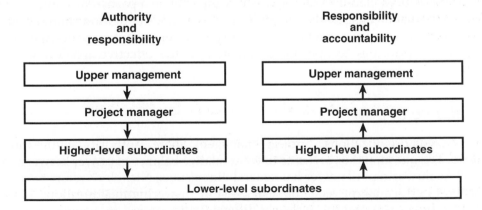

Figure 2.4   The flow of authority, responsibility and accountability

Exercising authority

To illustrate the exercise of authority: the upper management of an organization is aware of the tremendous benefits resulting from the application of project management to operational projects, and has stated as a matter of organization policy that project managers are here to stay. The appointment of a project manager becomes a delegation of responsibility and authority. This occurs when the complexity and size of a task to be accomplished is large enough to place the accountability for successful completion on one person. Either an informal memo is circulated, or formal publication is made of the project manager's appointment to the position.

Practically speaking, this means very little to the newly appointed manager. The project manager is in a similar situation to a fisherman who wishes to catch fish. Although success as a fisherman cannot be achieved legally without a fishing licence, no fisherman is deluded into thinking that the issue of a licence means anything more than the legal right to try.

In the project management situation, a piece of paper may say that the manager has the authority to manage, but it does not supply the ability to do so. In reality, the project manager has potential but not actual authority. Before gaining that real authority, the manager must:

- influence others without commanding, through the use of expert power and charismatic authority such as charm, personality, appearance, friendship and alliances;
- exercise project authority by making decisions about project objectives, policies, schedules and budgets;
- be backed up by authority through the relationship with the project sponsor and a formal or informal project charter appointing the project manager and communicating this to the organization.

As a project manager builds authority, the need to resort to formal authority mechanisms reduces. Because authority is based partly on a particular manager's reputation for sound and consistently correct decisions, a good reputation should be a major goal. In turn, consistently correct decisions are partly dependent on a manager's correct assignment of priorities to specific problems and the effective resolution of those problems.

The balance of power

In projectized organizations, project managers share authority with functional managers. The question thus arises as to what relative balance of power between them is optimal? As the concept of power has several dimensions, Nicholas[67] refers to characteristics of best performing projects that can assist in answering this question: 'In the best performing projects, authority is clearly differentiated: project managers are given the power to obtain the backing of top management, to procure critical resources and coordinate work efforts, and to mediate conflicts; in contrast functional managers are given greater power to make decisions over technical problems and the technology used.'

Despite the considerable responsibility that most project managers carry, they generally do not have the formal hierarchical authority to deliver projects. Rather, they have project authority, empowering them to make decisions about project objectives, policies, schedule and budgets, but cannot give direct orders to back up the decisions.

This balance of power is further described in Chapter 1, in terms of project manager and functional manager joint accountability and performance evaluation.

PROJECT MANAGEMENT METHODOLOGIES

Methods are the techniques or arrangements of work in a particular field or subject. A methodology is a system of methods and principles used in a particular discipline.

The practice of project management, as in any other discipline, requires a sound management approach based on consistent and repetitive processes. Process alone does not form a methodology. For a methodology to be complete, it must contain a system of methods, rules, processes and document templates.

An organization's development in project management is often reflected in the consistent application of a project management methodology. Benefits flow from the repetitive application of an organization-wide methodology, suited to the needs of the projects and the culture of the organization. For example, applying a rigid and detailed methodology in a creative, 'blue skies' type of environment will soon be resisted and will lose credibility.

Methodologies must focus equally on the business as well as on project requirements. A methodology that leans too much in one direction or the other tends to misdirect the efforts of project participants. Inexperienced project managers will place a greater emphasis on applying the methodology meticulously, irrespective of the cost to apply it and without consideration of benefits. Detailed application of methodologies invariably requires core team members and other project participants to plan, monitor and report at too fine a level. Protests soon arise as an inordinate amount of time is spent on project management requirements and too little time on project work.

Rather than over-emphasizing detail, a series of steps arranged as a guideline will allow project managers the latitude to adapt and modify the steps without compromising consistency.

Standardized methodology advantages

Toney and Powers, in their research report *Best Practices of Project Management Groups in Large Functional Organizations*[87], discuss the advantages of standardized methodologies under the following headings:

- **Efficiency** – A methodology improves the project organization's efficiency, resulting in a favourable impact on the business bottom-line. Project delivery on time, within cost, and meeting user needs ensures that the return on investment specified in the business case is achievable. Each project does not have to reinvent the methodology every time project planning is undertaken.
- **Reduced training** – The time to train new and inexperienced project managers is reduced considerably as there is a common approach and process in place around which the training can be structured.
- **Improved project predictability** – Business planning relies on a high degree of predictability in operations. Projects, on the other hand, experience a high degree of variability. Having project delivery predictability brings stability to the planning and management of the business.
- **Stakeholder confidence** – Project success can only be measured by stakeholder satisfaction. Stakeholder confidence is essential in building favourable perceptions. A clear and appropriate methodology that is correctly applied builds confidence and creates an aura of certainty.
- **Project success** – Methodology application is about risk reduction and increasing the probability of goal achievement. Many different industries have experienced improved goal achievement associated with methodology application.
- **Common terminology** – A standardized methodology provides a common vocabulary, including key terminology. Improved communications enhance project efficiency and stakeholder perceptions. The potential for errors is reduced and project participant demoralization associated with rework is minimized.
- **Common frame of reference** – It provides a common frame of reference for all project participants. When disputes arise over interpretation, the common frame of reference is important in the process of resolution.
- **Easy to understand** – Business and projects are complex enough without the addition of complexity and ambiguity in a methodology. Project participants at times envelop the project with jargon, creating an environment where only those 'in the know' feel comfortable. An easy to understand methodology will avoid this behaviour.
- **Professionalism** – A well-developed methodology presents a professional image internally as well as outside the organization. Structured presentations and proposals are easy to prepare and deliver. It aids project managers in easily presenting the concepts and status of the project to stakeholders.
- **Evaluation** – The formalized steps of the methodology make possible a common frame of project evaluation. For example, business case development can now be compared and evaluated across several different types of projects. Results of project audits across the organization can be compared, and meaningful interpretations and conclusions can be made.

There is a tendency to regard a single tool, such as a critical path analysis (CPA), as a methodology. CPA is a tool that could form part of a methodology, but it cannot itself be the methodology. This tendency causes the perception that specific planning software packages are complete methodologies. The impression is that they endow the project practitioner with all that is required in respect of a methodology.

A sound methodology should address each of the nine areas of project knowledge across the project life cycle. It should be capable of adaptation and integration into other business processes and procedures. It must be acceptable to those who will use it and, above all, it must be simple to follow. Rather than being prescriptive, a good methodology will be more of a guideline. It will be systematic and logical and each part should fit together to form a cohesive whole. Objective Directed Project Management (ODPM™), which is described in Part III, is based on the above criteria. ODPM supports the Business Focused Project Management (BFPM™) and Wrappers™ approach to form a total methodology to handle the business of projects.

The Project Management Institute's PMBOK® Guide[73] contains a set of processes which, when logically linked, create part of a methodology. With the addition of templates, tools and techniques, a methodology can be developed. The PMBOK® Guide leans heavily towards the use of critical path analysis as a planning tool and most of the processes revolve around its use. It serves its purpose admirably as a guideline to the background, bodies of knowledge, and processes of project management. It provides a set of best practices of project management. The authors have based much of the detailed project planning phase of ODPM on the contents of the PMBOK® Guide.

Although the PMBOK® Guide[73] process is comprehensive, it is less explicit in the areas of the business interface and the integration of project outputs into the business. The value of project management is that it better positions the organization to achieve stated business objectives and hence its strategies. Project managers have at times alienated business functions by imposing methodologies and process detail that are inappropriate. This creates the impression that project management is all about filling out forms and process control rather than facilitating the delivery process and integration with business. The following In Practice case expands on this concern.

In practice...

Aligning methodology with project management maturity

The authors witnessed a situation in a large service-driven organization where a Project Support Office (PSO) was established to assist with the project management of an important national programme. As the organization had little experience in project management, and no methodology and systems in place, the PSO faced a major challenge.

The need for immediate assistance was high as the three-year programme was well into its first year. While supporting a large number of project managers with varying needs, it became clear that a methodology was urgently required as each project was required to go through a similar process. An important input to the design of the methodology was a project management maturity (PMM) survey done across all sections and levels of the organization. The PMM of an organization is determined or assessed through applying a process and model that considers the project management tools, techniques and processes used in the management of projects. The survey revealed that, on a scale of 1 (ad hoc project management) to 5 (sustained project management), the organization's PMM was somewhere between 1 and 2.

Despite the PMM survey results, the PSO developed a methodology more suited to an organization at level 4 or 5. The methodology developed was based on best practice project management. This was understandable from the PSO's perspective as they were a group of dedicated professionals whose purpose was to deliver best practice project management support to all projects, while pursuing excellence in project management.

As the programme unfolded it became clear that the project management methodology requirements were too onerous and that project managers were reluctant to apply them. The methodology was comprehensive and detailed, requiring considerable data input, and the resulting reports focused on detailed numbers and not on results. Comments from project participants were that the methodology was like 'using a four-pound hammer to drive in a tack'.

The PSO's response to the above was perhaps predictable: 'The projects must be slipping behind schedule because of poor project planning and the lack of diligent methodology application. If only the programme manager would issue an instruction that all projects must conform to the PSO standards and methodology.'

The programme manager would issue repeated instructions compelling all to use the methodology. In spite of this, the adherence to the methodology was haphazard and sporadic. The programme manager called a meeting with the PSO to assess the situation.

The meeting revealed that the customers of the PSO services had not been consulted on what an appropriate methodology should contain. This is not an unusual situation when an organization is new to project management, as inexperienced project managers would be hard pressed to state what their needs would be in terms of a methodology. Also, in their enthusiasm the PSO staff had not designed at, say, PMM level 2 with a process improvement strategy for the next few years.

On the programme manager's instruction, the PSO developed a new business-focused project management methodology that was owned by the organization project managers and implemented nationally. The new methodology was targeted at PMM level 2 to 2.5 and is delivering the type of benefits expected. The PSO has regained its credibility and is now delivering excellent support organization-wide.

Important lessons…

1. Always be driven by customer needs, even when the customer is not knowledgeable. The responsibility of those who are knowledgeable is to guide the customer who is new to concepts and methods of project management.
2. Customer ownership of new processes and methods is essential. Unless the client perceives value, the project management methodology will not be used.
3. When developing a new methodology, consider the organization's capability to implement it effectively.

4. Enforcing a methodology that aligns poorly with the needs and culture of the organization will not yield the desired results.
5. The PSO must guard against their own enthusiasm when developing the methodology, as it must meet the customers' needs and not their own.
6. Resistance to the application of project management methods should not be brushed aside as 'because the methodology is not being followed correctly, their project is in trouble'.

THE ORGANIZATIONAL LEVELS

In project management, as in general management, various levels can be identified. The following three levels are used in this book:

● strategic (upper management);
● tactical (project and functional management);
● operational (project team level).

At the strategic level, a project is integrated into the overall business by defining how the project's purpose meets business objectives and strategies. At this level, the change required is specified. The strategic level is the owner or upper management level – they are concerned with the formulation of strategy. Strategy brings about change, and change is implemented through projects. The owner or upper management manages change.

At the tactical level, tactics for achieving the purpose or change are developed. The flow of results or deliverables is defined and managed by the project manager and functional manager. Project management is concerned with the tactics required to implement the changes (projects) specified by the top level. Project managers manage a series of results (objectives) which, when achieved, will take them closer to the final objective – the change required. The functional manager is concerned with resourcing specialists to the project and the technical inputs to the project.

At the operational level, an operational plan (sequence of activities) is developed for achieving each element (result) of the tactical plan. This level is primarily the domain of the project team. The project team is responsible for actually executing the work (activities) needed to deliver the results required. Functional managers manage team members who deliver work to achieve project activities.

The levels themselves do interface with each other and often overlap, depending on the management style of sponsors and project and functional managers. It is important to note that there is close communication between the levels but as a rule no interference by one level in the objectives of the other.

These organizational levels form part of the Wrappers model explained in Chapter 4. The strategic level spans the Strategic and Business Wrappers, while the tactical level is within the Project Wrapper. The operational level is contained in the ODPM process at the heart of the model.

BRINGING PROJECT MANAGEMENT PARTS TOGETHER

In this section, the five distinct parts of project management, as discussed in Chapters 1 and 2, are brought together as shown in Figure 2.5. The parts are interpreted from left to right as follows:

- *Management.* The first block shows the functions of management (PLOCC). The capacity to manage is a prerequisite of project management.
- *The project management knowledge areas.* The next block shows the nine project management bodies of knowledge. These are the areas of knowledge that a competent project manager should possess. They are also the dimensions that must be managed effectively.
- *Organization.* This block represents the organization levels within which the project must operate, as explained in the previous section. As projects are temporary and flexible, these levels do not precisely align themselves with the permanent functional structure.

   The two triangles in the background signify the top-down and bottom-up nature of project management and project communications. They also indicate the delegation of authority and responsibility down the project organization, and responsibility and accountability up the line.

   The horizontal lines separating the levels indicate a delineation of function and absence of interference between the levels. The two-way arrows indicate firstly the communications between the levels and secondly that these levels are permeable in terms of roles. They also show that all formal communications between operations and upper management/owner occur through the project management level – the project management level is the integrator.
- *Time and phases.* The project life-cycle diagram shows the basic project phases and how resource requirements change over the project's life.
- *Process.* The process line running from beginning to end indicates that project management is a process or series of related processes. It also indicates that the project management process is what threads all the components of the diagram together from start to end.

Finally, project management is the process-driven management (PLOCC) of all areas of the project (PMBOK®), its context and environment, at all organizational levels over time and through all phases. Viewing project management in this wider context develops an appreciation of the challenges that project participants face in delivering and integrating projects into the business.

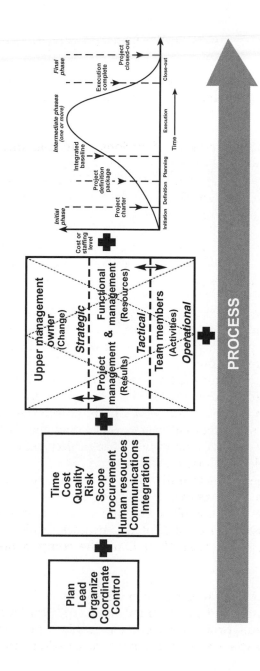

Figure 2.5 Integrated project management

Part II

Focusing Projects on the Business

3

Projects and strategic linkages

The invisible assumption of management is the focus on doing. People are selected because they get things done. But, while doing is variable, being is constant. The trouble is that the being of people and organizations is hard to move. As long as people's radar are tuned into doing, you have no place to get hold of the underlying issues.

Richard Pascale (1938–), US management educator and author

INTRODUCTION

Part I of this book focused on the basic building blocks of projects and project management. It viewed a project as being singular and tactical. Part II of this book focuses on bringing the business of projects and operations closer together, using processes already owned and driven by the organization. Projects are viewed as being plural and strategic. Part II consists of three chapters covering the following topics:

- This chapter identifies the need for linking projects to strategy and introduces the concept of Business Focused Project Management (BFPM). It also addresses the paradoxes that upper management and project managers face in the management of projects. These paradoxes lead us to a number of best practice rules that can generally be applied to a wide spectrum of projects.
- Chapter 4 discusses BFPM in more detail and introduces the Wrappers™ concept. This concept models the project processes as they flow from organization imperatives to business strategies and on to project approaches.

● Chapter 5 provides guidelines, processes and techniques for introducing and using BFPM in an organization.

THE NEED FOR STRATEGIC LINKAGES

Within business enterprises, projects seldom exist in isolation. Business projects originate as a result of change initiatives arising from the organization's strategic and business plans and, as such, exist alongside operations and within a portfolio of other projects. If projects are to be focused on the business then the linkages between the organization's strategic and business plans need to be placed in context and their importance recognized.

In developing a business focus for projects, organizations must consider a wide range of issues and follow a process that enables the correct projects to be undertaken in support of organization strategy. These issues include:

● upper management support for project management;
● cross-functional interface with projects;
● project selection and prioritization;
● portfolio management;
● upper management interface with project managers;
● the project support office (PSO);
● project manager career paths;
● the learning organization.

Organizations that do not adequately address these issues or do not formalize the linkages between strategies and projects find that projects seem to pop up across the organization in an uncontrolled manner. This results in confusion and consequent failure to achieve the desired project results. Confusion and failure arises from:

● a lack of clarity as to how projects align and link to the organization's strategy;
● the apparent absence of a business process for selecting the projects;
● project priorities constantly changing;
● upper management's apparent lack of awareness of the number, scope and benefits of the projects being undertaken.

The arising confusion and project failure rate results in:

● project participants feeling that they are working not only on many unnecessary projects but also at cross-purposes with other areas of the business;
● projects being seen as black holes into which money and people disappear and from which, with a bit of luck, something may emerge;
● organizations attempting too many projects outside of their capacity and capability;

- a general weariness with projects and a lack of motivation to complete them (project fatigue);
- a misunderstanding of urgency vs. priority;
- doing the 'wrong things, right' instead of doing the 'right things, right';
- doing 'less with more' rather than doing 'more with less'.

Project success and failure are discussed in Appendix C, as well as a set of typical project problems and solutions, and the reader is referred to that appendix for a fuller discussion of project success and failure. An understanding of project success and failure adds to the learning about what to focus on to enhance the value projects bring to the organization.

Linking projects and strategy gives projects a strategic and business focus that goes a long way towards resolving many of these problems. Combining a strategic focus with a business process for selecting and prioritizing projects is an important step in creating an environment for successful projects.

The authors have developed an approach, Business Focused Project Management (BFPM™), to achieve effective management of corporate projects from their conceptualization through to the delivery of the desired business outcomes. BFPM takes an organization-wide view of project management – focusing on the needs of the owners, while integrating closely with the requirements of executives and upper managers.

WHAT IS BFPM?

Simply put, Business Focused Project Management is the application of project management to projects linked to the organization's strategies in order to deliver those strategies in an effective manner – in effect, managing the organization by projects.

Paul Dinsmore, project manager and author, in an article 'Toward corporate project management' (*PM Network*, March and June, 1996), describes this philosophy as follows: 'Managing Organizations By Projects is an organizational mindset. It is a way of thinking about business. It means the company is project-driven, that corporate goals are targeted and achieved by managing a web of simultaneous projects, including operational improvement and organizational transformation programs as well as traditional development projects.' He goes further to say: 'From the MOBP view, organizations are "portfolios of projects". Therefore, the aggregate result of an organization's projects becomes the company's bottom line. Mission, visions, strategies, objectives and goals are transformed into company-wide programs that translate corporate intentions into actions. These programs are, in turn, broken into projects to be managed by corporate staff or professional project management personnel.'

BFPM subscribes to this definition and implements it through the Wrappers™ model (Chapter 4) and the ODPM™ project management process (Part III). Benefits and advantages experienced by organizations applying BFPM include the following:

- a more goal or objective-oriented organization; this mindset permeates through the organization from the strategic level, through the tactical level, to operations;
- a speeding up of, and greater contribution to, the implementation of the organization's strategic objectives;
- a strengthening of the project environment by providing structures and processes to conceive, execute and validate projects effectively;
- the dynamism of the organization is facilitated through the provision of the means to adjust project strategies to changing scenarios through project selection and prioritization;
- allows all levels of management and the core project team to contribute to the achievement of the organization's strategies;
- allows for the measurement of both project performance and progress towards achieving strategic goals.

What businesses need is focused strategic planning coupled with disciplined action through projects and this is essentially what BFPM offers.

The following highlights the major differences between BFPM and traditional project management:

BFPM	Project Management
Strategic	Tactical
Integration, coordination and control of multiple projects (plural)	The management of a project (singular)
Organization-wide and cross-functional	Project-wide and not necessarily cross-functional
An operating environment or framework	A discipline
A business philosophy	A specialist function

BASIC CONCEPTS AND DEFINITIONS

In order to gain a better understanding of BFPM it is necessary to define three basic concepts: strategy, project selection and prioritization, and project portfolio. These concepts are expanded on in subsequent chapters.

Strategy

Strategic effectiveness is achieved by setting the right objectives or goals and implementing them. Some form of strategic planning of this nature is done at all levels of organizations. For clarity and simplicity, the authors have adopted the following terminology in this book:

- Strategic planning at the organization level results in a set of organization imperatives.

- These are converted into business strategies by the business managers.
- Business strategies are in turn carried out through projects whose strategy is the project approach or plan.

A discussion of strategic management is outside the scope of this book, but the interface between strategic management and project management is relevant.

Organization and business strategies are essential to BFPM. If they are not present or well defined, then there cannot be projects focused on the business.

Project selection and prioritization

Project selection is the process of evaluating individual projects or groups of projects and then choosing to implement some of them so that the strategic objectives of the organization will be achieved.

Project prioritization is the ranking of the selected projects into some order of importance or urgency. It defines the projects' order of execution and prioritized demand on the organization's resources such as people and money.

The criteria against which projects are tested for selection and prioritization are derived from the organization and business strategies in place at the time. Since these can change depending on changing scenarios, the project selection and prioritization processes need to be applied continuously against all projects in an organization, whether initiated or not.

Project portfolio

The project portfolio represents those projects that best meet the strategic/business needs of an organization. The projects contained in the portfolio arise from the project selection and prioritization processes. The portfolio is managed in a manner similar to that of an investment portfolio; projects are added, 'invested' in, replaced and terminated in accordance with the value or expected business impact the portfolio delivers to the organization. The project portfolio is continuously monitored and evaluated as well as continuously being passed through the project and selection and prioritization processes.

PROJECT PARADOXES

The authors have spent more than 25 years lecturing, training, consulting, practising and mentoring in the field of project management. During this time, they have observed thousands of managers involved in developing and implementing projects. These observations revealed a pattern of management contradictions experienced in the delivery of projects. On closer analysis, the authors discovered that these management tensions were largely similar across different industries, yet they varied in the extent of the challenges they posed to the organization. In established project industries, such as engineering, the contradictions created fewer problems, while in the newer project areas, such as business, they posed considerable obstacles.

Rather than regarding the contradictions or tensions as dilemmas, viewing them as a set of paradoxes reveals some insights into project management and highlights best practice principles useful in the business of projects.

What are paradoxes?

> The way of paradoxes is the way of truth.
> Oscar Wilde (1854–1900), playwright, toast of London, convict

The *Collins English Dictionary and Thesaurus* (1998) defines a paradox as a 'seemingly self-contradictory statement that is or may be true'.

Religious tenets have often been expressed as paradoxes. They encourage people to reflect deeply on seeming contradictions and, in doing so, to reach deeper understanding and meaning. The same principles can be applied to project management. Two opposite tensions, thesis and antithesis, will develop a synthesis. What must be understood is that the synthesis is not merely a compromise of the two extremes but could be a novel solution.

In his book *The Age of Paradox* (1995, Harvard Business School Press), Charles Handy states that business paradoxes will increase both in number and in kind. When faced with a paradox, Handy's advice to managers is that they 'can, and should, reduce the starkness of some of the contradictions, minimize the inconsistencies, understand the puzzles in the paradox, but [they] cannot make them disappear completely, or escape them'. The authors concur with this view.

Paradoxes in the project context

Project paradoxes appear to have the same characteristics as those stated by Handy. The starkness of the paradox can be reduced through an improved understanding of project processes and the business context in which they operate. In an environment of uncertainty, the paradoxes bring some focus and balance to opposites and create a platform of better understanding for the wise project manager to build on.

The challenge is to manage the paradoxes and not to avoid them in the early stages. If the paradoxes are viewed as too difficult and therefore not addressed, the project will move down a path that is not sound. Later, the project team will have to deal with the consequences of this avoidance, and often it is too difficult or expensive to change course. The difference between a competent project manager and a novice is the deeper understanding of these management tensions.

Delivering project change in the fluid, fast-moving business environment requires some form of stability, which leads us to the First Paradox.

Paradox 1: Project change requires stability

In the absence of essential elements of stability, change will result in confusion and turmoil on the project. Project sponsors and managers need 'islands of stability' to guide teams and to ensure the integration of project deliverables into the organization. Without this stability, project results will not align with organization strategy and stakeholder expectations. Project participants and stakeholders will have difficulty comprehending the project's contribution to the organization's vision, resulting in unproductive activity and high levels of frustration and demotivation.

Typical elements of stability are:

- a sustainable organization vision, mission, critical success factors (CSFs), goals and objectives;
- a recognized organization culture;
- a project mission, CSFs, and objectives that are aligned with organization strategy;
- a clear understanding of what the organization will change to as a result of the project;
- a well-developed change strategy that maps the transition from the current state to the future state;
- clear communication on what will not change and how the project will contribute to this.

The first point above, and largely the second, is usually present in the organization and automatically flows into the project core team's attitude and understanding. The remaining points are the responsibility of the sponsor and core team to develop, communicate and facilitate.

These islands of stability will assist the project as it navigates through uncharted and often treacherous waters. They form the basis of project strategy or general approach, ensuring that planning is objective directed (ODPM process as discussed in Part III).

BFPM recognizes that business projects grow from fuzzy to clear through progressive elaboration (see Chapter 1), thus leading us to the second paradox.

Paradox 2: Clarity is achieved by embracing fuzziness

BFPM is different from the classic project management approach taken in construction/engineering projects, which have a relatively high degree of certainty at early stages.

In business projects, team members often find themselves moving around in fog, searching for guiding beacons to point them in the right direction, as discussed in Chapter 1. As the team reaches each consecutive beacon, the fog progressively lifts, revealing more light. The project team needs to accept this fuzziness as a normal state in the project process.

The project team's recognition of the fuzzy to clear concept is essential for building a stable project, but to ensure project results the executive, upper and functional management must also understand and support the concept. A cultural change will be required to shift from the rigid approach of fixing time, cost and performance at early stages, to one where the project team is encouraged to develop the project from fuzzy to clear.

A fuzzy to clear approach requires:

- progressive elaboration on what business results the project will deliver;
- project sponsor and upper management understanding and support;
- an organization planning process that is guided by strategy and sets the business direction for the required changes;
- supporting and protecting the project team from the pressure of delivering something that is perceived to be correct rather than taking the time to elaborate the project;
- a fine balance between the extent of research and planning and implementing the project.

The fuzzy to clear concept does not imply that project scope is allowed to change freely with no limitations; rather it is reviewed and improved at important points along the project life cycle. This approach also requires business case benefits and costs to be reviewed at the same points, with 'go/ no-go' decisions rigorously applied at the important points along the project life cycle.

Another characteristic of construction/engineering projects that distinguishes them from business projects is that the major outputs or deliverables are tangible. In cross-functional business projects, the outputs are often intangible and dependent on the experiences and perceptions of stakeholders. Such projects include restructuring an organization, customer service improvement programmes, management development training and business process improvements. In these projects, changes are sought in people's actions, organization culture and stakeholder perceptions.

BFPM enables us to build our project management plans around owner-defined business requirements, which are measurable in terms of business results. The focus is on aligning the project results with the organization strategies, rather than on project management processes, which leads us to the third paradox.

Paradox 3: Business results are the measures of project success

This third paradox directs us to where our focus should be. Project success must be perceived and measured in terms of business results (effectiveness), supported by the project process (efficiency). An efficient process is necessary but alone is insufficient to ensure success.

Karl von Clausewitz, in *On War*[92], offers much food for thought. His theory of war is just as applicable today as it was 150 years ago. It states: 'The key to success is correctly identifying those few crucial, limited areas on which outcome depends. And then concentrate overwhelming, superior force at those decisive points whilst being defensively protected elsewhere.'

It is a known fact in business that most attention is paid to the things that get measured. The same is true for projects. Therefore, a project must align with organization strategy, identify its own strategies, develop critical success factors (the things that must go right), undertake risk analyses and establish performance measures that are results focused. It is then the role of upper management to focus efforts on those crucial areas of success.

From then on, monitoring, measuring and taking corrective action are needed to ensure that the critical areas are achieved and project results delivered. Project measures that merely evaluate project management efficiency and not business results will misdirect upper management, the sponsor, the project core team and stakeholders.

When organizations have many cross-functional initiatives, functional staff may work on several projects as well as undertaking departmental work. As well as facing extra stress, staff often perceive their career promotion opportunities and personal growth to be in jeopardy. This environment is not conducive to team work as individual loyalties lie with their functional department. Project work is strongly reliant on teams, yet it is the individual member that makes the difference. BFPM recognizes the fourth paradox.

Paradox 4: Build teams by focusing on the individual

In order to build teams, individual motivation needs to be understood and nurtured. Nicholas[67] describes project work as stimulating, satisfying, and providing a sense of achievement. The project mission, objectives and critical success factors are achievement motivators, while project participation encourages decision making that enhances participative ownership. Tools and techniques such as the deliverables breakdown structure, milestone objective chart, milestone responsibility matrix, critical success factors, risk analysis and contract development can also be motivators if team members are closely involved with their development. When these motivators are combined and personal rewards are in line with personal and career aspirations, the result is a set of powerful personal motivators. These tools and techniques are discussed in Part III, ODPM, and in Appendix B.

The constant pressure of achieving project products and results is highly motivating to many people. This, combined with participation in decision making, helps to avoid the stress and conflict that will exist in a non-participative environment or one that exerts excessive pressure.

Peter Viall (in *Managing Business and Engineering Projects*, Nicholas[67]) studied a large number of teams that 'perform at levels of excellence far beyond those of comparable systems'. The consistent factor was that these teams knew what they had to do and were committed to doing it. Team members must be clear why the team exists and what their role is.

Viall identified time, feeling and focus as the three characteristics always present in the behaviour and attitudes of leaders and members of high-performing teams. He encouraged would-be leaders to 'Seek constantly to do what is right and what is needed in the system (focus). Do it in terms of your energy (time). Put your whole psyche into it (feeling).'

In successful teams, the leaders and members devote a large amount of their energy and time to the task, with full commitment for the duration of the initiative. They feel strongly about the achievement of the objectives and their purpose. They openly defend the project and the benefits it will deliver. They focus on critical areas, important issues, and have a clear list of priorities.

BFPM recognizes that the goals of individuals and those of the organization must be in reasonable harmony if project results and personal growth are both to be achieved. Upper management, project sponsors and managers need to be sensitive to team member aspirations and their motivational needs in terms of rewards and growth.

Although projects are achieved by vigorous horizontal management, minimizing the vertical role has serious consequences on project performance. This challenge is introduced in the fifth paradox.

Paradox 5: Integrate horizontally with a vertical focus

BFPM assists us in managing cross-functional projects in organizations that deliver services and create products.

Irrespective of the roles project managers and functional managers play in a project, there are always horizontal and vertical interfaces. BFPM clearly recognizes the need to include in the project process functional managers who will be either directly responsible for performing project work or responsible for providing resources to be directed by project managers. Functional managers are the custodians of resources in their areas; however, they may also be responsible for delivering part of the project work.

When functional managers perceive that the project manager is cutting them off from the project through lack of communication, not seeking subject matter expert advice, or by taking decisions that rightfully belong in functional areas, they will withdraw support for the project. Regaining their trust and support thereafter can be a difficult and time-consuming undertaking. For project managers this is an experience to avoid, as it can considerably diminish the chances of project success.

The challenge to upper management is to find a structure that meets the needs of the project as well as those of the functional departments. Structure has an important influence on culture and behaviour, accountability, authorities, roles and responsibilities, functional boundaries, policies and procedures. From a project management perspective, the interface between the temporary project structure and the permanent organization structure, and more specifically with the functional managers, is of utmost importance. Chapter 1 discusses organization and project structure.

In Chapter 1, the authors discuss uniqueness as an important characteristic of projects. The unique factors of a project are often new or unknown to the organization. Unless the unknown is explored and understood, the project core team will not be able to plan and deliver the project with certainty. This introduces the sixth paradox.

Paradox 6: Focus on the unknown to achieve certainty

The most distinct difference between projects and operations is the unknown and there-fore uncertain aspects of projects versus the familiarity and repetitiveness of operations. In the experience of the authors, which is validated by post-implementation audits, poor project performance is directly linked to the inability of the project leader to identify and manage uncertainty.

Focusing on uncertainty requires a continual search for 'what is different', 'what has not been done before that can harm the project' and 'unique factors that need addressing through a proactive risk approach'.

The challenge is to seek out carefully what is new or different in terms of people, products and processes. These will form natural risk areas requiring concentrated management and continual evaluation during project execution.

Managing and integrating uncertainty or risk is one of the fundamental competencies of project leaders and team members. Focusing on those areas of uncertainty aids in the achievement of certainty.

Managing these paradoxes is not easy, yet they are crucial to successful project outcomes. Flexible yet focused project management is essential to manage effectively the changes required to lead organizations into the new millennium.

In practice...

Project measures align with business

The authors witnessed a project that involved amalgamating two major production facili-ties 200 km apart into one facility. As a project it was challenging, complex and unique in many ways. Neither of the two facilities' management teams had any experience of a project of this size and complexity. A project sponsor, manager and team were appointed from within the facility where the amalgamation was to take place. The project team was trained in the basics of project management, with a good dose of time, cost and quality criteria and trade-offs. Project management software was purchased and time planning became a major focus, supported by detailed cost analysis and quality control of project work. The project manager and team felt that they were on top of the situation.

Weekly project reports were professionally drawn up and presented promptly to the project sponsor, who was also head of finance. The sponsor, project manager and team had a cordial relationship, and all went well for the first six months, while the project was in definition and design stage. When construction commenced there was a marked increase in conflict between the plant production and the project participants. Access to areas for construction was not available as promised, contractors were delayed and the requests for extensions of time began. Production staff complained about the state of the environment in areas where project work was being undertaken. This conflict situation led to the major stakeholder calling a meeting of the key project participants and production managers.

The CEO of the major stakeholder set out in no uncertain terms the problems that production staff were experiencing, and demanded action from the project team. The sponsor defended the project position, explaining that they were trying to deliver the project to budgeted time and cost and thus position the facility to achieve the business case benefits as promised. It was then that the difference between process performance measures and business performance measures dawned on the project manager. The CEO pointed out that it would not matter if a perfect project was delivered on time, at cost and to quality if the combined production output of the two facilities was not maintained, or quality was impaired by the construction work. The customer impact and the associated market share loss would make any project success irrelevant. The priorities had clearly been set, and stakeholder performance criteria determined.

Life on the project changed after that meeting. Production output and quality took precedence over project process performance measures. Project reports concentrated on measures such as production output and quality in areas where construction work was under way, and included input from production managers. Project criteria of time, cost, quality and scope were still reported on but within the context of the business. They became supportive measures rather than the leading measures.

The project was delivered successfully, notwithstanding a 10 per cent cost overrun and 20 per cent time overrun. The stakeholder was delighted that the customers from the two plants were not affected by the amalgamation, and market share had remained at expected levels. The efforts of the project participants and the production staff were publicly acknowledged.

Important lessons...

1. Determining stakeholder success criteria is far more important than success criteria determined by the project team.
2. Each project is unique in terms of:
   - the changes it brings to an organization;
   - stakeholders and their interests;
   - the mix of team members;
   - its relationship with the parent organization.

   Therefore, effort is required to understand what criteria stakeholders value.
3. Project teams must clearly understand why their project exists in the organization: to position the organization to achieve its business objectives.

And the trouble is, if you don't risk anything, you risk even more.

Erica Jong (1942–), writer

4

The Wrappers™ model

Just to conceive bold new strategies is not enough. The general manager must also be able to translate his or her strategic vision into concrete steps that 'get things done'.

Richard G Hamermesh

INTRODUCTION

This chapter presents a model, the Wrappers™ model, that links strategy, business process, project management and a project delivery process. This model, shown in Figure 4.1, represents the Business Focused Project Management (BFPM™) approach discussed in the previous chapter and was designed to assist in alleviating the concerns expressed in that chapter.

THE WRAPPERS MODEL

The Wrappers model provides a framework for the integration of the organization's strategic, business and project management levels. At the core of the model is the Objective Directed Project Management (ODPM™) process. Each level 'wraps' its functionality around the immediate inner one in an integrated and linked manner.

Other than providing a framework for integration, the model serves a number of additional purposes as follows. It:

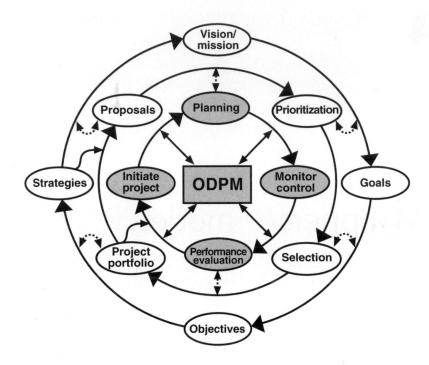

Figure 4.1 The Wrappers model

- provides a framework for the building of an enterprise-wide project management environment;
- places all the components of a business-focused project management approach into context and perspective;
- shows the path to be taken for the effective and fast transformation of strategies to business outcomes and project outputs;
- indicates what metrics must be in place to measure effectively the delivery of results and achievement of goals;
- provides a discipline for the delivery of strategic objectives through the execution of projects;
- shows how projects are progressively elaborated (Chapter 1) from concept to delivery;
- when populated with processes, templates, tools, techniques, dashboards and systems, it forms a complete methodology for Business Focused Project Management.

The implementation of BFPM guided by the Wrappers model in an organization is discussed in the next chapter and in Part III.

The following sections explain each wrapper layer in the model.

You've got to put your heart in the business and the business in your heart.
Thomas Watson

THE STRATEGIC WRAPPER

Where there is no vision the people perish.
The Bible, Proverbs 29:18

Figure 4.2 The Strategic Wrapper

The outer wrapper is the Strategic Wrapper representing the organization's vision, mission, goals and objectives and is primarily owned by the executive level of the organization, who are responsible for setting organization strategy.

An organization's strategic planning develops the vision, drives the mission, and states which objectives/outcomes are necessary for success. Organizational strategy is converted into action through business strategies (general approach/direction), which in turn enable goal setting and identification of a potential portfolio of projects.

The Strategic Wrapper further defines the relationship between the organization and its environment, identifying the organization's strengths, weaknesses, opportunities and threats (SWOT). The context includes social, technical, economic and environmental issues, political/public perceptions, and operational and legal aspects of the organization's functions (STEEPOL). The SWOT and STEEPOL analysis forms an integral part of organizational strategic planning.

In the absence of organizational strategic planning, projects will deliver results that are not aligned with desired business outcomes. Portfolio and project performance measures will exist in a vacuum created by the lack of strategic direction.

THE BUSINESS WRAPPER

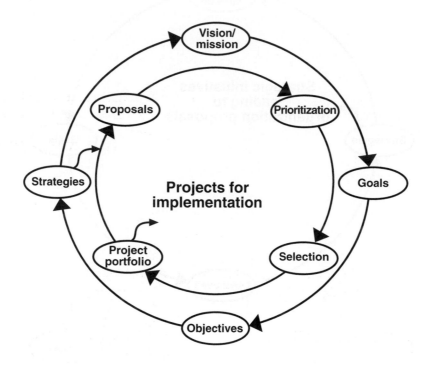

Figure 4.3   The Business Wrapper

The middle wrapper is the Business Wrapper and is owned by upper management. It receives project proposals from operations and functions, and considers them in a selection and prioritization process. These proposals are prepared in support of the organization's strategic imperatives and are generated by departments or at the executive level.

The result of the selection and prioritization process is a portfolio of projects. The executive or board sanctions the portfolio of projects, thus committing organization-wide resources. The chief executive officer (CEO) champions the complete portfolio, while executive members or upper management sponsors have the responsibility for ownership of individual projects. This ownership is of utmost importance to successful project delivery.

A Portfolio Council, comprising representatives of the executive and upper management, manages the project portfolio. Portfolio Council members usually own the organization-wide resources required to deliver the projects and therefore have a strong interest in ensuring that only well-scrutinized (selected and prioritized) projects are approved.

Chapter 5 discusses the Portfolio Council role in more detail and the important interface it creates between the executive and the project level. Chapter 5 also covers the selection and prioritization process and the development of proposals and business cases.

THE PROJECT WRAPPER

Faster in almost every case is better. From decision-making to deal-making to communications to product introduction, speed, more often than not ends up being the competitive differentiator.

Jack Welch, CEO, GE

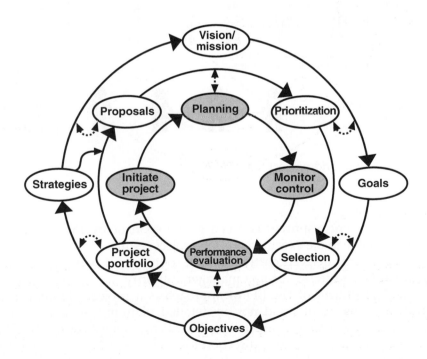

Figure 4.4 The Project Wrapper

The next wrapper is the Project Wrapper, representing the project management level. It is jointly owned by the project sponsors, project managers and participating functional managers. It is here that projects are initiated, planned and executed, and project results integrated into the business. The project manager and core team members primarily manage this level. Subject to the functional managers' mandate, core team members represent their functional areas and coordinate project work in their functional areas. This is illustrated in Figure 4.5.

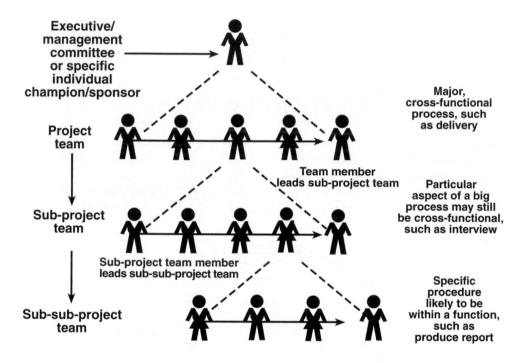

Figure 4.5 Functional and project teams

Authority to implement resources is given to the sponsor by the executive, and the sponsor is accountable to the executive for the project results. Project manager authority to manage the project is derived partly from the sponsor and partly from interpersonal influences. Chapter 2 addresses project manager authority.

An essential component of the BFPM approach is a project planning process that focuses on measurable results and not on detailed planning, which belongs at team level. These results are objective directed as described in ODPM (Part III). They link to the performance measures and give direction to team-level planning. Project managers and team members expand these results to the next level – the task deliverables. Team members can now focus on the work required to achieve the deliverables.

Team members take on the responsibility for planning the work to achieve the deliverables. These deliverables lead to project results, which in turn contribute to the intended business outcomes.

From this planning will flow an understanding of what each individual contributes towards a deliverable, and how their individual performance is measured.

THE ODPM™ PROCESS

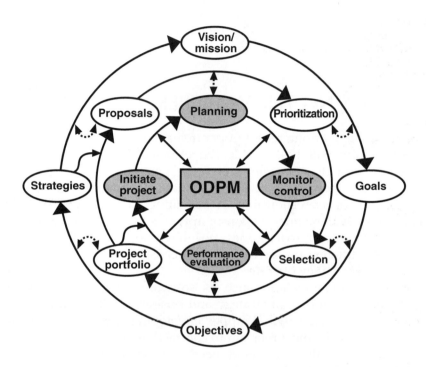

Figure 4.6   The ODPM process

At the heart of the Wrappers model is the Objective Directed Project Management (ODPM™) process. Outputs from the application and management of this process will be project deliverables that are to be handed over to the Project Wrapper and ultimately to the Business Wrapper to be integrated into the business or operationalized. The ODPM process is discussed in detail in Part III.

Effective individual assignment

Effective individual assignment relies on, firstly, a clear understanding of contribution to deliverables, and secondly, a personal commitment to delivering the work assigned. The contract between sponsor, project manager and functional managers facilitates and ensures individual commitment to performance. This is covered further in Part III, Chapters 7 and 8.

Through ODPM, an environment is created where each person on the project understands what he or she must deliver and how his or her performance will be measured. This avoids the uncertainty that often permeates a project as it approaches critical delivery times.

This approach integrates the project deliverables and clearly demonstrates contribution towards business outcomes. It crystallizes cross-functional authority and performance accountability, especially when team members come from various functional areas of the organization.

USING THE WRAPPERS MODEL

Projects making up the portfolio reflect upper management's decisions on the combination of initiatives that will best enable the organization to achieve its strategies. Proposals become projects once they enter the portfolio and a project sponsor is appointed to oversee the project at upper management level. The sponsor in turn appoints a project manager responsible for managing the project process. The ODPM process is activated when the project sponsor appoints the project manager.

The entire Wrappers approach does not have to be applied to all projects. Organizations have different business planning needs, depending on the industry and market segment in which they operate.

For purely project organizations such as software development companies and contractors, the outer wrappers of strategy and business belong mainly in the client's domain. The Project Management Wrapper enveloping the ODPM process and the ODPM process itself are the most relevant to contracting organizations.

Other organizations, on the other hand, need to apply all the levels of the model, as they strive to convert strategies into projects into outcomes.

The conceptualization, selection, prioritization and initiation of projects moves from the outside of the sphere inwards, as do the control mechanisms. The results delivered by the ODPM process are assimilated into the business by moving from the core of the sphere outwards. Likewise, monitoring and reporting move outward from the core. These flows ensure that upper management and the executive are kept informed. Such reporting enables the organization to assess project progress against business cases, ultimately leading towards the achievement of strategy.

Through the progressive elaboration nature of the Wrappers concept, which is also the basis of the ODPM process, BFPM is capable of delivering business-focused results from projects in a fuzzy to clear manner (see Chapter 1).

PERFORMANCE MEASURES ACROSS THE WRAPPERS

> I think it is an immutable law in business that words are words, explanations are explanations, promises are promises – but only performance is reality.
> Harold Geneen (1910–), former Chief Executive,
> International Telephone and Telegraph Company

Performance measures are drawn from organization objectives and goals, and built into the project business case. These measures guide the project team and give direction to results-focused planning. Project performance measures require consideration in terms of the project management process as well as project results.

There is a danger in imposing project management methodologies that direct team members to measure how well the project management process is delivered (efficiency) rather than how well the project business results are being achieved (effectiveness). Although a balance of both is required, project success is determined by stakeholder perception of success. Delivering projects on time, within cost and to specification is only part of the picture. This indicates efficiency, but it is the stakeholders' perception of value to the organization that determines overall success.

Process performance measures are typically (output focused):

- timeliness of deliverables;
- budget versus actual costs;
- product produced to functional specification.

Project business performance measures include (outcome focused):

- project results achieved and integrated into the business;
- contribution to organization goals, objectives and strategies;
- stakeholder satisfaction with process and results.

Technical project managers tend to focus more on process, while business project managers are more concerned with business results. Ideally, a balance between the two is required, determined by the project type, organization culture and systems.

Upper management, and specifically sponsors, must ask for project measures that are wider than the usual process measures. Measuring business results will ensure that both the project core team and functional managers focus on what is important to the organization. Reporting to key stakeholders will become more meaningful and build a positive perception.

An approach to the measurement of both business and process-focused attributes is the use of a project balanced scorecard. This could consist of the following measurements:

- financial measures such as growth, economic value-add, return on capital employed, cost savings, etc;

- project process measures such as cost/time performance, quality, use of resources, etc;
- client measures such as satisfaction, use of product, new clients, retention, market share, etc;
- learning and development measures such as motivation, empowerment, training, team satisfaction, productivity, etc.

The project core team should guard against accepting responsibility for delivering results that they cannot achieve. This is often the case where only operations are in a position to achieve the business results. However, it is the responsibility of the project team to deliver to operations the products that will enable them to achieve the business results. There are exceptions, particularly where a project creates a new product or service, and the project team becomes a new operations section. In this case, the project team effectively hands over to themselves.

In practice...

Software or a solution?

Soft Solutions Ltd is a small, but highly successful, software solutions group. Their focus is to seek business opportunities and develop systems solutions to maximize business opportunities. In the past three years, they have grown from the two founding partners to an organization of 150 people. The organization adopts a flexible, informal approach to management, flowing from the style adopted by the two founding partners. In any organization, growth of this nature is fertile ground for the proliferation of internal and external projects, as business methods, policies and procedures are immature and subject to variability and random application. It was no different at Soft Solutions Ltd.

At present Soft Solutions Ltd is running approximately 40 projects, of which up to 10 are classified as important external projects, and the remainder are medium to small, internally focused projects. The managing partner, Paul, became aware that over the past three months the company performance seemed to have flattened out, and the cash flow position in particular was becoming strained. He figured this was probably attributable to the two large new development projects, which were absorbing considerable resources. This would probably rectify itself once the next progress payments were received.

Being a proactive person, Paul took to the corridor and paid a visit to the financial director. To Paul's surprise, the financial director informed him that the large payment had already been received and captured in the current financial figures. A feeling of disquiet came over Paul as he knew the business well – historically the organization had always been cash flush, but recently it was experiencing a few difficulties in meeting commitments. Walking back to his office, he met one of the project managers who was working on an important internal project. Enquiring about how the project was progressing, he was surprised to hear that in the past six weeks it had stalled, and that the project manager was on a new IT initiative. By the time he reached his office, Paul had decided to request a quick inventory of all current projects, listing the projects as well as the responsible project managers. Within three days the inventory was completed and presented to the two partners. They were surprised at the number of projects under way and spent some time discussing the impact that these projects had on the company. It was clear that all these projects, not just the important external ones, were competing for limited resources. Paul expressed his concern to his partner, Ian, that they did not know where all these projects were in terms of achievements, costs, and what benefits they would deliver and when. They agreed that perhaps they needed some external advice in the area of project management.

A reputable consultant was contacted with experience in advising CEOs on project management within a strategic and business framework. She agreed to meet with Paul and a few managers from his organization.

The meeting was held a week later in Paul's office. Paul, his business analyst, Geoff, and IT Department project manager, Susan, were present. Anya, the consultant, joined the meeting.

Paul: 'My concern is that I don't know where projects in the organization are in terms of delivery, and even worse, I don't know what each of these projects is supposed to deliver to the business. My partner and I need to get a grip on projects, as they are consuming vast amounts of resources. How do I know that the company can sustain all these projects, and, more importantly, should we be undertaking all of them?'

Anya: 'Paul, do you know which projects are mission critical, which are there to support important projects, and which are necessary to keep the company growing, such as R&D initiatives?'

Paul: 'We do know which are our important projects in terms of sales, but that is as far as it goes. We have grown rapidly but our management systems have not. Perhaps Geoff and Susan can expand.'

Geoff: 'Although we have some idea of what's happening in projects, from a business analysis point of view we're at sea. IT appears to be on top of projects, and we supply information as needed. There is no process whereby business analysts' input is mandatory; consequently, we feel projects are at risk. Also, we feel vulnerable that there is no person from the business leading projects.'

Susan: 'We do have a rough idea where all our projects are, and we do use a software package to schedule our projects. What we don't have is some consistent methodology and process that will bring discipline to planning and reporting. Also, I believe that we should have a champion for each project.'

Anya: 'Would it be useful to have a top-down view of all the current projects, grouped into a portfolio of projects? These projects could then be evaluated, prioritized and selected in terms of the value they bring to the organization. The selection process will consider the resource impacts on departments, as well as the cash flow effects on the business. Once a project is selected it is handed over to a champion or sponsor who takes ownership for the business results. The sponsor then appoints a project manager to deliver the project.'

Paul reflected for a moment. How did she know about the resourcing and cash flow pressures? Perhaps the pattern was familiar for fast-growing companies.

Paul: 'That all sounds interesting, but I have a company to run. What I want is a simple system that will tell me where all the initiatives are, so that I can exercise control over this important part of the business.'

Anya: 'We must guard against going down the path of a quick-fix solution, as we would find that such an approach would not deliver the required results. Systems to track project time and cost progress are plentiful – our challenge is to find a high-level top-down approach that gives direction to a portfolio of projects, and then focus on the management of this portfolio. Simultaneously, attention can be given to establishing a simple project management method and process that will assist project participants, project managers and sponsors, and yourself at upper management level.'

Geoff: 'How will this approach bring more business focus to our projects?'

Anya: 'The portfolio of projects ensures that only projects that are aligned to the business strategy, and thus add value to the business, are undertaken. The upper management responsibility to manage the portfolio will ensure that project focus is on business results and not only on a project management process. Recognizing that technology delivers to the business is an important shift that upper management needs to make. Training and educating business project managers is a key strategy required if organizations are serious about business leading technology projects. In the past, too many technology projects have taken on a life of their own and become runaway projects, resulting in major cost overruns, late delivery, and often less functionality. I am not laying the blame at IT's door, but rather at the inability of upper management to lead and control projects in the business.'

Susan: 'I agree with Anya that a major weakness in our organization is the lack of project ownership or sponsorship by the business managers. As we in IT are familiar with the process of developing projects, we tend to move on in the direction we believe to be correct. If the business does not provide direction the project will become technology driven rather than business focused.'

Paul: 'This is all becoming complex. All I need is a simple project management system that will deliver to my needs. Why do we have to get involved with portfolios, sponsors and business project managers? All this jargon is new and could potentially be resisted in the organization. Is there no other way of meeting my needs?'

Important lessons…

1. It is often only when upper management feels uncomfortable about project-related information and impacts that the need for project management is identified. Pressure on business performance, together with the realization that they do not know where key organization initiatives are at, prompts the sudden interest in project management.
2. Upper management, when confronted with a new situation relating to projects, tend to want to grab the nearest and best software package so they can rapidly print out some information. This will give them a feeling of comfort and demonstrate that they are in control.
3. If an organization is serious about projects delivering to the business, business project managers will need to be developed to lead the IT and other cross-functional project members through the process of project management. They will also need to demonstrate key project management competencies, as discussed in Chapter 1. Project management will become an important and valued competency in the organization.
4. The differing project management needs of the various participants and key stake-holders have to be carefully considered in the development of a meaningful project management solution. Paul's desire to have a simple project management system to meet his objectives is driven by the need for rapid information, as he cannot wait for a comprehensive strategy that could take months or years to implement. Anya has an interesting challenge on her hands.

CONCLUSION

Strategies and projects go hand-in-hand. Projects achieve strategies but do not create them. Projects can only be initiated as a result of business needs and strategies. The authors have noted that many organizations devote much time and effort to formulating strategies and business plans, but relatively little to their implementation through projects. Strategies need to be rapidly translated into daily work if they are to have any effect. The ability to execute strategic initiatives quickly and effectively is fast becoming a critical business attribute as companies respond to a rapid pace of change.

Building an environment that supports project management is essential for organizations that are serious about project management. The processes represented by the Wrappers model are vital and should not be ignored if an environment conducive to successful project management is to be created. The Wrappers model cannot effectively operate in an organization that does not value and support project management as a key managerial competency. As a model, Wrappers lives through the sincere and honest actions of upper management and the committed support of project and functional managers.

A corporation without a strategy is like an airplane weaving through stormy skies, hurling up and down, slammed by wind, and lost in the thunderheads. If lightning or crushing winds don't destroy it, it will simply run out of gas.

Alvin Toffler, American lecturer and author of
The Adaptive Corporation (1995)

5

Implementing Business Focused Project Management

Knowing is not enough; we must apply.
Willing is not enough; we must do.

Johann Wolgang von Goethe (1749–1832), German writer

INTRODUCTION

Chapter 4 introduced the Wrappers™ model that placed strategy, business and projects in context. This model enhances the business understanding of projects, particularly in the areas of project performance measures, accountability, and the critical relationships between sponsor, project manager and core team members.

Successful projects, and hence successful implementation of an organization's strategic initiatives, require an environment that fosters a project management approach. Upper management has a crucial role to play in building an organization platform from which projects can effectively be delivered. Recognizing that project managers have limited ability to command resources and influence functional managers, upper management must create an environment that supports and rewards the cross-functional delivery of project work.

This chapter provides guidelines for the implementation of such an environment in the context of BFPM and the Wrappers model. It also focuses on the most important aspects of the Business Wrapper – project portfolio management and the selection and prioritization processes.

The layered model shown in Figure 5.1 illustrates the implementation of BFPM in an organization. The model is interpreted from the bottom up, commencing with 'Awareness and support' up to 'Project delivery', with 'Measurement' and 'Learning' being common to all layers.

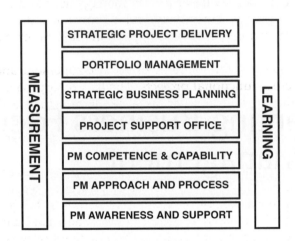

Figure 5.1 Implementing a BFPM environment

From the model it would appear that implementing BFPM in an organization is a discrete step-by-step process. Although there is a general sequence to the steps in the implementation as each is layered in, many of these occur in parallel. BFPM does not occur in a revolutionary manner but rather in an evolutionary manner. An organization starts with the application of project management (awareness, approach and process) and, through a process of realization of the value that it brings to the organization, the organization progresses through the layers. The authors have on many occasions consulted to companies who have jumped in by first creating expensive and sophisticated project support offices, only to find that they have realized no real improvement in their ability to manage projects. Invariably, the authors' findings are that the underlying layers of awareness and support, and competency and capability, are lacking. They may have implemented the best project support office with sound approaches and processes but, since there is no awareness and support of or competence in project management, project management is not accepted throughout the organization and therefore not effectively applied. The old proverb applies – 'you can take a horse to water but you cannot make it drink'.

RELATING THE LAYERS TO REALITY

To illustrate how the layers build, the following describes how they lay in an organization in a generic manner:

- An organization becomes aware of project management and starts to apply it. As a result of early successes, awareness and support for its continued use grow. However, the approach and processes applied are not uniform across the organization.

- The organization realizes the value of project management and begins to attempt larger and more cross-functional projects. The lack of approach and process uniformity causes confusion and conflict, as a result of which a decision is taken to formalize the approach and processes and to implement them organization-wide. The organization's confidence in its ability to apply project management grows, and more ambitious initiatives are attempted.

- Due to the growing number of cross-functional projects, more and more people at all levels of the organization become involved in projects. Their enthusiasm, however, does not make up for a lack of competence. There is a danger that projects could begin to fail due to a lack of expertise at all levels. The organization addresses this by instituting project management training as part of people development programmes at all levels. Competence increases as a result, and projects mushroom throughout the organization, overloading the limited resources.

- To gain control of what appears to be a runaway situation, and to provide overloaded project managers with relief from some of the administrative tasks, the organization implements a centralized project support office (PSO). This requires that all projects be registered and executed in a consistent manner. It also provides the organization with a view of the load projects are placing on the organization's resources.

- As a result of the improved understanding of what projects are being executed, brought about by funnelling projects through the PSO, management begins to realize that many of the projects are perhaps not delivering value to the organization or are not in line with corporate strategy. To gain more value from fewer projects, the organization introduces the approach of developing business cases and proposals for all projects prior to their initiation. This requires the organization to critically examine their strategic and business planning processes. Changes are made to these processes to link them with those of project management, and to make them more objective (goal) oriented and more capable of being projectized. This broadens the scope of the PSO's functions.

- To further enhance the executive view of projects and to ensure that value delivery is maximized, a selection and prioritization process is introduced which selects and ranks project proposals based on merit (value), resource limits and contribution to strategy. This results in a portfolio of projects being maintained which represents those projects that will best deliver the strategy of the business. Fewer projects are now being executed, but more value to the organization is delivered. The organization focuses on managing its project portfolio at executive and upper management level.

● BFPM has now been implemented in the organization at all levels, and the organization is now focused on its strategy and its delivery through the projects making up its portfolio, effectively 'managing the organization by projects'. Projects now commence in the 'boardroom' and are delivered back to the 'boardroom'.

● Throughout this evolutionary process, the organization continued to measure the performance and outputs of the projects. As each layer was transitioned, more measurement criteria were added. Project measurements were supplemented with measures of human performance, then business performance and, finally, strategic performance. The important common denominator is that the measurements are against project, business and strategic objectives in a linked manner.

● In a similar evolutionary manner, what the organization learnt from transitioning each layer has been applied back into the organization, thereby facilitating the building of the next layer. The learning never stops. Once all the layers are in place, the layering cycle repeats itself by revisiting each area and making improvements, resulting in new experiences and learning. In this manner, the application of BFPM in an organization is constantly being honed and focused, thereby improving the overall performance of the organization.

> Not everything that can be counted counts, and not everything that counts can be counted.
>
> Albert Einstein (1879–1955), relativity genius

RELATING THE IMPLEMENTATION LAYERS TO THE WRAPPERS MODEL

Table 5.1 relates each of the layers to the relevant wrapper and component. This assists in the understanding of how BFPM is implemented in layers, yet guided by the Wrappers model. From the table, it is also possible to see the progressive implementation of BFPM through the Wrappers model.

The layers are further discussed in the sections that follow. Measurement is not specifically discussed in this chapter as it is implied throughout. It is dealt with in Chapters 4 (measurement across the Wrappers model) and 11 (measurement of project performance).

Figure 5.2 (opposite) shows the Wrappers model as described in Chapter 4.

PROJECT MANAGEMENT AWARENESS AND SUPPORT

In non-projectized organizations (function-focused ones), upper functional managers manage project managers. When upper managers appoint project managers to deliver

Table 5.1 Relating the layers to the Wrappers model

Layer	Wrappers model
PM awareness and support	ODPM and the Project Wrapper
PM approach and process	ODPM and the Project Wrapper
PM competence and capability	ODPM and the Project Wrapper (starts there and permeates throughout the whole Wrappers model)
Project support office	Project and Business Wrappers
Strategic and business planning	Business and Strategic Wrappers
Portfolio management	Project, Business and Strategic Wrappers
Strategic Project delivery	The complete Wrappers model
Measurement	The complete Wrappers model
Learning	The complete Wrappers model

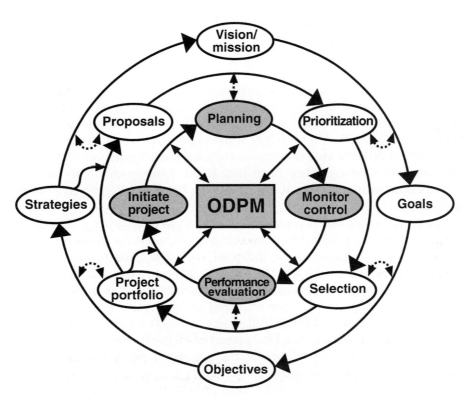

Figure 5.2 The Wrappers model described in Chapter 4

results in a cross-functional manner, but then give minimal support to the project when conflict between the functions and project arises, project management is undermined and devalued. This reinforces traditional behaviour, and rewards functions for giving projects lower priority than functional work. In this environment, projects will fail and project management will be perceived as not adding value to the business.

Project participants know well the truth of the expression 'actions speak louder than words'. Upper management must not only be sincere in what they say, but more importantly, they must be honest in doing what they say they will do. Graham and Englund[34] refer to upper management authenticity and integrity as the glue required to create a successful project environment. Sponsors who demonstrate honesty and sincerity while leading by example become a pillar of strength for the project managers and team members. Their actions send a strong message to functional managers that projects are a priority and important to the survival and growth of the organization.

Organizations that truly wish to embrace project management as a way of doing business require someone in upper management to champion the change. This champion will likely face opposition, as traditional management resists change. Organizations that have successfully implemented a project management approach have achieved this through a champion who has been able to demonstrate the benefits by delivering projects considerably more effectively than before.

An awareness of how project management can benefit the organization must be introduced. Key personnel must be trained in the concepts, philosophies, tools and techniques of project management and its importance to the successful actioning of organization strategies.

Without the support of an upper management champion, the probability of successful implementation is slim. Conditions conducive to an upper manager taking on the challenge exist when management is progressive and realizes that projects are an important component of future growth. Alternatively, if management is slow to introduce change, a stocktake of failed projects and the impact they have on organizational performance and staff morale will soon convince them that action is necessary. This stocktaking is part of normal business in projectized organizations, but is the exception in non-projectized (function focused) ones.

The results of a stocktake usually surprise, and at times shock, upper management as they realize the number of projects that are being undertaken. To drive home the point, a sound stocktake will also estimate the total resource impact of all the projects. Additional information that highlights the need for project management is a list of projects completed in the past few years, including their costs and timeliness. This information is usually compelling, as the costs incurred are generally significant and timely delivery is the exception. If resistance still exists amongst upper managers, a further powerful way to demonstrate the need for project management is to assess the business benefits recovered through projects versus the business case promises made. At this stage, most resistance is usually overcome.

Many organizations have one or more critical projects that are either out of control or heading down that path. The authors' experience indicates that often these projects have a major technology component as part of the total scope. Managers responsible for delivering the project conveniently blame technology for the problems and state that if 'technology was known' at inception, the project would be on track. Research into project success and failure (refer to Appendix C) demonstrates that the majority of project problems are attributable to management, organizational culture and planning. The choice of which technology platform, operating system and contractor to select is a managerial problem, and not driven by technology itself. Highlighting an out-of-control project and the reasons for its state can present a strong argument for implementing an organizational project management approach.

Upper management must appreciate that support does not imply 100 per cent consensus. Provided a substantial majority supports the initiative, it should proceed.

After the comprehensive stocktake described above, the astute upper manager will have realized that the current mix of projects may not align with the organizational strategies, resulting in a less than optimal use of resources. Support will be gathering for the establishment and management of an organization-wide portfolio of projects, as well as effective project management of individual projects.

Another approach to creating upper management awareness is to ensure that they attend training courses with project managers, requesting them to take a sponsor role in the training exercises. The training course must address the alignment of projects with organization strategies, and encourage teams representing various levels of the organization and functions to work together. This helps the managers realize their responsibilities on projects and the problems that their lack of support creates for project participants. Carrying out an anonymous evaluation of project-related problems in the organization, at the end of the course, provides further persuasive data for the need for project management. An anonymous evaluation avoids the problem of staff unwillingness to challenge upper management.

PROJECT MANAGEMENT APPROACH AND PROCESS

To implement an organizational approach to project management, the question of which project approach is the most appropriate for the organization, and how it will be implemented, must be considered. Upper management, functional resource managers and project managers are all involved in resolving this issue.

Organizations have set up taskforces, working groups or steering committees to manage these issues. The authors recommend setting up a Project Management Initiative Group (PMIG). Membership of this group comprises a cross-section of upper and project managers. A major objective of this group is to ensure that management at various levels in the organization have ownership of the new approach. Having an executive member chair the group will demonstrate high-level support for the change.

To consider the operational question of what approach is appropriate and how to implement it, a different sub-group can be set up to research and draw up proposals. Many organizations will have departments or project managers who have developed their own project management approach out of necessity. Research into these, as well as external best practice methods, will be essential inputs to this sub-group's work.

Care must be taken to avoid the pitfall of recommending an approach that is comprehensive and mature in application but does not fit the requirements of the organization. Typically, the more mature and rigid approaches of construction and engineering do not fit well in a flexible business environment.

One of the sub-group's first tasks must be a survey of the organization's project management capability level. This capability level is often referred to as the project management maturity level and is measured on a scale of 1 to 5, where 1 is ad hoc and 5 is sustained project management. Once the maturity level is established, a target maturity level for the medium to longer term is determined.

The sub-group can now develop a project management implementation plan for the organization. After agreeing on the appropriate project management approach, the sub-group needs to address the establishment of a project management system that will support that approach. Part of the sub-group's task is to gather adequate inputs from those who will be affected by the project management approach and resulting system.

Part III sets out the ODPM process that would typically underpin a project management system. The challenge for the sub-group is to determine which components are essential, which are nice to have, and what to omit at this stage. Although upper management is championing the new approach, it will not succeed if it is too complex or is perceived to add little value to projects.

PROJECT MANAGEMENT COMPETENCE AND CAPABILITY

This layer is extremely important, at two levels: 1) at the higher level the challenge is to develop upper management's ability to manage and support project managers, and deliver the business benefits; 2) at the project level it is to develop project managers capable of delivering project outputs and enabling business benefit uptake in the organization.

The most critical development is that of upper management's ability to sponsor projects and manage project managers.

To illustrate, the authors observed an organization in the service industry that appointed sponsors and project managers to manage and deliver their projects. Project managers in this organization experienced frustration through a lack of sponsor focus and support during project execution. As the organization had an entrenched hierarchical structure, and upper management's performance was measured by the achievement of functional objectives, project objectives had become obscured and less important. Sponsors still focused on functional objectives, although projects were vital for achieving organization strategy. When conflict arose between functions and projects, the sponsors supported the functional objectives that reflected favourably on their performance evaluation.

A survey was undertaken in this service organization to establish upper management's understanding of a project sponsor role. The results varied from reasonable to low levels of understanding. This information was presented to an upper management executive meeting, together with the impact that poor sponsor performance has on projects and the organization's performance.

The CEO was surprised at the results and disturbed by the clear consequences of weak sponsorship. A programme of upper management training in project management, with a strong emphasis on sponsorship, was instituted, and a taskforce appointed to review management objectives and their alignment with project objectives. The CEO had realized that if projects were the vehicles to deliver organizational strategies, it was imperative that functions must align with service delivery and project objectives. The turnaround was remarkable. Sponsors took real ownership of the project objectives by writing them into their yearly objectives, and actively supported the project managers in achieving them. This was not surprising, as people in business tend to perform tasks that get measured. Project managers reported a higher level of job satisfaction as their contribution to the organization's performance and growth was evident and valued.

The following issues will need to be considered.

Sponsor development

Sponsor development should ideally form part of the organization's management development programme. Critical inputs to this management training will be the selection and prioritization process, and the project management approach and process. The training must simulate real organizational conditions and role-playing should enhance the learning.

Developing management abilities is time consuming, yet upper managers have limited time to devote to training. The training arrangements must recognize these factors. A programme spread over a few months is preferable to a lengthy, concentrated period, as long as the training results in skills and knowledge that can be used immediately on projects. As in any training, the managers will need time to practise their new skills. Only when the new skills are perceived as adding value will other managers become enthusiastic about attending the training themselves.

Project manager development

Project manager and sponsor development should ideally take place in tandem, so they can jointly attend parts of the training and participate in the role-playing. This will result in improved understanding and appreciation of each other's roles and the responsibilities of projects. It will also highlight the interaction between project managers and sponsors.

The training can be a combination of courses, conferences, mentoring and consulting. The course structure and content should be developed in consultation with upper and project managers, using outlines from other courses with organization specifics added. A typical course would cover:

- an overview of portfolio and project management;
- upper management and project roles and responsibilities;
- the Project Management Body of Knowledge (PMBOK®)[73];
- the project process;
- integration of project management into the organization's business;
- workshop exercises and simulation exercises.

Quality simulation exercises provide an opportunity for sponsors and project managers to experience team building, stakeholder management, project trade-offs, conflict management and benefits realization. Such exercises help the two groups realize that successful project delivery is strongly dependent on supporting each other, especially when things go wrong. Problems experienced in the training and simulations provide an opportunity to discuss solutions and decide on which components should become organization practice.

Project management development includes the above training, as well as specific training on the detailed management of a project. Such a course would cover:

- project management tools and techniques, including planning, estimation, risk management, scope development and objective setting;
- application of tools and techniques within a project management process;
- developing a project definition plan, as shown in the definition stage of ODPM;
- behavioural components, including team building, motivating team members, conflict management, managing sponsors and managing stakeholder expectations;
- organization issues, such as dealing with cross-functional management and how to deliver a project in a weak matrix structure;
- business fundamentals, such as how an organization is run, how decision making affects direction and profitability, and how to manage a project as a small business;
- customer focus and marketing skills, as projects deliver products and services to both internal and external customers.

The Project Management Institute (PMI®) Standards Committee's *A Guide to the Project Management Body of Knowledge*[73] forms an excellent foundation for project manager development. This publication and the Project Management Professional certification examination, offered internationally through the PMI, have become standard in many organizations and industries. Executive and upper management should encourage project managers to undertake this examination and pursue certification. The Association of Project Managers (APM) is the United Kingdom arm of the International Project Management Association (IPMA), and it also undertakes certification of project managers. For IT project managers, an international organization, CompTIA, offers the IT Project+™ certification.

Project managers can further develop themselves by attending university courses at master's degree level at both business schools and engineering schools. Technical institutions also offer practically focused project management courses.

Some organizations may not have the resources to develop project management competencies in-house. Many providers of project management training can meet this need, as long as the training is managed effectively. Upper management and project manager development is not negotiable if the organization is serious about organization project management.

Making project management a key management competency

Organizations that value project management will ensure that project management is a key competency in all managers' job descriptions. Purely project organizations may go further and make project management a career position. In service and production industries where projects constitute an important part of the business, project management is increasingly viewed as an essential management competency, necessary to advance in the organization.

One government service organization undergoing a major restructuring was faced with the task of reviewing all positions and developing a set of competency-based evaluation criteria for position descriptions. The restructuring presented an opportunity to change the existing evaluation system and send a message to the organization that upper management was serious about change. Business would be conducted differently in future. As project management had been applied to projects in the past, management insisted that all management levels would need to demonstrate some level of competency in the skill of project management. Consultants were appointed to develop the competencies, resulting in the following requirements in the position descriptions:

- Middle managers were to demonstrate competency in managing small projects with limited interfaces across other functions.
- Upper managers had to manage competently large projects with interfaces across many functional areas.
- Senior upper managers were required to prove competency in managing a programme of projects consisting of many related projects delivering major benefits to the organization.

Executive members were required to demonstrate competency in managing portfolios of projects containing programmes of projects as well as a range of individual projects delivering broad-based benefits to the organization.

Also included in the job descriptions were project, programme and portfolio sponsorship roles at the relevant levels.

This sent a clear message to all managers applying for jobs, that scoring a '10' in operations and a '3' or '4' in projects would no longer suffice. In the appointment process that followed, some 'experienced' managers did not make the grade. Years of service and operational knowledge were no longer enough. A shock message went out through the organization. Functional managers are now more supportive of project managers and, in certain instances, are willing to take on project management roles to improve their competency and strengthen their CVs. The organization's approach elevated the role of project management and increased the demand for project management training and education.

The competitive edge of the future will be in business practices, project management and functional expertise. Organizations that fall behind in any of these areas will experience difficulty in retaining a leading role in industry. Business practices and functional expertise have received considerable attention and development over recent decades, while project management is still immature in many organizations.

Upper management must ensure that project management is both a valued and sought-after position, and that it becomes the 'school for leaders of tomorrow'. Fleming[28] reinforces the business role that project managers will play in future.

The authors recommend that some form of human performance measurement on projects be included in organizational performance systems. Such an approach must set project management performance objectives for sponsors, project managers and team members.

THE PROJECT SUPPORT OFFICE

As an organization builds and matures in its application of project management, it requires project services such as project administration, project facilitation, project management coaching and mentoring. These services are required to further bolster the application of project management and to provide consistency in the approach. The provision of these services relieves the pressure on the project manager and team, allowing them to focus on producing results. Other than services, the project environment requires that project processes are applied consistently, document contents are complete and administered through the process, and that the quality of project management throughout the organization is assured. At the executive/upper management level, there is a need for a single portal for, and view of, all corporate projects.

The project support office (PSO) or an equivalent function takes on these roles in the organization. If an organization only undertakes projects occasionally, a permanent project office may not be needed. However, as organizations invest more resources into projects, a disciplined approach is required to avoid costly errors and the development of a different project methodology for each new project.

As the practice of project management has grown, many projectized organizations have recognized the need for a PSO to support the project management initiative across their organization. The PSO should be staffed by project management professionals. The duties and functions of PSOs vary by organization, but include some or all of the following:

● Supporting the project team in administrative tasks for project scheduling; report production and distribution; project management software support and maintenance; issue and risk database tracking; and the creation and maintenance of a 'visibility room', where plans, charts, diagrams and reports are displayed for viewing.

- Providing the organization with project management consulting and mentoring. As organizations become more projectized, personnel who can serve as internal project management consultants and mentors will provide skills, knowledge transfer and sound advice that will contribute to the organization's ability to deliver projects effectively.
- Developing and maintaining project management methodologies and standards for the organization. Consistent application of common methodologies and standards will benefit the organization. These must be developed to meet business needs, and to ensure ownership of the methodologies by upper management.
- Providing employee training in project management as a prerequisite for the adoption of project management in the organization. The PSO can develop and deliver the training or obtain the service externally, whichever is the most effective.
- Providing the organization with competent managers to run projects. PSOs can contain a pool of project managers who can be assigned to carry out the organization's projects as the need arises. This approach can work well in large organizations that run many projects (Block and Frame[10]). However, the authors have found that for most business projects a more effective approach is for business managers to manage projects, assisted by the PSO and project consultants.
- Acting as the custodian of the organization's project portfolio management systems.

The PSO can also be responsible for administering project proposals, including:

- receiving and logging the proposal;
- providing an initial evaluation of the proposal for completeness of information;
- arranging reviews of proposals by finance sectors and any other relevant parties;
- facilitating the selection and prioritization process;
- communicating with all relevant parties about the process;
- assisting in the research and preparation of the project proposal;
- maintaining a library of accepted and rejected project proposals and business cases;
- assisting with conversion of proposals and business cases into projects and ensuring that information is maintained on them.

This book does not discuss the PSO functions in detail, nor does it discuss the detailed implementation of a PSO. Numerous journal articles and books on the subject are available. Such a book by Block and Frame[10] covers the subject effectively in an easy to assimilate reference. Given below, however, is a brief list of steps and actions normally taken to implement a PSO:

- Approval and support
  - Define the purpose and concept.
  - Find a sponsor or champion.
  - Obtain executive/upper management support and initial approval.
- Assessment
  - Assess and document the organization's project maturity level, application of project management practices.

   - Conduct a needs analysis.
- Design
   - Design the PSO structure, project management systems and processes.
   - Develop a roll-out plan.
   - Develop a communication plan.
   - Formulate the PSO budgets.
   - Document the design and develop the business case.
   - Present business case to executive/upper management and obtain support and approval to continue.
- Implementation
   - Implement facilities (tools, staff, documentation, systems).
   - Conduct awareness campaign.
   - Roll out the project management systems and processes through the organization.

STRATEGIC AND BUSINESS PLANNING

Corporate strategy and business planning takes cognisance of the organization's capability to deliver its objectives effectively through projects. Strategic and business plans are described as projects to be implemented in support of, and in addition to, operational initiatives. The organization's executive, with support of the project support office, manages the strategic and business projects as a portfolio.

Strategic planning must be done before any business planning can take place. There are many approaches to strategic planning and a discussion of them is beyond the scope of this book. It suffices to say that the output from any strategy planning exercise must deliver at least a vision/mission, goals and objectives and strategies to address them. Answers to at least the following questions should be established:

- What business are we in?
- Who are our competitors?
- How are we performing?
- How is the market we are in changing?
- What is our position or desired position in the market?
- How are we changing to fit the market?
- What are our strategic objectives and goals, and how are we going to achieve them?

Once the strategy has been developed, business plans and proposals are formulated to action them. Proposals are potential forerunners of the business case. If the executive/upper management accepts a proposal, it usually undergoes elaboration to become a business case that is put forward to the executive for approval. Proposal content, therefore, is usually lighter than in the business case document.

Given below are some typical components and approaches to proposals and business cases. It is up to the proposer, sponsors and project managers, however, to determine the extent to which a proposal is developed, as well as the subsequent business case.

Background/situation

Describes the background or situation relating to the problem or opportunity that has arisen. This sets the context for the proposal. It must be brief and precise; only factors related to the specific problem or opportunity are discussed. The purpose is to focus the project participants and obtain support from upper management. It should describe how the project will contribute to organizational strategy. This linkage creates some stability in the 'shifting sands' environment that typifies projects. If the proposed project is about service or product improvement, the background should include a description of current services, costs and similar factors.

Organizational need

Stated in one or two paragraphs, the organizational need description is crisp and concise. The need could be both a problem and an opportunity. It is a high-level state-ment that must aim to 'sell' the project. The rationale must be logical and encapsulate the potential benefit(s) to the organization. This part is often referred to as 'the case for change', and it is the responsibility of upper management and the sponsor to enthuse the organization with the benefits resulting from the change.

If the case for change is poorly articulated, the potential benefit will not be under-stood, which invariably causes implementation difficulties as individuals resist change they do not understand or believe is not in their interests.

Options and alternatives

Upper management and the executive require a high level of assurance that proposals have been thoroughly investigated, and that a range of alternative options for maxi-mizing the opportunity have been explored.

A brief discussion on each option will place it in context of the proposal and the expected performance. The preferred option must be indicated, along with a rational argument demonstrating why it is chosen.

Project purpose

This states the project purpose as a clear and concise goal. The intention is to provide a clear focus for the proposal. This purpose is agreed to by the proposer and sponsor. Once a project is declared, the purpose is debated and, if necessary, altered to suit the needs of the project team, as they must 'own' it. Typically, a purpose statement will contain:

- identification of the problem or opportunity;
- reference to a proposed solution to the problem;
- a link to the strategic intent of the project.

A well-conceived and developed purpose statement consists of one or two paragraphs.

Objectives, strategies, rationale

Objectives simply state what the project aims to achieve. Well-defined objectives are simple, concise, results focused, achievable, measurable and time bound. At the proposal stage, objectives may be less explicit than in the business case, but the measures of these objectives must be clear. Generally, projects should not have too many objectives (say, three to five), or the team members will lose focus. If these objectives are achieved, the organization is well positioned to achieve the desired outcomes. For each objective, a few (five, say) critical success factors must be developed (the few things that must go right).

Upper management has an interest in understanding the strategies or approaches to be taken to achieve the objectives. This needs to be described in general terms, focusing on sound approaches that engender confidence in the proposal. The strategies described should be sufficient to allow independent assessment of the feasibility of the approach. Once a project is initiated, the project team will draw heavily on the strategies and build upon them.

Proposals need a clear indication of the rationale and calculations on which the projected benefits and costs estimates are based. This analysis has an important impact on the assessment of the proposal and must be carefully prepared.

Stakeholder analysis and communication strategy

Every important initiative requires stakeholder interaction and support or 'blessing'. Typically, stakeholder analysis includes:

- identification of key stakeholder groups;
- consideration of the benefit and risk to the stakeholders resulting from project implementation;
- assessment of their ability to influence the project.

Following the stakeholder analysis, the proposal for large initiatives must suggest a simple but robust communication strategy that can be implemented should a project be launched. Chapters 7 and 8, Part III, expand on stakeholders' analysis and communication strategy.

Benefits retrieval strategies

Service organizations undertaking projects frequently experience difficulty in retrieving the promised benefits set out in business cases. In some organizations, benefits retrieval is not measured or reviewed as a way of doing business. The result is that projects are perceived as initiatives that absorb large amounts of human resources, with limited benefits realization for the organization.

It is crucial that the project sponsor becomes accountable for benefits retrieval. The project team delivers the project results and positions the organization to achieve the business outcomes, while the sponsor accepts responsibility for the business outcomes.

The group responsible for selecting and prioritizing business cases (the portfolio management group) is keenly interested in reviewing and understanding how the business case benefits are to be recovered. A proposal promising attractive benefits that are difficult to retrieve will not be viewed favourably. An example would be a restructuring project that, when implemented, cannot make the intended savings due to contractual conditions of employment, which prevent redundancies under certain conditions.

Proposals would generally not go as far as setting out the benefits retrieval methodology, unless this is well established in the organization. Business cases need to address this important aspect, as without a robust methodology the benefits will not be recovered.

It is important that the proposal explains which areas of the organization will receive the intended benefits. If this is not explained, the department(s) taking on the project products will reasonably assume that savings achieved in their area are available for their use. In addition, the organization needs clarity on how the savings will be reallocated via business plans or through other instruments of the ongoing business.

Scope

A general statement of the project scope should be written up in a few paragraphs. Scope boundaries must be stated as clearly as possible, considering what is appropriate for a proposal. Agreement with other affected projects is important to avoid duplication of initiatives.

The scope section must indicate which other projects are affected by this proposal. The portfolio management group will be cautious with any proposals that could derail mission-critical projects, and will carefully consider the associated risks before making recommendations to the executive.

Upper management is responsible for supporting the project manager and encouraging the elaboration of project scope, resulting in a sound plan during project initiation, discussed in Part III. This will place the project team in a sound position to achieve the expected results.

Potential constraints and limitations

Constraints must be stated, as well as their impact on the project and details of how they will be managed. Potential constraints may include time, resources, cost, quality and legislation. Limitations relate more to the quantum of product delivered through the project. Both constraints and limitations must be addressed in the proposal.

Indicative time frame

Most proposals contain indicative time frames as to when the project will be completed. These time frames are improved upon later, as the project is elaborated. Delivery times should be estimated with caution, as stakeholders always seem to remember the promised delivery time, cost and what the project will deliver. Conditions attached to the promises, however, are seldom remembered! 'Fuzzy' projects with high uncertainty and a range of delivery times is one option to manage expectations.

Key assumptions

Any assumptions made in developing the proposal must be recorded. A proposal founded on shaky assumptions is unlikely to gain approval from the portfolio management group.

Risk factors

Proposals should cover the key high-level risks to the project, and the business case must supply more detail. It is useful to assess the probability of the risk occurring, as well as the potential impact of each risk. Following this with a sound risk mitigation strategy will increase confidence in the proposal.

Evaluation of factors considering value and risk

Evaluation factors are discussed below under the heading 'The appraisal factors of value and risk'. Proposers need to address these factors in detail, as they form the basis for weighting and scoring in the prioritization and selection process.

PROJECT PORTFOLIO MANAGEMENT

Three major components of the Business Wrapper are the selection, prioritization and project portfolio. The combination of these components is referred to as project portfolio management. Project portfolio management is the pivotal link between the Strategic Wrapper and the Project Wrapper. It creates a vehicle that informs executives and upper management on the proposed initiatives being investigated, the resource and change impacts, and the financial viability of the proposals, as well as which combination of projects will best deliver optimum strategic results.

Applying a flexible but disciplined approach to project portfolio management will result in an appropriately resourced portfolio of projects. This is sometimes referred to as a programme of projects (discussed below under the heading 'Managing multiple projects as a programme'). The authors prefer the portfolio concept, as a portfolio can include individual projects as well as programmes of closely related projects. Projectized organizations deliver both programmes and individual projects in pursuing business improvement.

Projectized organizations encourage proposals from all levels across the organization. The project selection and prioritization process tests these proposals against a set of predetermined factors and acts as a filter or gateway system through which the proposal must pass. Project portfolio management can be described as consisting of four major functions as follows:

- *solicitation*, which defines how business cases and proposals are to be evaluated by the organization's decision makers;
- *selection*, which defines how business cases and proposals are added or removed from the project portfolio;
- *prioritization*, which defines how projects are ranked relative to pre-defined criteria;
- *registration*, which defines how proposals and business cases become projects and are registered in the portfolio.

The portfolio management processes are typically executed in the sequence given above. Business cases and proposals are created and submitted for approval (solicitation). Those proposals that meet pre-defined criteria and which are deemed to be of benefit are approved and added to the portfolio (selection). The selected business case/proposals in the portfolio are then ranked in order of urgency, importance, and demand on organization resources (prioritization). The prioritized business case/proposals contained in the project portfolio are then registered as projects to be actioned.

Once built, the project portfolio does not remain static. New projects are continuously added and existing projects either stopped, removed or completed through the functions of solicitation, selection and prioritization. In this manner, the project portfolio represents the 'inventory' of an organization's projects as well as its investment in effecting its strategy.

It is obvious from the above that a weak or incorrectly applied project portfolio management process leads to confusion over the relationships between projects and strategies, and increased conflict over resource priority for projects. It is upper management's responsibility to ensure robust and consistent project portfolio management.

Although the project portfolio has been referred to in the singular above, organizations can have multiple project portfolios. Multiple portfolios result from the approach that an organization adopts in structuring the outputs from its strategy planning process. An example might be a telecommunications company which may have as its strategic objectives major components such as, amongst others, marketing, infrastructure, distribution and human capital. If the strategies for each are complex, a separate portfolio may be built for each component to allow ease of management but consolidated into one for executive/upper management purposes.

Proposal and business case documents, the inputs into selection and prioritization, were discussed in the previous section. The selection and prioritizing process is covered in more detail below in the section 'The selection and prioritization process' (p 103). Project registration is primarily done by the PSO and is discussed above.

In this and earlier sections, executive/upper management was referred to as the 'approvers' of business case/proposals and it was implied that they are the project portfolio management group. An appropriate organization structure for project portfolio management is shown in Figure 5.3 (a single portfolio is assumed). The roles shown in the structure are explained below.

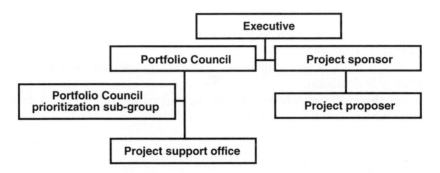

Figure 5.3 Prioritization and selection structure

Project proposer

The person or group who initially proposes the project is the proposer. Their responsibilities include obtaining sponsorship, preparing the project proposal and business case, and managing the proposed project until a project manager is appointed.

Project sponsor

A sponsor is an upper manager in the organization who will champion the project, as described in Chapter 1. Their responsibilities in this early stage typically include supporting the project proposer, approving any initial expenditure for costs incurred in information gathering, analysis and preparation of the project proposal and business case, and presentation to the Portfolio Council and executive. Once the project obtains approval, the sponsor provides ongoing sponsorship and support to the project manager and team.

Portfolio Council prioritization sub-group

This sub-group is responsible for the initial evaluation and scoring of all project proposals. Their primary responsibilities include the following:

● Analysing and interpreting project proposals. This requires a disciplined approach, assessing all proposals against set criteria.

- Carrying out the scoring and initial prioritization. Each member of the sub-group scores every proposal independently. This leads to an individually prioritized list of projects.
- Drawing up a ranked list of potential projects. The sub-group meets and jointly draws up a recommended prioritized list.
- Making recommendations to the Portfolio Council.

The Portfolio Council prioritization sub-group should comprise no more than six managers. It should represent upper and functional management as well as various departments of the organization. This cross-functional composition will ensure that proposal influence, impacts and benefits are assessed in the widest possible context.

Typically there should be at least one representative from each of the following areas:

- finance;
- strategy and planning;
- policy (in government agencies);
- information technology;
- region or district (national companies).

The prioritization sub-group should also be able to co-opt any other specialist knowledge necessary to make informed judgements on relative priorities and proposal content. Occasionally, more than one member of the sub-group could have a direct interest in a particular proposal. Requiring members to declare their interest in proposals will allow the potential problem of undue influence to be managed.

Portfolio Council

This group, chaired by a member of the executive, is responsible for finalizing the prioritization list received from the prioritization sub-group. The council's main responsibilities are:

- strategic analysis of project proposals;
- reviewing the prioritization sub-group's scoring;
- finalizing the prioritization list;
- making recommendations to the executive.

Executive Committee

This is the group responsible for making the final 'go/no go' decision on all project proposals. The executive's responsibilities include:

- discussing the prioritization list;
- reviewing representations or presentations from project sponsors;

- making decisions such as full approval, partial approval, rejection or deferral;
- communicating the decisions through the project sponsors to the organization.

STRATEGIC PROJECT DELIVERY

Once all the preceding elements have been implemented, the organization can truly say that it is delivering its strategic and change initiatives in the most effective way. Projects become the 'way' the organization shapes itself.

Measurement of the organization should now be in all areas, and particularly strategic, business, project and human performance. Balanced scorecards should be in place for all these dimensions. Personnel have measurable objectives that when achieved deliver projects; projects have objectives that when achieved facilitate business objectives which in turn, when delivered, achieve the strategic objectives.

What information are executives looking for? Generally, senior executives look for information that will help them make sound business decisions as well as position them favourably in terms of their personal and professional growth. For example, they look for ways to measure and increase the return on their organization's investments and reduce expenditures, while containing risk. These outcomes tend to be tied to corporate strategy, as well as individual project outputs.

Once BFPM is in place, executive/upper management will have views of all these dimensions and strategic decisions can be taken in all areas to guide the organization towards its objectives.

Learning

Project learning is frequently spoken about in meetings, forums and project audits, yet it rarely progresses any further. Everyone agrees on its importance, but few ideas are actually implemented. Learning through projects demands a disciplined approach, requiring an upper management mandate and project participant commitment.

Project participants naturally enjoy celebrating project achievements and then moving on to new challenges. Capturing information on critical areas of projects is often seen as a tedious burden they can well do without. Yet the information that project participants carry in their heads is both extensive and enormously valuable to the organization. Information on what went well, what was new and different, and what tripped up the project will position individuals and the organization to improve performance and competitive edge. If this is so valuable, then why the reluctance to institute a system to capture and use it? It does not appear to be a cost factor, as once such a system is set up and operating effectively, the marginal cost to feed information in periodically appears to be minimal.

The problem seems to be deeply rooted in the culture of today's organizations. The pressures to deliver new products and services at an ever-increasing rate, within tight time and cost frames, and successfully first time, create an environment that is intolerant of errors. Managers may express their desire for people to learn from their own and others' mistakes, yet they do not reward or encourage open and honest project reviews and information sharing. Compare this approach to many Eastern cultures, which take a substantial amount of time discussing, consulting and learning from each other before implementing a project. Each participant's input is valued, and the learning comes from sharing the vast knowledge each contributes.

Until upper management demonstrates that they are both sincere and honest about a learning organization, nothing much will change. A culture of not encouraging and rewarding those who have made mistakes is deeply set in both society and at an organizational level. Experience has shown that communicating failure is fraught with dangers, and individuals will naturally protect themselves from this risk as there is too much at stake from a personal and societal point of view. The irony is that this behaviour is not sustainable as mistakes are invariably uncovered, leading to management interference and organization exposure.

True learning in organizations requires leadership that challenges traditional culture. Leadership that values learning as much as traditional performance measures will face pressure from managers who wish to retain the status quo. It will take a strong visionary champion to mandate the behaviour change and ensure that managers are supportive of a learning environment.

For a project-learning organization to be successful, upper management must build an environment where mistakes are openly discussed and learning is rewarded. Projects are risky and therefore more prone to mistakes than ongoing business. Mistakes in this uncertain environment are part of a discovery process that leads to better understanding. Learning from the errors enhances the organization's risk management capability, resulting in better future performance.

The Project Management Initiative Group should investigate the best way to establish and operate a learning approach that meets the needs of all project participants, as well as the organization.

THE SELECTION AND PRIORITIZATION PROCESS

The project selection and prioritization process is principally a method for assessing the relative merits of potential projects and ranking them against predetermined and weighted factors. The objective is to help upper management maximize the benefits that projects bring to the organization's business performance, and to make well-informed decisions on the allocation of limited resources.

Any such process must allow for flexibility that reflects the realities of the organization, or support will not be forthcoming from the important decision makers. This does not imply that discipline is no longer required, but rather that the relationship between discipline and flexibility is a paradox that the prioritization process must manage. Excessively rigid application of the process can lead to the process becoming more important than the outcome.

The Project Management Initiative Group should delegate a sub-group of its members to develop a robust selection and prioritization process that meets the requirements of the organization. This sub-group must also consider different categories of projects, and research various selection and prioritization models used in other organizations and industries.

A suggested project selection and prioritization process is shown in Figure 5.4.

BENEFITS OF A SELECTION AND PRIORITIZATION PROCESS

The selection and prioritization process goes beyond some traditional methods of project appraisal by including non-financial factors, and thereby seeking to identify projects with the greatest impact on business performance. In doing so, the method attempts to assess the total value of a project to the business.

J D Frame in *The New Project Management*[30] makes the following argument for an effective selection and prioritization process:

> A big problem with offhand project selection is that it leads to the ineffective use of resources. Support of a project to satisfy short-term exigencies may lead to long-term fiascos. Those making the decisions often forget that by committing resources to a poorly conceived project idea, they are tying up those resources. They have not taken into account the opportunity costs of their decision. If a truly good project prospect arises in the future, they may no longer have the resources to pursue it because their resources are tied up in marginal undertakings.

All levels of the organization benefit from implementing the process. Some of the more important benefits are:

- a rigorous approach to proposal preparation;
- involvement of all relevant parties during the prioritization process;
- greater transparency in decision making;
- better information available for decision making;
- building up a library of knowledge in a central database, to make future project proposals and approvals easier;
- an audit trail for project approvals.

Projects that are launched rapidly without the discipline of selection and prioritization are difficult to defend when things go wrong. Project participants and staff become confused and frustrated, as the functional areas do not share the priority of their work. Such projects are primarily driven from high up in the organization, and consequently their priority is imposed rather than established or demonstrated. Enthusiasm then resides mainly in the person driving the project on behalf of an executive member, and resources are often reluctantly supplied.

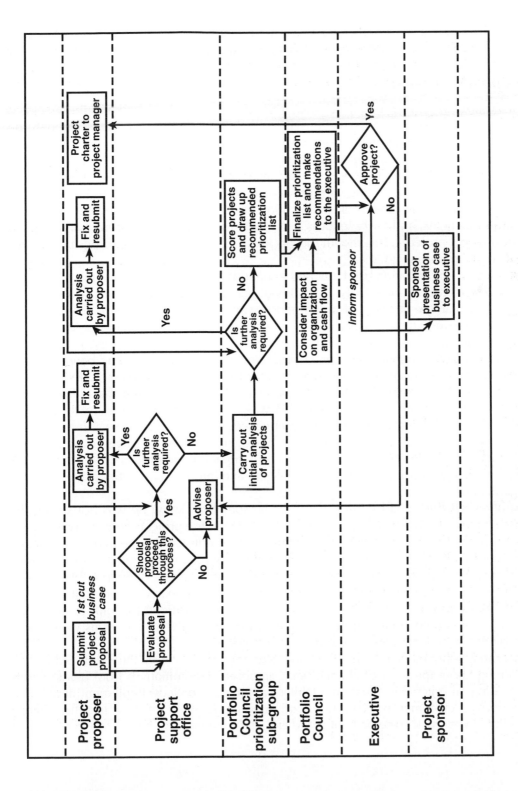

Figure 5.4 Organization project prioritization and selection process

All proposals are good!

After a 70-hour working week, John was not looking forward to spending the weekend reading board papers. He resigned himself to the task and started to wade through the forest of paper. The operational reports were familiar, covering operational performance, financial performance, customer satisfaction surveys and complaints – all the usual stuff. He wondered how often these reports were 'massaged' to meet reporting requirements. Still, these appeared to be in line with previous months. What really got to him were the development proposals. Reams of paper addressing purpose, scope, objectives, CSFs, deliverables, benefits, and a whole lot of jargon that the development group had come up with for national projects. This month the stack was particularly high, and his appetite for reading was diminishing rapidly.

Ever since the organization had launched its national change programme, the quantity of paper had increased exponentially; a sentiment echoed by his fellow executives. By the time John had read the first two, his mind started wandering. At 11 pm on Sunday evening, he stopped. The unread proposals would be skimmed through on the plane tomorrow; that would have to do.

The Board was in progress and agenda item 'New project proposals' had been reached. Individual project sponsors or managers delivered eloquent presentations, followed by discussions on the wonderful benefits the projects would deliver, and the brilliant technology the organization would receive. This was followed by questions relating to the benefits and how the project would be implemented. The proposals were approved more out of the belief that the project sponsor or manager appeared to have covered all the bases rather than the Board understanding the full impact of the proposal. Most proposals focused on strategic advancement, service delivery and improved operational capability of the organization.

John often felt frustrated by the process, as he somehow knew he was not seeing the complete picture. However, as he had little knowledge in the projects area, he was unable to raise important issues and argue them. Many of his co-directors appeared to be relaxed and frequently his protestations were misinterpreted. Surely, these initiatives must affect the organization in many dimensions, yet there was no big picture of the portfolio of projects. The CEO championed the change programme and appeared to be well informed about its status and performance. This made it even more difficult for John to query the proposals, as he could appear to be obstructive. Consequently, all proposals were good! Each provided excellent benefits and manageable risks.

Concerned, John reflected on the mood and messages out in the field. Staff were complaining about the level of change being imposed. The initiatives from headquarters were creating an untenable situation. Deliver operational services, implement new initiatives, improve customer service, but with funding reduced to pay for the change programme. When will there be light at the end of the tunnel?

Important lessons...

1. Executive ownership of the changes brought about by projects is often lacking, as they do not understand the impacts and influences a single project can have on the organization.
2. Proposal prioritization, together with an analysis of limited resources required to deliver the portfolio, is essential to avoid over-promising and under-delivering. An organization-wide view of the resources required to deliver the proposed projects will avoid overloading staff and will improve the quality of services delivered.
3. Approving projects must be done within a framework of clarity rather than pressure. Essentially, all projects will deliver some form of benefits. The important issue is which set of proposed projects will deliver the optimum portfolio of benefits.
4. Sponsors championing their projects will unwittingly 'sell' the project at the expense of other proposals. Without a process that assesses which proposals will deliver maximum benefits, organizations will continue in this unfocused manner.
5. One has to invest in projects to obtain the benefits downstream. This can cause a severe drain on an organization's human resources. Careful consideration must be given to the amount of project work placed on staff, as well as the level of change visited upon staff at any one time.
6. Approving projects without full understanding affects organization cash flow. It is not sufficient to view only the cost of undertaking the portfolio of projects. Just as important is the stream of funds returning from the projects. Delays in achieving financial benefits can place the organization under a cash flow strain. Large organizations running many projects simultaneously can be exposed to serious cash flow problems through delayed returns on project investments.
7. A selection and prioritization group or committee will ensure an unbiased list of prioritized proposals. This role is pivotal to support the Portfolio Council.

WHEN TO PRIORITIZE

Prioritization should take place at least quarterly, preferably monthly, and as often as weekly in organizations undergoing intense change. The prioritization sub-group needs to meet regularly, with frequency depending largely on the number of current initiatives. The prioritization timetable must also take account of business planning dates such as yearly budgeting, business strategy development and board reports. The information flowing from the prioritization sub-group is vital to assess the proposed level of change the organization faces.

Quick start initiatives

Certain projects may need to proceed without going through the formal prioritization process. These will often occur in times of crisis, or in response to a political statement or legislation that demands immediate response either to mitigate damage or to demonstrate progress. On these occasions, one of the following two situations could occur:

● The Portfolio Council prioritization sub-group can be convened at short notice to consider the proposal. If it measures favourably against other projects, it can be added to the prioritized list. Often this means that some other project or pending project is reprioritized, temporarily suspended, or even cancelled.
● Project approval to proceed is rapidly obtained from the CEO or executive, and then the project is subjected to prioritization at the next formal meeting. Although this process will not necessarily change the project's priority, it will place it amongst the remainder of the prioritized list.

PROJECTS IN THE CONTEXT OF PRIORITIZATION

In the context of prioritization, projects are an investment over a fixed or long term from which a stream of benefits is expected. While many definitions of 'project' focus solely on 'capital' expenditure as the defining factor, the investment view ensures that projects involving significant amounts of 'operating' expenditure are treated in a similar fashion to capital projects. Projectized organizations in the service delivery and manufacturing fields typically invest large amounts of personnel and operating resources in projects.

To consider a project proposal in the context of an investment, the executive must set certain thresholds that a proposal must meet. These typically include estimates of personnel, operating costs and capital costs. Proposals can then be tested against the thresholds in the selection process.

If the thresholds are met, the proposal can be allowed to proceed through the prioritization process. Certain projects may continue through the process even if they do not fit the criteria. These might be essential to implement because of their political impact on the organization or because of their public or customer importance. The selection and prioritization process must also be able to evaluate these types of projects.

APPRAISAL CATEGORIES

Appraisal categories provide a basis for a balanced assessment. By incorporating a number of factors, the degree of risk and uncertainty associated with each project can be evaluated. This allows an assessment of whether the organization has the necessary readiness and resources to overcome the possible barriers to effective implementation of the project.

Examples of appraisal categories are financial, strategic, organizational/management and technical, and there may be several factors in each category. For each factor, a positive (value) or negative (risk) weighting is determined by upper management and the executive. Weightings must be carefully considered to reflect the business objectives over the short to medium term. If the organization finds itself in financial turmoil, a relatively higher weighting can then be assigned to the financial contribution of a proposal, and contribution to strategy will receive a relatively lower weighting.

The authors recommend that a maximum of 12 factors be used at any one time in order to keep the prioritization process manageable. An example set of 12 factors is discussed below in the section 'The appraisal factors of value and risk'.

In practice...

Democracy in selection and prioritization: 'One proposer – one vote'

Selection and prioritization had become a major headache in the IT department of a large organization. IT had approximately 35 initiatives either as current projects requiring further funding or as new proposals for delivering improvements to operations. James, the IT director, decided to discuss the problem with Mary, the PSO manager. It is early Thursday evening in James's office.

James: 'In IT we have serious problems over which proposals to fund, which projects should continue, the impact of a tight financial climate – as well as operations demanding more IT support across the organization. The proposers of new initiatives and the project managers of current initiatives are all insisting that their initiatives are essential for service delivery and achieving future strategies.'

Mary: 'You're not the only one with problems – all areas of the business face similar decisions. I do agree, though, that as IT has a major focus on supporting new business initiatives, you will be one of the worst affected. What do you think the real problem is?'

James: 'Probably my constrained IT resources and budget, the organization's limited ability to fund new projects, and the expectation that IT will deliver on all proposals. The executive also seems to expect that IT will support all proposals they approve.'

Mary: 'We have a selection and prioritization methodology that you may find helpful. In this process, proposals must be submitted to a selection and prioritization committee for independent assessment and scoring of all proposals. The committee then recommends a prioritized list of proposals to the executive, indicating which should be funded.'

James: 'The project teams work long hours and are dedicated. It is tough to tell them that their initiatives or projects will not receive new or further funding. Maybe the proposers should score their own projects based on the selection and prioritization methodology. They will then be able to recognize if their proposals don't stack up when presenting them to the senior IT managers.'

Mary: 'I have serious doubts about that idea. My recommendation is that you stick to the methodology.'

James: 'I have already asked my project managers and project proposers to present their proposals on Monday morning at 9 am. I am going to give them the PSO selection and prioritization methodology straight away and get them to score their proposals for Monday.'

It is Monday morning, 9 am. The project proposers look tired. As expected, most had worked through the weekend preparing their presentations.

Mary sat back and relaxed. What could possibly come from this session? No surprises! Virtually all proposals scored maximum points, meeting all criteria, and each presenter argued passionately for his or her proposal. The IT director and senior managers were none the wiser.

This was certainly 'one proposer – one vote'. Mary wondered where all this was heading. What would be the next suggestion?

Important lessons...

1. Implementing a prioritization process requires discipline.
2. Proposers will all score their own projects at the highest level possible. It is essential to separate the proposers from the evaluation and scoring process.
3. Business managers (sponsors) should present the proposals, as they will own the change resulting from the project. Technology is there to enable the business to achieve proposed improvements.
4. Functional heads cannot manage the prioritization process. The appropriate structures must be used for selection and prioritization.
5. Releasing a methodology without the appropriate structures, training and understanding of organizational impacts is not recommended.

THE APPRAISAL FACTORS OF VALUE AND RISK

This section discusses a set of 12 factors suitable for a public sector organization. Each factor is described and the value or risk of each factor leading to suggested weightings is discussed. Organizations may wish to develop their own set of factors for proposal evaluation, using these as examples.

Financial

1. Overall financial evaluation (value)

The overall financial evaluation appraises the likely impact of the proposed project on the organization's financial performance. Some calculations are important in evaluating the financial impact, as explained below.

A cash flow summary illustrates the costs of obtaining the complete product or service and integrating it into operations, including the operating costs related to the product or service. Similarly, the expected financial benefits returned over the operating life of the product or service are reflected. This will provide some clarity on the retrieval of benefits to the organization. A diagram placing time on a horizontal line with costs and benefits indicated at year-end is a useful analysis tool.

Net Present Value (NPV) is the money amount of all outlays (costs) and inflows (benefits), over the life of the service or product, discounted at the organization's cost of capital. This will result in a positive, zero or negative monetary amount, indicating whether the investment is financially sound for the organization. A positive NPV indicates that the proposal exceeds the organization's minimum return on money invested. Discounting merely allows future funds to be viewed at today's value.

The benefit:cost ratio is calculated by dividing the NPV of the benefits by the NPV of the costs. The result shows whether the investment is financially viable for the organization. A ratio of greater than one is usually considered favourable.

A useful resource to assist readers is the *Introduction to Cost Benefit Analysis for Program Managers* (Second Edition) published by the Australian Department of Finance. This document discusses different approaches to cost benefit analysis and interpretation. It is important to apply the most appropriate approach when analysing proposals, as a lack of knowledge can unwittingly create an incorrect impression.

Other books on financial analysis can provide guidelines and methods on topics such as payback, net present value, discount rates and financial portfolios.

Strategic

The strategic factors relate to the likely impact of the proposed project on the organization's strategy. The following factors contribute to this evaluation.

2. Contribution to strategy (value)

This measures the degree to which the proposed project relates to or achieves approved organizational goals by contributing to the critical success factors and improvement of operating efficiency and effectiveness. Projects, and hence the portfolio, must contribute to the organization's three- to five-year goals, while recognizing the constraints facing the organization in the next year. Proposals must clearly describe their strategic contribution.

3. Political/public perception gain (value)

This factor assesses the degree to which the project will provide a social advantage or a benefit to the community and, if appropriate, meet political expectations. The advantage is measured by the degree to which the project enhances services and meets public or political expectations.

4. Contestability advantage (value)

Public and private sector organizations today operate in an environment where significant areas of the business are contestable. This factor measures the degree to which the project enhances the organization's advantage over its service delivery competitors.

Organizational/management

The organizational/management factors appraise the likely impact of the proposed project on the organization's culture and employee satisfaction.

5. Organizational culture (value)

To a greater or lesser degree, each project will contribute to the cultural shift taking place within the organization. Positive influences on the organization's culture in line with organizational goals are important to the overall success of business strategies. The project proposal must consider the impact on the organization's culture shift.

6. Contribution to employee satisfaction/support (value)

This factor measures the degree to which the proposed project contributes to the job satisfaction of staff. Typical projects that contribute to employee satisfaction are those aiming to improve service delivery, enhance staff safety and health, reduce paperwork, or improve process efficiency. As with any change project, there will be resistance by those who perceive that their position is under threat. The proposal must clearly explain the level of change and potential benefits to staff.

7. Change management (risk)

This factor focuses on the ability of the organization to implement changes required by the project. To determine the degree of risk associated with achieving maximum project benefits, the following are assessed:

● management's ability to facilitate change;
● the existence of management processes to facilitate change;
● the likelihood of change acceptance by certain groups within the organization.

The project proposal will need to assess the risk level of these points.

8. Pace of change (risk)

This factor considers the organization's ability to absorb high levels of change without having a negative influence on operations. As each project moves from design to implementation, ownership of the project outcomes moves from the project participants to operations, thereby affecting service delivery capability. Branches of the organization may also have their own project initiatives that influence service delivery.

The Portfolio Council will assess this factor, considering information from operations across the organization. The organization's training plan is also an important gauge of proposed levels of change. Effective assessment of this factor requires considering which other projects will be implemented simultaneously with the proposal.

9. Execution capability (risk)

This measures the degree to which the project depends on new or untested skills, management capabilities or specialist expertise. For example, placing an inexperienced project manager on a large and complex project will significantly increase the risk of later delivery and cost overrun. Having an inexperienced or non-influential sponsor with a poor understanding of project roles and responsibilities will compound this risk.

The project proposal must address this risk, which requires tactful interpretation, as management ability is under the microscope.

Technology

Technology is an important tool in the achievement of business improvement projects, and the following factors need to be evaluated.

10. Compatibility with corporate architecture (value)

This factor assesses the degree to which the technology component of the project fits the organization's current information and technology architecture.

11. Definitional uncertainty (risk)

This assesses the degree of information and technology risk in project implementation. Projects lacking specification certainty or with a high probability of future changes will subject the organization to increased risk. Information and technology projects that intend to deliver results over an extended period also carry considerable risk.

12. Technical uncertainty (risk)

This assesses the project's dependence on the introduction of new or untried technology, and hence its inherent risk. The level of dependence on the following needs to be considered:

- application software;
- hardware dependencies;
- operating system software;
- third parties.

Organizations also often have to consider the value that a project will deliver against the chance of success (risk). The combination of these two factors results in projects varying between 'time-wasters' and 'gambles'. Table 5.2 illustrates this range.

Table 5.2 Chance of success vs. value

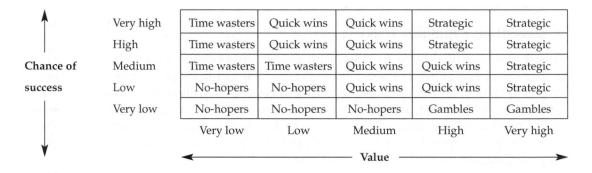

		Very low	Low	Medium	High	Very high
Chance of	Very high	Time wasters	Quick wins	Quick wins	Strategic	Strategic
	High	Time wasters	Quick wins	Quick wins	Strategic	Strategic
	Medium	Time wasters	Time wasters	Quick wins	Quick wins	Strategic
success	Low	No-hopers	No-hopers	Quick wins	Quick wins	Strategic
	Very low	No-hopers	No-hopers	No-hopers	Gambles	Gambles
		Very low	Low	Medium	High	Very high

Value

WEIGHTINGS OF FACTORS

Upper management and the executive are responsible for reviewing all the factors and agreeing on the factor's significance to the organization. After considering current business strategies and organization circumstances, the executive and upper management award a weighting of between 0 and 10 to each factor. Value factors are assigned a positive weighting, and risk factors a negative weighting. It is important that the weightings are reviewed periodically to reflect the organization's changing environment. Review periods could vary from three months to a maximum of one year.

Each of the above value and risk components is scored in the range 0–5. These factor scores are then multiplied by the weightings to establish the score for the component. These individual component scores are added to establish the project score.

An example of an analysed proposal, showing assessed value/risk scores, relevant weightings and total scores, is shown in Table 5.3.

Table 5.4 shows an example of a prioritized list of project proposals. This list is drawn up by the Portfolio Council prioritization sub-group and reviewed by the Portfolio Council. The Portfolio Council in turn submits the list to the executive for the final decision. The line separating proposals C and D in Table 5.4 represents the funding threshold. This prioritized list also reflects the human resource capacity available to deliver the proposed projects. A further snapshot of the human resource loading per quarter will further assist executives with decision making. This line is shown between proposal B and M.

Table 5.3 Project value and risk analysis proposal for project A

	Value Risk	Weight (0–10)	Score (0–5)	Total
1. FINANCIAL				
1.1 Overall financial evaluation	Value	10	4	40
2. STRATEGIC				
2.1 Contribution to strategy	Value	10	5	50
2.2 Political/public perception gain	Value	5	4	20
2.3 Competitive advantage	Value	3	3	9
3. ORGANIZATIONAL/MANAGEMENT				
3.1 Organization culture	Value	8	4	32
3.2 Contribution to employee satisfaction	Value	5	5	25
3.3 Change management	Risk	−8	2	−16
3.4 Pace of change	Risk	−9	5	−45
3.5 Execution capability	Risk	−6	1	−6
4. TECHNICAL				
4.1 Contribution to corporate architecture	Value	5	5	25
4.2 Definitional uncertainty	Risk	−5	3	−15
4.3 Technical uncertainty	Risk	−5	3	−15
Total value score				201
Total risk score				−97
VALUE – RISK SCORE				104

Figure 5.5 is a graphical representation of the prioritized projects showing the relationship between value and risk scores for the proposed portfolio of projects.

The graphical analysis shown in Figure 5.5 enables the executive to view its portfolio strategy and decide which mix of projects will deliver the maximum benefit to the organization. Certain projects that are mission critical or contractually committed are usually prioritized ahead of service improvement, research and development, and discretionary projects.

It is important to maintain the right perspective of selection and prioritization. It is an important management tool, but is no more than that. It cannot replace sound management decision making. However, in a complex, rapidly changing environment it provides some clarity. Accountability of upper management and the executive is sharpened, as decision making has a more definite foundation and is more objective. Without adequate information, accountability for decisions is arguably 'watered down'. The responsibility for ensuring that the most appropriate methods of information gathering are used for decision making ultimately rests with the CEO.

Although an organization may have carried out a sound selection and prioritization analysis, the external environment may affect the portfolio in many ways. For example, the organization may experience an unexpected cash flow problem, necessitating a re-evaluation of the portfolio. In Table 5.4, projects A, H, K, L and M require capital funds

Table 5.4 Prioritized list of project proposals

Project Prioritization List

Project ref.	Project name	Project description	Project category	Value score	Risk score	Priority score	Priority	Capital or operating funds	Xxxx year capital budget	Xxxx year operating budget	Cumulative xxxx capital budget	Cumulative xxxx operating budget	Xxxx budget	Xxxx+1 budget	Total budget
	Project A	To develop and implement a …	1. Executive mandated project	201	-97	104	1	Cap.	1,550,000	0	1,550,000	0	0	0	0
	Project H		3. Service improvement project	120	-23	97	2	Cap.	150,000	0	1,700,000	0	0	0	0
	Project F		3. Service improvement project	149	-57	92	3	Op.	0	180,000	1,700,000	180,000	0	0	0
	Project I		2. Contractually committed project	95	-12	83	4	Op.	0	375,000					
	Project J		4. R&D project	129	-75	54	5	Op.	0	312,000	1,700,000	867,000	0	0	0
	Project K		5. Discretionary project	106	-66	40	6	Cap.	2,235,000	0	3,935,000	867,000	0	0	0
	Project L		5. Discretionary project	119	-83	36	7	Cap.	645,000	0	4,580,000	867,000	0	0	0
	Project B	Upgrade the current …	1. Executive mandated project	72	-37	35	8	Op.	0	350,000	4,580,000	1,217,000	0	0	0
	Project M		5. Discretionary project	104	-83	21	9	Cap.	500,000	0	5,080,000	1,217,000	0	0	0
	Project C	Redesign and implement the … process	1. Executive mandated project	105	-94	11	10	Op.	0	230,000	5,080,000	1,447,000	0	0	0
	Project D		4. R&D project	154	-155	9	11	Cap.	220,000	0	5,300,000	1,447,000	0	0	0
	Project E		2. Contractually committed project	120	-113	7	12	Cap.	2,500,000	0	7,800,000	1,447,000	0	0	0
	Project N		5. Discretionary project	75	-69	6	13	Cap.	1,350,000	0	9,150,000	1,447,000	0	0	0
	Project G		3. Service improvement project	85	-86	-1	14	Cap.	75,000	0	9,225,000	1,447,000	0	0	0

▪ ▪ ▪ HR capacity available

▬▬ Capital fund limit

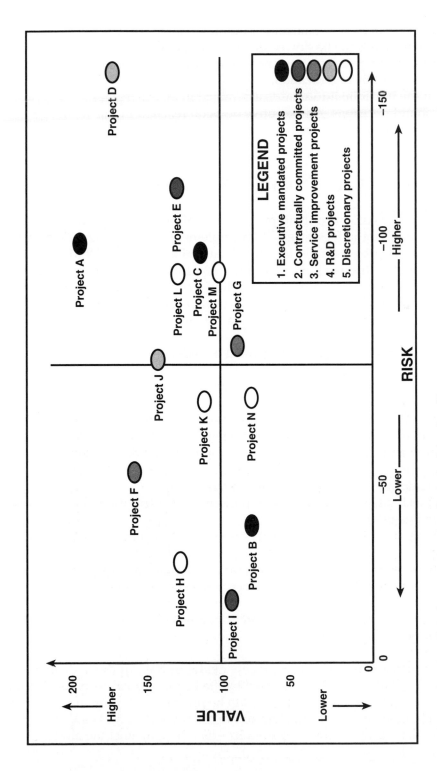

Figure 5.5 Graphical representation for prioritization list

and would place pressure on organization funding. Potentially, projects K, L and M may individually or jointly have to be slowed down or deferred, depending on the severity of the funding situation. Reprioritization and ranking will need to be undertaken to reflect the current impacts on the organization.

It is here that the portfolio information assembled in an orderly fashion assists executives to make sound decisions. An executive decision reached in this manner will stand up to scrutiny much better than the typical 'shoot from the hip' decision making.

MANAGING MULTIPLE PROJECTS AS A PROGRAMME

A portfolio of projects consists of both programmes of projects and individual projects, making up the total initiatives selected to implement the organization's strategies. Managing individual projects is discussed in detail in Part III, the ODPM™ process.

This section briefly discusses the discipline of programme management – implementing business strategies to provide maximum benefits for the organization, while controlling risks. The PMBOK® Guide[73] defines a programme as 'A group of related projects managed in a coordinated way. Programs usually include an element of ongoing activity.'

Aspects of effective programme management include:

- focusing on managing strategic initiatives through multiple projects and the associated benefits and risks;
- focusing management attention on a defined set of benefits, which are understood at the outset, managed throughout the implementation of the portfolio (programme), and delivered and measured during implementation and at completion;
- assisting upper management to set priorities, evaluate and choose options for action, and allocate resources for implementation;
- creating a mechanism for ensuring that projects are contributing to the achievement of expected business benefits;
- guiding an organization in achieving its strategic shift from where it is now to where it wants to be;
- ensuring that the impacts of programme-driven changes on business operations are coordinated, and that the transition to operations is well managed.

The definition and planning of how the programme will contribute to the change in business operations is of utmost importance. This process includes:

- preparing and maintaining a clear process model of the improved business operations, ensuring that the model is 'owned' by the business areas responsible for operating the products or services and is seen to be practical, relevant and achievable;
- ensuring that objectives and priorities of the constituent projects are clearly driven by their impacts on the business operations – test them against the model.

Developing the programme's scope is an essential building block to achieving success, and covers the following components:

- identifying relevant strategies and change initiatives, assessing their impact on the business areas and defining the benefits sought;
- identifying candidate groupings of projects and evaluating them for business benefits, economies of scale and compatibility with support services such as IT infrastructure, human resources and financial systems;
- selecting a programme consisting of a group of projects that allows the best balance between strategic objectives, operational impacts and affordability, and that is achievable within an acceptable level of risk;
- defining and documenting each grouping as a programme, and obtaining authorization for the business case.

Structuring the programme is an important sponsor and upper management function, and includes:

- organizing the roles and responsibilities at both programme and project levels;
- dividing the programme into projects and then sub-projects to facilitate its management, synchronizing planning and funding cycles and the delivery of benefits;
- coordinating the deliverables from each project with the aim of achieving some of the planned benefits at the earliest possible time;
- planning review points (islands of stability) between project phases and deliverables to review progress, direction and the achievement of benefits;
- ensuring that plans for and changes to support facilities such as IT and human resources are coordinated across all the projects.

Managing the programme to balance the dimensions of risk, quality and change includes:

- assessing and managing risks associated with the programme, its projects and the planned changes to business operations;
- ensuring that the assessments of quality and fitness for purpose fully meet the requirements of the business;
- ensuring that progress reporting is open and effective, so that risks can be foreseen and mitigated in the most appropriate manner;
- being aware of developments external to the programme (such as legislation or policy changes) and taking action to accommodate them;
- managing the programme impact on business operations – for example, to avoid any reduction in customer service during the transition implementation;
- involving personnel in affected business areas to prepare them for change, for example with training, awareness communications and procedure planning;
- managing the transition of the project deliverables to business operations;
- ensuring that support services such as human resources and IT are able to accommodate changes in the business operations.

Programme managers must ensure that the programme delivers its planned benefits, by:

- looking for measurable improvements in business operations;
- identifying benefits from the programme as a whole, as well as those from individual projects;
- actively managing benefits delivery and recovery throughout the programme;
- providing time at the end of each project or major deliverable to reassess benefits achieved and evaluate any adjustments that need to be made to the programme.

Programme management is thus a specific management function that gives direction to projects and spans the project process. It receives deliverables from projects and assists in integrating them into the business. The overall aim of a programme is to better position the organization to achieve its strategic objectives.

In practice...

Selection and prioritization meets upper management – an uncomfortable experience

Judging by the number of projects launched in addition to the existing programme of projects, the situation at ABC Business Services Ltd appeared out of control. Both programme management and project teams were constantly under pressure and conflict was becoming the norm rather than the exception.

The recently established project support office (PSO) identified the problem and undertook the design and development of a project selection and prioritization model, which would enable the executive, functional and project managers to make better decisions.

As the model developed, the impact and importance of such a selection and prioritization methodology became clear.

There were always a large number of proposals vying for the organization's limited resources, and naturally all proposals promised attractive returns and benefits. The finance department operated the *de facto* selection and prioritization system by allocating funds or recommending to the executive which projects should be funded. This situation became untenable, as informal influences at both executive and finance department levels formed the basis of prioritization.

Sponsorship of the selection and prioritization development initiative project was at the deputy CEO level. Finance and IT team members had been brought into the development of the model. Initially, finance staff were not supportive as they felt that the PSO was 'meddling in their affairs'.

Once the process was developed and the methodology completed, presentations were made to senior managers in order to obtain feedback and support. The sponsor was supportive and encouraging throughout.

A selection and prioritization paper was drawn up and circulated to committee members. The impact of the paper became clear to the top end of the organization, and an interesting reaction followed. Executive members representing national areas perceived it as interfering with the resource decision making. Although planning and finance staff were consulted and had actively contributed to the proposal, their upper management was clearly not committed to the process. They perceived it to be interfering with the informal system that had been operating for some time. The PSO staff held urgent meetings and discussions with the sponsor.

Finally, the sponsor withdrew the paper; the PSO staff and manager were disappointed and disillusioned. How was it possible that a system which would be operated by functional heads, owned by the deputy CEO, administrated by a neutral project support office and prioritized by an independent committee could not get support?

The PSO manager, reflecting on the series of events leading to the decision to withdraw, concluded that organizational culture changes slowly, and is fraught with multiple interests, hidden agendas and other pitfalls. Changes of this magnitude require consultation and ownership by the executive and operational line managers. The dilemma was how much consultation was required. Where did one draw the line?

Important lessons...

1. Processes and systems that change the way organizations do business must be owned by the internal stakeholders at an early stage in the project process. Had the executive members bought into the selection and prioritization process at the outset, the process would in all probability have been accepted and implemented.
2. Upper management, like most staff, resist changes to the way that business is carried out. This resistance is often based on fear resulting from a lack of input early in the process. Fear of losing control, or of the shifting of decision-making power, will usually be resisted until managers can see benefits for themselves and their staff.
3. Making assumptions about stakeholder needs without consulting them, and then promising a system that will 'meet their needs', is likely to fail.
4. Having a senior sponsor will not always guarantee success if the stakeholder strategy and communication are not sound.

In practice...

Holding the baby!

The establishment of the Business Development Group (BDG) was a great opportunity to fill a critical gap in the area of business research and development. As the work of the group influenced the future direction of the organization, senior management had a keen interest in the performance of the BDG. So much so, that one of the key result areas (KRA) of the organization's strategy read: 'The Business Development Group will develop new organization strategies and implement these via projects that will result in improved business performance'.

The group had both a clear mandate and a direction from the executive, as well as being licensed to undertake 'blue skies' thinking. Enthused by the challenge and wide mandate, the group took to the task with purpose and focus. An enormous amount of research in visioning, operating models and business strategies was undertaken in the first year. Cases for change and business cases were also developed for a series of major redesign projects. Some operational inputs were received through the secondment of staff to the projects; however, the majority of the 'grunt' work was undertaken by BDG staff.

Design work, workshops and implementation planning required another six months, resulting in business cases that were ready for prioritization. Following a prioritization and selection process, a prioritized list of projects was presented to the executive for consideration.

The executive, after studying the business cases and considering the recommended prioritized list, approved three business redesign projects for implementation across regions. These projects would create a significant change in the way that regions delivered services.

The BDG was now faced with the challenge of implementing the redesigns. The BDG manager found that no implementation strategy existed to guide the implementation teams in regions. A strategy was rapidly cobbled together to become part of the implementation plan. An implementation pilot was to be undertaken in one of the regions, under the sponsorship of the regional manager, and managed by an operational project manager.

Although the sponsor of the three projects was the General Manager Operations, a senior member of the executive, the regional managers had a great deal of autonomy. They managed their own budgets and operations staffing, as well as holding full accountability for service delivery and implementation of national projects in their regions. It was accepted from early on that the implementation of the projects would affect service delivery.

When the project team arrived in the pilot region, they discovered a lack of support at both management and staff levels. Life on the project became progressively more difficult, leading eventually to open hostility.

The regional manager was beginning to realize the extent of the changes the projects would create. Staff were resisting the changes, demonstrating this by a lack of contribution to workshops. The regional manager, sensing the resistance, stated that implementation would not continue until the managers were convinced that the proposed project changes were sustainable within current resource limitations. This sent a clear message to the staff that regional management did not really support the projects.

The implementation team became more isolated, as they effectively reported to the regional manager (who was acting as the implementation sponsor) but did not receive any support from him. The message coming back to the project team and BDG was 'Don't conceive and leave us with the baby. Don't expect us to foster your children'.

By the end of the second year, the BDG manager was disillusioned. None of the redesign projects had been fully implemented. The BDG was criticized for designing projects at great expense yet delivering nothing! The team became defensive and morale slipped. Although the BDG worked long hours with passion, their performance was perceived as being ineffective. Internal audit had been less than complimentary of the BDG's performance – ratings against the KRA were poor.

Understandably, the BDG manager did a lot of soul searching, and finally had to come to terms with the fact that projects in a strongly decentralized organization can, at best, only be conceived by a business development group. Early ownership by those who will own and operate the products resulting from projects is critical to success. Delivering the baby, and then expecting regions to adopt and raise it, is not the best policy in these types of organizations.

Changes to the BDG have now taken place, with improved role clarification and all national projects being decentralized. The KRAs have been altered to better reflect the BDG's role in the process. Projects are now primarily driven by region staff, with the BDG in support and offering a consulting and mentoring role.

Important lessons...

1. Project performance measures must be achievable by the project team. In this case they were not. If the measures had reflected that BDG performance would rely on executive and region support for business cases, and that regions would then be responsible for detailed design and implementation, BDG performance would have been attainable.
2. Executive approval of a business case relies heavily on advice from both the project sponsor and BDG manager. The regional managers were not represented on the executive, and were therefore not party to the approval.
3. Those who have to own and operate the project outputs (products and/or services) should present the business case and defend it to the executive. They will then be committed to achieving the promised benefits.
4. Project sponsorship is crucial to project success. The moment that support is perceived to be waning, those who resist change will feel encouraged and undermine the project.
5. A project team should be protected from harassment. Team members must be supported and protected, as their job is tough. Others will observe or hear about the difficult working environment on projects, which will give projects a bad name in the organization and make it difficult to recruit teams in the future.
6. Upper management can be sincere in that they mean what they say, but if they meet resistance to change, they cannot meet the honest requirement – doing what they said they would do. In the real world, circumstances change rapidly, and in the 'fuzzy to clear' approach, where not all important factors are clear at the project initiation stage, it is often difficult to foresee all events and influences downstream. Thus, the criteria of honesty can be difficult to meet.

Part III

Objective Directed Project Management (ODPM)

6

Introduction to ODPM

WHAT IS ODPM?

Objective Directed Project Management (ODPM™) is a process developed by the authors. It consists of a series of interrelated steps, tools and techniques sequenced in a systematic and logical manner to provide a process for initiating, defining, planning, executing and closing-out a project. ODPM forms the core of the BFPM™ approach and is at the heart of the Wrappers™ model.

ODPM was developed to provide effective planning tools in the early phases of a project and to allow a better focus on the business outcomes that projects deliver. The authors found that the then traditional project management tools did not achieve these goals. The seeds of the solution were found in the influential book by Andersen, Grude and Haug, *Goal Directed Project Management*[2]. The idea was germinated further by a paper titled *A Workshop Approach to Project Execution Planning* by Claudio Pincus, in which the author discusses the use of facilitated workshops to develop a project execution plan. In particular, the paper gave a number of guidelines to be considered when developing a plan of execution; these are quoted below:

What are the specific objectives to be met?
What is the work breakdown?
Who must do what, where, when?
What are the obstacles in performing the work?
What are the major decisions which must be made? (When and by whom?)
What is the sequence of work?
What is the difference between the execution of this job and normal procedures?

How must the involved groups interrelate?
How will the accomplishments in achieving specific targets and goals be measured?

The paper further advocates the use of an 'intensive workshop approach' that brings together the key project participants, during the early stages of a project, to:

1. Formulate the plans, strategies, organizational structure, and relationships for successful execution according to requirements and with the participation of the involved parties.
2. Obtain a cohesive project team in which members understand their specific responsibilities, authority, and standards of performance as interpreted by the project manager and in accordance with the requirements of the parent organization.

Andersen, Grude and Haug[2] provide a list of important factors for avoiding pitfalls in projects. This list can serve as a 'requirement specification' for a project management process. The list is quoted below:

- The project must work on tasks which are important for the base organization. There should be a close correlation between the business plans and the objectives of the project.
- The base organization should have principles and policies of project work.
- Project methods and tools must compel those involved to spend time on defining project objectives and goals, i.e. what the project should achieve.
- Project methods and tools must compel those involved to focus on giving the project a composite goal, which encompasses matters relating to people, systems (technical matters) and organization.
- Project planning must take place at two levels; global or project level, and the detail or activity level.
- Short-term, controllable intermediate goals must be set.
- A plan must be clearly represented on a single sheet of standard-sized paper.
- Those who draw up the plans must know that they themselves will have to live with the consequences of them.
- There must be an understanding of the fact that change processes take time.
- There must be an understanding of what control is, and how important this task is in project work.
- A plan must be formulated in such a way that it both facilitates and promotes control.
- The project manager must be given authority in his dealings with the base organization.
- Procedures for reporting must be established.
- There must be an understanding that a project can be organized in several different ways.
- The lines of responsibility in a project must be clearly described.
- Binding agreements for releasing resources for the project must be drawn up.
- Line management and project members should be highly motivated.
- A project manager with the right qualities must be selected.
- Concrete work must be done to create good conditions for cooperation in the project.
- Common methods must be selected for work on the project which also encourage communication between the experts and users.
- Changes in project objectives and goals must be made after careful consideration.
- There must be quality control throughout the project.

After considering all the above in the context of their own experience in teaching and practising project management, the authors developed ODPM as a project management process and tested it in industry. With the publication in 1996 of the Project Management Institute's (PMI) *A Guide to the Project Management Body of Knowledge* (PMBOK® Guide) [73], ODPM was tested against the processes given in that publication and was refined to ensure closer alignment with the PMI standards.

Since its inception in 1990, ODPM has acquired a faithful following of project management practitioners in South Africa, New Zealand and Europe. Since then, the process has undergone many changes and refinements and has evolved as the delivery component of the BFPM approach. To date (2002), over 3,500 people have been trained in its use and it has been used on a variety of projects: large and small, complex and simple.

Because of its strong focus on results or objectives, ODPM can be and is being effectively used to plan and manage 'fuzzy' projects that do not respond well to the more scientific project management tools, techniques and processes. Such 'fuzzy' projects commonly exist in business, information technology, human resources and culture change or transformation projects.

CHARACTERISTICS OF ODPM

In addition to addressing the points and considerations given earlier, ODPM, as a project management process, has the following broad characteristics:

- is driven by results and objectives more than by activities – focusing on what the project is to achieve as well as how it is to be achieved;
- fosters commitment, ownership and buy-in during the early stages of a project;
- uses sound principles of management and is structured in an integrated, systematic and logical manner;
- places the traditional project management tools and techniques in their rightful place in the project management process, and introduces practical tools and techniques that are easy to assimilate and use;
- allows planning and management of 'fuzzy' projects and uses the principles of progressive elaboration and fuzzy to clear;
- allows for understanding of and participation in the project by all players: upper management, sponsor, project core team, functional organizations and other stakeholders, without them needing to become involved in the technical aspects of the project;
- ensures that the concepts and principles of authority, accountability and responsibility are applied and adhered to, without dictating an organization structure (such as matrix, functional or projectized);
- enables the project to be aligned with the business objectives and encourages project participants to take a business view of the project;
- allows creative thinking to be applied at all levels and by all participants.

OVERVIEW OF THE ODPM PROCESS

The ODPM process follows the project management life cycle as described in Chapter 1. The process begins with initiation and ends with the closing-out of the project. It starts once the BFPM process (Project Wrapper) has indicated that a project is required and ends when the required project outcomes have been delivered to the business or organization.

Although the ODPM process is continuous and sequential, it is subdivided into five distinct project management life-cycle phases: initiation, definition, planning, execution and close-out. The authors have found that project practitioners are inclined to approach project planning in an almost 'shotgun' manner, somewhat haphazardly applying tools and techniques. The ODPM process is designed to be followed step by step, from start to finish, with each step producing an output that is required by the next step, thus applying the principle of progressive elaboration. The steps are logically sequenced in a common-sense manner, but rather than being rigid, it becomes flexible and practical with use.

The project manager takes responsibility and accountability for the project management process and therefore has authority over its application. Steps in the process may be ignored or not applied but the accountability for the consequences of the omissions will always lie with the project manager.

Flexibility

The ODPM process is sufficiently flexible to allow it to be modified to suit a particular organization or type of project. Steps can be added and tools and techniques supplemented or replaced, provided the outcome of the step is not compromised. For example, the tool or technique for performing a stakeholder analysis can be any one of a number, but the output must always be a list of stakeholders and their involvement with the project. Similarly, the tool used for time analysis does not have to be limited to critical path analysis, but could be a technique such as line-of-balance, time-location charting, Gantt charts or activity schedules. Irrespective, the outcome must be that the project has been appropriately analysed in terms of time.

The flexible and generic nature of the ODPM process allows it to be used to manage projects, sub-projects, project phases and programmes in a consistent manner. The process remains the same, although the tools and techniques may vary or certain steps may, after careful consideration, be skipped. Similarly, the same process may be applied for complex or simple, large or small projects. The process remains the same; however, the tools, techniques and intensity of their application may vary.

Definition phase

There is, however, one phase of the ODPM process – the definition phase – that cannot be compromised and that must be applied in its entirety, including the use of the tools specified. The definition phase is relatively short, with very specific objectives, and within it lies the uniqueness and strength of the ODPM process. Skipping or diluting the definition phase removes much of the power of the ODPM process and weakens its contribution to successful project management.

Summarizing the ODPM process

Table 6.1 is a summary of the ODPM process, subdivided into the project management life-cycle phases.

The remaining chapters of Part III describe each phase of the ODPM process, and explain the steps within the phase. Excerpts from a case study, *The conference project*, are shown at appropriate points in the discussion of the process. The case study is given in full in Appendix A. The authors suggest that readers become familiar with the case study before reading the remainder of Part III. It is also assumed that the reader has covered the Introduction and Chapters 1 and 2, as many of the concepts outlined in those chapters are applied in the next five chapters. Some of the tools, techniques and basic concepts referred to in the following chapters are further described in Appendix B.

Note that the ODPM process is discussed in the context of a project, and that term is used throughout. However, the process and steps described could apply equally to programmes, sub-projects and project phases, and so the word 'project' also applies to them in context.

Table 6.1a ODPM process summary – Project initiation phase

STEP	DESCRIPTION/COMMENTS	TOOL, TECHNIQUE, TEMPLATE
1. Select project manager	Identify and select the best person to lead the project.	Competency assessment
2. Scrutinize the documentation	The project manager must scrutinize all documentation relating to the project, such as the business case and feasibility studies, to ensure completeness.	Business case and supporting documentation
3. Stakeholder verification	Verify the stakeholders who should be represented at the project definition workshop. Stakeholders should have been identified and analysed when preparing the business case.	Business case and supporting documentation
4. Produce the project charter	The project charter document is produced and signed by the sponsor and project manager. The project manager accepts accountability for the project.	Project charter
5. Inform all parties	Inform all parties of the start of the project by circulating the project charter to all affected and involved parties.	Project charter

Table 6.1b ODPM process summary – Project definition phase

STEP	DESCRIPTION/COMMENTS	TOOL, TECHNIQUE, TEMPLATE
1. Convene project definition workshop	Convene the project definition workshop on a suitable date and at suitable venue. Inform all and appoint a facilitator.	Project definition workshop (PDW) nomination form
2. Brainstorm and categorize issues	Brainstorm, categorize and document the issues. Anything not related to the project is put on a 'parking lot' list.	Issue lists Parking lot
3. Determine project purpose or mission	A concise statement is drafted, which describes the purpose of the project and acts as a focus for the participants.	Project purpose and objectives template
4. Determine objectives and performance measures	Document the measurable objectives and performance that must be delivered by the project. This will contain measurables for the project as well as the organization.	Project purpose and objectives template
5. Project approach	A general description of the intended approach to the development and delivery of the project, and the integration into the business.	Flow chart of the project Project life cycle
6. Determine the deliverables breakdown structure (DBS)	Determine the tangible deliverables that the project is to produce. Develop the deliverables breakdown structure (DBS).	Mind-mapping Deliverables breakdown structure (DBS)
7. Establish scope, assumptions, constraints and limiting criteria	Establish and document any constraints, assumptions and limiting criteria. Determine the scope, particularly what is in and out of scope.	Initial scope, assumptions, constraints and limits template
8. Determine result milestones and initial time estimates	Determine the result milestones and place them in a logical sequence. Determine the best initial time estimates.	Milestone objective chart (MOC)
9. Determine the responsible entities and project responsibilities	Determine the core team and other entities that will drive the project forward. Determine decision-making power. Determine and document who is accountable for achieving which milestone and who has the responsibility for doing the work.	List of responsible entities Contact lists Milestone responsibility matrix (MRM)
10. Prepare communications plan	Develop a communications plan or strategy to meet the information and communication needs of the stakeholders.	Outline communications plan
11. Perform project risk analysis	Identify the risks to the project and analyse them in terms of impact, manageability and probability. Formulate responses to the risks identified.	Risk evaluation template
12. Calculate initial cost estimate	Calculate the costs based on the information and data established up to this point. Produce an initial cost estimate (order of magnitude estimate).	Cost estimating Cost estimate template
13. Produce project definition report (PDR)	Prepare all the documents relating to the above steps and collate them into one document.	Project definition report

Table 6.1c ODPM process summary – Project planning phase

STEP	DESCRIPTION/COMMENTS	TOOL, TECHNIQUE, TEMPLATE
1. Organize planning work and convene any planning workshops	Verify who will be accountable for doing the detailed planning work (normally indicated by the milestone responsibility matrix). Convene any required planning workshops.	Work package responsibility matrix
2. Determine work involved at detail level	Break down the project work to be done to detailed (activity) level. Construct the work breakdown structure (WBS).	Mind-mapping Work breakdown structure (WBS)
3. Perform time analysis	Carry out a time analysis on the project activities using an appropriate method.	Gantt chart Critical path analysis Activity schedules Computer package
4. Perform resource analysis	Allocate resources to the activities and perform a resource analysis.	Resource analysis
5. Perform cost analysis	Calculate the costs based on the information and data established up to this point. Produce a detailed cost estimate.	Cost estimating Cost estimate template
6. Prepare quality plan	Prepare the quality plan.	Project quality plan
7. Prepare communications plan	Prepare the communications plan.	Project communications plan
8. Prepare human resources plan	Prepare the human resources plan.	List of responsible entities Project human resources plan
9. Prepare procurement plan	Prepare the procurement plan.	Project procurement plan
10. Integrate project plan	Ensure that all planning work for all work packages is integrated and all cross-checks are performed. Ensure integration of all aspects (cost, time, quality, scope, risk, etc). Project manager takes accountability for the project plan.	Integrated project plan baseline
11. Do cash flow analysis	Prepare the cash flow graphs and perform a cash flow analysis.	S-curve graphs Cash flow schedules
12. Produce integrated project plan baseline	Collate all project documentation as at this point and produce the integrated project plan baseline.	Integrated project plan baseline
13. Determine control mechanisms, project management information system (PMIS), and key performance indicators (KPIs)	Determine the control methods and mechanisms. Establish and document the KPIs for managing project performance. Ensure that the PMIS can produce management information.	Performance analysis

Table 6.1d ODPM process summary – Project execution phase

STEP	DESCRIPTION/COMMENTS	TOOL, TECHNIQUE, TEMPLATE
1. Hold kick-off meeting	Hold meeting to officially kick-off the execution phase of the project and to ensure that all are aware of what needs to be done.	
2. Establish monitoring and control systems and project infrastructure	Set up the processes required to monitor and control the project as well as to establish any infrastructure required.	
3. Monitor and evaluate project performance and progress	All aspects of the project (time, costs, quality, changes, risks, etc) are monitored regularly. The monitored information is evaluated and reviewed on a regular basis. Identify and flag any deviations.	Earned value reports and schedules Cost reports Activity progress reports Key performance indicators (KPIs)
4. Produce progress, status and performance reports	Produce regular progress, status and performance reports for the project. Circulate to all who need to know.	As above, attached to a formal progress report
5. Apply control, feedback and problem solving	Act on any deviations to the plan. Address any day-to-day problems.	Control, feedback and problem-solving techniques
6. Revise baseline if required	If changes are made to any aspect of the integrated project plan baseline, then the document must be updated to reflect those changes.	Integrated project plan baseline

Table 6.1e ODPM process summary – Project close-out phase

STEP	DESCRIPTION/COMMENTS	TOOL, TECHNIQUE, TEMPLATE
1. Plan completion	Plan the completion of the work.	Gantt chart Critical path analysis Activity schedules
2. Deliverable vertification (client acceptance)	This has been taking place throughout the execution phase. Ensure that all deliverables have been accepted and signed off by the client.	Acceptance certificates
3. Review performance criteria	Review the measurable objectives and performance criteria agreed during the project definition phase. Has the project achieved what it set out to do?	Performance analysis
4. Release resources	Release any resources from the project. Advise all resource managers that they are relieved of their commitments to the project.	
5. Contractual aspects and final accounting	Ensure that all the contractual aspects have been settled and that the final accounting has been done.	
6. Complete all documentation	Ensure that all project documentation is collated and filed.	
7. Post implementation review (PIR)	Conduct a post implementation review (PIR). This establishes what went well, what did not happen according to plan, lessons learnt, etc.	
8. Write final project report	Write a final project report summarizing the history of the project and evaluation of the performance.	
9. Terminate and archive project	End the project and archive all documentation. Advise all of the completion and termination of the project.	

7

The project initiation phase

INTRODUCTION

The project initiation phase is the first phase of the project management life cycle. It is the start of a process that takes the project brief, as developed, selected and prioritized using the BFPM™ approach, through to the delivery of the project's outcomes back into the business.

The major input into this phase is the business case and supporting documentation developed using the BFPM approach.

The most important objectives of this phase are to ensure that:

- a project manager is selected to lead the project;
- the project manager is briefed on the project;
- the project manager accepts accountability for the project;
- authority is given to the project manager to deliver the project;
- all parties are made aware of the project and of the project manager's authority.

The major outcome of this phase will be an authorized and briefed project manager who can take the process further.

Two people play major roles during this phase: the project sponsor and the project manager. The sponsor must have the authority from upper management to deliver the project. The project sponsor is responsible and accountable for the selection of the best person to lead the project. The sponsor must then brief the project manager. Once the project manager accepts the brief, the sponsor delegates the authority, accountability and responsibility for project delivery to that project manager.

Each of the steps in the project initiation phase are outlined and discussed below.

SELECT THE PROJECT MANAGER

The first step in the process is to identify, select and appoint a project manager to lead the project. This is the sponsor's task. As the sponsor and project manager will work closely for the entire project, a certain balance should exist between their strengths and weaknesses. They should, where possible, complement each other, and an honest, up-front understanding of each other's strong and weak areas will benefit the project.

The project manager is selected primarily for his or her ability to manage a range of people to get things done. The ability to lead and motivate teams is of cardinal importance. These two qualities are required as well as a certain level of competency in project management. The profile, competencies and attributes of a project manager are discussed in Chapter 1.

There is a tendency to appoint a person with the most technical expertise or knowledge of the business to the position of project manager. Although often unavoidable, such appointments can place a project at risk. The appointee may have a high level of technical expertise and business knowledge, but may lack the necessary project management competencies.

There is also the danger that an appointee with a high level of technical expertise may become more involved in the technical aspects of the project at an operational level rather than focusing on management issues. This can mean that not only is the project managed ineffectively, but may also result in project team members feeling threatened or demotivated if the appointee becomes technically involved and begins to direct the technical approach at a detailed level. In addition, appointing a person with high technical expertise as project manager may deprive the project of that person's technical ability, which could be more valuable at an operational level.

It makes sense, therefore, to appoint a person with strong project management competency, and who has reasonable knowledge of the project technology rather than the other way around. It is important to note that project managers tend to be generalists rather than specialists.

Another point for discussion is whether an organization should appoint a project manager from within the organization or from outside. Some years ago, organizations would have been hard pressed to find a project manager with the right attributes internally. The situation, however, has reversed dramatically over recent years, as many organizations have improved their competency in project management through training and development programmes. The authors have been involved in project management training since the 1970s and can attest to the phenomenal growth of this area, both in the number of courses offered and in the number of attendees. The trend, therefore, is towards developing competency in project management and appointing project managers from within as a first option.

Externally appointed project managers have, in the authors' opinion, always experienced problems of authority in their dealings with internal upper management and staff. This causes conflicts and an increase in tensions, which could place the project in jeopardy. A further problem is that when externally appointed project managers complete the assignment, they walk away with the experience and knowledge of the project that should remain with the organization.

What then can be done if the organization has limited competency in project management? The answer is straightforward – develop it! This can be done by appointing an internal project manager with some competency and then bringing in an external project management consultant to act as mentor or adviser to the appointee.

Being selected by the sponsor as the project manager does not mean that the nominee must accept the role. The person can either accept the brief – subject to certain conditions – or decline the role, depending on whether he or she is confident that the project is attainable in terms of parameters such as feasibility, cost, time and scope. Further, the project manager must believe that he or she will have sufficient influence over the parameters that drive the desired project outcomes. Before accepting the role, the nominee needs to scrutinize the business case and other supporting documentation that was developed using the BFPM approach.

SCRUTINIZE THE DOCUMENTATION

If the project arose through the BFPM approach, a business case and supporting documentation would have been generated (see Part II). The nominee project manager must scrutinize this documentation for completeness and validity. The sponsor is the custodian of this documentation and will probably lead the nominee through it. This allows the nominee to obtain a first-hand view of what the project entails.

The nominee project manager has an obligation to the organization and to the project management role to review the documentation before accepting the role of project manager. Too often, unattainable commitments in respect of time, cost and scope are specified in business cases by their authors, who may not necessarily have been the nominee project manager or the sponsor. By accepting the project brief and therefore the commitments made in the documentation, a project manager becomes accountable for delivering the desired outcomes and achieving the performance. Many project managers have found themselves committed to the delivery of someone else's unattainable promises. This is why it is vital for a nominee project manager to scrutinize the documents and ensure that upper management has applied due diligence in developing the case for the project and its prioritization. Decisions to accept project briefs are very often based on undocumented assumptions or incorrectly conveyed perceptions of other stakeholders, including the sponsor or upper management.

Scrutinizing the documents is made easier if a formal process, methodology or approach exists through which an idea or initiative passes before becoming a project to be delivered – such as BFPM. Typically, the most important document to flow from the business processes to the project team is the business case document in some form or other. This could be supported by various other documents, such as feasibility studies, vendor proposals, situation reports, as well as any instruments of authorization, such as minutes of meetings and letters of appointment.

What happens if:

- there is no documentation or the documentation is inadequate or incomplete?
- it is apparent that the project has not been well thought through from a business view?
- it appears that business processes have not been followed to select and prioritize the project?

It is then the nominee project manager's prerogative to decline the brief or to accept it conditionally. In most cases of conditional acceptance, the project manager will ask the sponsor to clarify the brief, or request that missing information be made available. If the missing information is not readily available, the project manager could request to be empowered to obtain the missing information. This could involve a change to the project manager's brief, the granting of additional authority, or access to potential sources of information.

A project manager cannot take ownership of a project without believing in it. If the project manager cannot buy into the project then there is little chance that he or she can influence other project participants to buy in.

The project brief should only be accepted once the project manager is satisfied that the project objectives and performance parameters are attainable and that the project brief has passed the business prioritization and selection gates.

STAKEHOLDER VERIFICATION

According to Obeng[68], 'Project success is and can only be defined by stakeholders'. It is essential, then, for the sponsor and project manager to ensure that the most influential stakeholders are represented at planning work sessions such as the project definition workshop (PDW), which is the first step of the project definition phase (covered in Chapter 8).

A stakeholder analysis is normally performed as part of the business case development, and this analysis must be available to the sponsor and project manager to help them determine which stakeholders should be involved. The purpose of this step, therefore, is to verify that a stakeholder analysis has been done and to select those stakeholders who have the most ability to influence the outcomes of the project. Stakeholders are discussed in Chapter 1 and stakeholder analysis outlined in Chapter 5.

If a stakeholder analysis has not been done as part of the business case, then it will need to be done before proceeding. The project manager cannot be held accountable for the robustness of the stakeholder analysis carried out in the business case development process.

A stakeholder analysis approach that the authors have found useful in the initial phases of projects is described below:

- Classify stakeholders as primary or secondary. Primary stakeholders are those that have influence over the project, and are affected by the project changes resulting from implementation. Secondary stakeholders are mainly affected by these project changes.
- Consider the risk(s) and/or the benefit(s) to each stakeholder, resulting from implementing the project.
- Reflect on the risk and benefit as described above, and develop an influencing strategy to keep the stakeholders engaged in the project objectives. This 'relationship building approach' is fundamental to developing a sound project plan permeated with strong stakeholder focus. An example of this relationship building: a key primary stakeholder could lose their position if the project fails. As project manager it would be important to build trust and a close working relationship with that stakeholder, thereby ensuring support on critical decisions and approvals.
- The above three factors are important inputs to considering what information the stakeholder requires to come along on the project journey. This information should form an integral part of project reporting, as discussed in Chapter 10.

The above four points are usually represented in tabular format, which can later be extended to form the outline of a communications plan.

The output from this step includes a list of stakeholders who should be represented at the project definition workshop. There will often be more interested stakeholders than would be prudent to involve in planning sessions. The rule here would be to include those who have the greatest influence over the outcomes of the project. Stakeholders who need only information or who should be consulted during later phases of the project can be brought into the project through the communication plan or responsibility matrices, as discussed in Chapters 8 and 9.

PRODUCE THE PROJECT CHARTER

Once the project manager has agreed to accept the project brief, project management authority over the project must be delegated to that project manager. This delegation can come from the sponsor (representing the client) or from upper management. This 'authority to proceed' is contained in a document aptly called the project charter.

The word 'charter' is defined in the *Collins English Dictionary and Thesaurus* (1998) as 'a formal document granting or demanding rights' and that is exactly the intention of the project charter. Apart from formally recognizing the existence of a new project, it serves to authorize (grant) the project manager to make use of the organization's resources (rights) such as people, equipment, materials and funds to deliver the project.

The project charter document is normally concise and should cover at least the following:

- the overall project purpose;
- the priority of the project relative to other initiatives in the organization;
- identification of the project manager and sponsor;
- the extent of the project manager's authority;
- important dates and estimated project duration;
- funds available (cost of the project);
- any other resource limitations;
- what benefits the project will bring to the organization.

The project charter is normally produced by the project sponsor in cooperation with the project manager and is signed by both parties – the sponsor authorizing and the project manager accepting. Only after both have signed can it be said that the project has been initiated.

It is imperative that the project manager does not proceed without a charter. Frustration, conflict and tension could arise if the project manager's authority is not recognized by stakeholders and resource managers. Many industries have the equivalent of a project charter contained in certain of their standard documents and contracts. An example of this is an engineer's letter of appointment or terms of reference in an engineering project or contract.

INFORM ALL PARTIES

All stakeholders need to be informed of the existence of the project and the project manager's authority. To achieve this, the project charter is communicated by any appropriate means to all stakeholders and organizations potentially affected by the project.

PROCEEDING TO THE NEXT PHASE

If all the steps outlined above have been covered, the outcome of the initiation phase will be an initiated project led by a committed sponsor and an authorized and well-briefed project manager.

The project now enters the project definition phase.

8

The project definition phase

INTRODUCTION

Once a project has been initiated, it needs to be further clarified, evaluated and planned. The project definition phase follows the project initiation phase, and is probably the most important stage in the life of a project, as it is during this time that the foundations of the project are laid. The result of the project definition phase should be a project that is well conceived with stakeholder buy-in. Poor definition often leads to project failure with inevitable stakeholder dissatisfaction and team disillusionment.

The project definition phase is not the time to make hasty decisions or rash promises. Rather, it is the time to apply rational, broad and clear thinking to produce an initial definition of the project.

During the project definition phase the project manager, sponsor and other project participants together develop the different components of the project definition report (PDR) – the major deliverable from this phase. The aim of the project definition report is to obtain approval to continue with the detailed project planning phase. This approval constitutes a major control and verification point in the life of the project.

The major input into the project definition phase process is the business case and any supporting documentation. These documents will contain most of the information required to define the project. As discussed in Chapter 7, if the business case or similar document has not been developed then the sponsor, in cooperation with the project manager, must develop the documentation before proceeding with this phase.

Most of the project definition phase process is executed as a single facilitated work-shop: the project definition workshop (PDW). The authors have been using project definition workshops to guide the definition phase process since 1990, and its importance cannot be stressed enough. Many project practitioners have moved in the direction of project definition workshops, although they may be called by different names.

The traditional image of project planning has always been that of a solitary planner toiling away at producing a plan while occasionally communicating with individual stakeholders, but this is now changing. The concept of commencing a project with such a workshop is now starting to appear in project management literature. Bill Quirke in *Communicating Change*[76] describes the reason for mixed group work as follows: 'By mixing people from different functions, [the] different viewpoints help to avoid a monolithic common group view that prevents the exploration of issues.'

This chapter describes the project definition phase step by step. Although the process is presented in sequence, information and detail discovered during later steps can mean that steps already completed must be revisited and modified. An experienced facilitator who fully understands the process will facilitate it in an integrated manner, moving up and down the process as required.

Note that the steps described in the sections 'Brainstorm and categorize issues' to 'Perform project risk analysis' are performed during the PDW, with the assistance of the facilitator. The steps 'Calculate the initial cost estimate' and 'Produce the project definition report' are performed by the project manager after the PDW. A PDW typically takes a day or two but can take longer, depending on the level of complexity of the project.

CONVENE THE PROJECT DEFINITION WORKSHOP

The project definition report is normally produced from information and input obtained by conducting a project definition workshop. This workshop acts as the kick-off meeting to the planning phases and fixes the official start of the project.

Besides the project manager and project sponsor, the workshop is attended by a client representative (who could be the sponsor) and representatives from each resource-providing entity (usually the functional departments that will be involved in the project). The main criterion for attendees is that they must be capable and authorized to commit the functional department or organization they represent. Key stakeholders must also attend, particularly if they have the ability to influence the project's direction and outcome.

A neutral facilitator whose function it will be to extract the necessary information and to handle the group dynamics must conduct the workshop. It is important to understand the concept of facilitation. Hunter, Bailey and Taylor in *The Art of Facilitation*[40] have, in the authors' opinion, concisely captured its essence:

> Facilitation is about process – how you do something – rather than the content – what you do. A facilitator is a process guide; someone who makes a process easier or more convenient. Facilitation is about movement – moving something from A to B. The facilitator guides the group towards a destination. Facilitation makes it easier to get to an agreed destination.
> Facilitate = to make easy or more convenient.

Why have neutral facilitators? It is normal for conflicts to arise during the workshop and the facilitator must be prepared for this. As well as gathering information, the workshop serves to identify and resolve conflicts at an early stage. To achieve this may require the facilitator to create conflict. If the project manager or project sponsor facilitates, the conflict will be directed towards them and this may create problems later in the project. In addition, the project manager and project sponsor are too close to the project. If acting as facilitator, they may unwittingly force their opinions on the group, or steer the discussion in a direction that suits them. Leadership, management and facilitation must not be confused during the PDW.

It is imperative that the client is represented at the workshop. If they are not, their expectations, covert objectives, hidden agendas and any potential conflicts cannot be successfully resolved. This also applies to key stakeholders.

The PDW is not a technical specification workshop; it is more of a business workshop where the tactics and strategy of the project will be defined. The presence of pure technical or operational people at the workshop can cause it to turn into a technical specification session, thus defeating the true purpose. The functional managers who are accountable and responsible for the project work will represent the operational view.

Andersen, Grude and Haug in *Goal Directed Project Management*[2] make the above point very clear. In the following extract, they discuss the difference between the level of planning performed during a PDW and detailed planning:

> The most common mistake is that [detailed] planning is concentrated on the level of detail specifications and crammed with special terminology. The plans do not provide an overview nor do they encourage discussions about the main thrust of the project. The plans only present details. This frightens off the line management and non-specialists. They feel that they have nothing to contribute. They lose interest in the project and disclaim responsibility for it.

As the PDW will involve people whose time may be limited, it must be kept as short as possible. Most workshops can be completed in one to two days of focused and dedicated effort, but some may take longer. The length of the workshop depends on a number of factors, including the complexity of the project, the number of stakeholders, the level of conflict and the number of issues that need to be resolved. Because of the time factor, there may be resistance from some stakeholders over attendance. The following incident illustrates this point and offers a possible solution.

In practice...

The reluctant attendees

The authors worked with a large information technology consulting firm that had introduced the ODPM™ process. Although everybody was comfortable with the process, there were problems getting functional managers to participate in project definition workshops.

The common excuse was 'we don't have the time' or 'we're too busy'. Non-attendance was reaching epidemic proportions and some action had to be taken.

A simple solution presented itself – why not issue, via the sponsor, a formal invitation to each attendee requiring them to RSVP? The wording of the invitation, however, is what did the trick. After the preamble stating the purpose, venue, time and date of the workshop, the invitee was requested to indicate acceptance of the invitation. Remember that most of the invitees were functional managers, and were fully aware that they would be required to commit to the plan arising out of the workshop. The acceptance part of the invitation read as follows:

Please RSVP to _____ (convenor) and tick one of the following options:
☐ *I will personally be attending the workshop.*
☐ *I will not be attending the workshop but have tasked _____, who will be authorized to take project-related decisions on my behalf, to attend.*
☐ *I will not attend the workshop but hereby grant the appointed project manager authority to take project-related decisions on my behalf.*

Attendance by functional managers or their deputies jumped to 100 per cent virtually overnight! The sting lies in that the invitation requires the functional manager either to be there or to delegate authority to someone else. Since accountability will remain with the functional manager even if the authority is delegated, a Catch-22 situation was the result. Personally attending was seen as the lesser of the three evils and delegating to the project manager was an option that was not even to be contemplated. Any protests that could have been raised regarding the second option, such as 'but I have no one I can trust in my department to whom I can delegate', would reflect poorly on the manager's ability to employ competent staff or the manager's poor succession planning or ability to delegate. Rather than risk being regarded as an inadequate manager, most functional managers who were perhaps 'guilty' of not delegating or not trusting selected the first option. The concepts of authority, accountability and responsibility can work in mysterious ways!

BRAINSTORM AND CATEGORIZE ISSUES

> People can only take new ideas on board when they have had a chance to offload some of their mental baggage.
>
> Bill Quirke, *Communicating Change*[76]

Whenever a group of people gather or something new is attempted, issues will arise. These issues could relate to the past, present or future and could be based on fact or perceptions. They could be personal issues, issues relating to the project, or issues created by the advent of the project. Many of the issues will relate to the play of power and politics in the organization as well as the organization's culture. The PDW brings together all the major stakeholders, who might be from different organizations, and there may be issues of integration, diversity and interface.

Such issues need to be identified and addressed as soon as possible. If issues are left unspoken, they tend to smoulder and will eventually spark some form of conflict, loss of focus, or alienation of project participants. If any personal issues arise that could influence the project, the project manager will need to address these outside the PDW.

The PDW begins with the brainstorming and categorizing of any issues, which are then displayed for the duration of the workshop. The intention is that the issues must be addressed and resolved as the PDW progresses. Not all issues will be project related or be within the mandate of the project participants to resolve. Such issues need to be placed in a 'parking lot' so as not to divert the focus of the group. This parking lot of issues can then be referred to the appropriate people. Issues on the parking lot typically relate to business, culture, organization politics and dissatisfaction with organization strategies, policies, procedures and standards.

During the brainstorming, the group's understanding and knowledge of the business and the project will emerge. It is important to allow enough time to create the issues list as it is an important input into the rest of the workshop proceedings. The astute facilitator categorizes the relevant issues into groups or areas of concern, which gives an indication of what has worked well in the past, as each participant brings the 'data base' of past experience. Knowing what has worked well in the past, when correctly related to the current project, serves as input to the critical success factors described in the following sections, and to risk analysis.

Brainstorming can be done either by the whole group or by breaking participants into smaller groups.

DETERMINE THE PROJECT PURPOSE/MISSION

The project mission statement is most valuable if there is a strong image or theme that provides a single focus to the project team and stakeholders. It is this unifying statement that gives the project team a sense of direction and the stakeholders a common understanding of purpose.

Using the business case, the issues list and through brainstorming and discussion, the workshop group must construct the project purpose/mission. This must be short, clear and to the point. It is a concise statement of the project's purpose or mission, including its strategic reasons. In essence, it is the project's primary objective. An effective project purpose/mission statement should relate to the intention and purpose stated in the business case, and contain the following elements:

● identification of the problem or opportunity;
● a proposed solution to the problem;
● a link to the business objectives of the project.

The business objectives are a subset of the organization's strategic objectives. Business projects are derived from business objectives, and established as vehicles of change which contribute to the achievement of business objectives.

The project purpose/mission gives the workshop group a clear business statement, which forms the basis of further project definition. It serves to focus the group's further discussions.

It is important to note that there is no right or wrong purpose/mission statement. The purpose/mission must be a mutually agreed statement that all in the group can commit to, thus achieving ownership and buy-in. This concept of no right or wrong, but rather mutual acceptance, applies throughout the PDW.

For the case study (see Appendix A), after much discussion, the following project purpose/mission was drafted:

Project purpose/mission

In order to contribute to the future growth of the ITM, the ITM Executive council has decided that a publicity campaign is required. A conference and exhibition is to be held which will generate funds for the campaign.

This will also create awareness and contribute to membership building, which is aligned with the marketing strategy of the ITM.

It is important to note that the purpose/mission is not the scope of the project nor the detailed objectives. These are still to be derived.

DETERMINE THE OBJECTIVES, PERFORMANCE MEASURES AND CRITICAL SUCCESS FACTORS

The objectives and performance measures add detail to the project's primary objective (purpose/mission). They are measurable results that confirm whether the project purpose/mission has been achieved. The objectives and performance measures must therefore contain two important elements: 1) identification of what objectives the project must achieve; 2) performance measures that verify whether the objectives have been achieved.

Effective objectives and performance measures will:

- focus the entire project team on the final results that must be achieved;
- further describe the project purpose/mission;
- collectively be the most important milestones of the project on which all planning must continuously focus (that is, they are part of the final project milestone);
- indicate the measurable end of the project.

In general, three to five objectives are sufficient for most projects. More objectives do not necessarily contribute to focus and clarity, but can shift thinking into lower levels of planning.

A question that all projects face during definition is how objectives are chosen. The mnemonic SMART can assist in determining the objectives. SMART represents the following in terms of objectives:

Specific	Must be clearly stated and not ambiguous.
Measurable	Must be quantifiable and capable of being measured.
Agreed	Must be acceptable and agreed by all relevant parties.
Realistic	Must be achievable within the time period agreed.
Time-bound	There must be a defined time period for achievement.

To further assist the project team in choosing objectives, distinction is made between objectives relating to products or deliverables of the project and the business results the project contributes to. In the case study (see Appendix A) extract shown in Table 8.1, four objectives are stated of which three are product focused and one is business enabling, namely, 'Increase membership numbers'.

A further aspect to consider is critical success factors (CSFs). When developing objectives there should be some reflection on 'what are the few things that must go right' to achieve the objectives. These assist the team in placing emphasis in a few critical areas to achieve success, as described by Karl von Clausewitz, in *On War*[92] (Chapter 3).

Each objective has a corresponding performance measure(s), whereas a CSF can relate to multiple objectives. The CSF 'Design a user-friendly, highly advertised Web site' relates to all four objectives.

CSFs, once identified, should permeate the definition planning and be continuously referred to during the process. For example, scoping of the project must reflect the CSFs. Also, the high-level risk analysis should contain the inverse of the CSFs, ie what will cause the project to fail?

The group should guard against stating objectives that could be regarded as obvious, such as: 'Successfully complete the project to scope, within cost and time budgets.' All projects should obviously have this as an objective.

Objectives must also not be outside the influence of the project team. For example, in the case study conference project, such an objective could be 'Retain current membership'. This is beyond the project as there is more to membership retention than running a conference and exhibition. An unpopular decision by the ITM Executive Council could cause existing members to resign, and this would not normally be a consequence of the project.

In the case study (see Appendix A), the objectives shown in Table 8.1 were agreed.

Table 8.1 Objectives, performance measures and critical success factors

Objectives	Performance measures	Critical success factors (CSFs)
● Hold a successful conference	● 80% or more delegate satisfaction level measured off evaluations ● Realize a net profit of $50,000 ● Attract at least 100 conference delegates	● Internationally acclaimed ● Excellent programme
● Hold a successful exhibition	● 80% or more delegate satisfaction level measured by exit survey ● 20 exhibitors ● 2,500 exhibition visitors	● Careful screening and selection of industry-representative exhibitors
● Increase membership numbers	● 20 new members within 3 months of the proceedings	● Add value to members both in run-up and at the conference ● ITM follows up potential new members prior to and after the conference
● Create a Web site in support of the conference and hand-over to the organization	● Number of hits on Web site ● Length of stay at the site	● Design a user-friendly, highly advertised Web site ● Research and appoint a professional and successful Web designer

ESTABLISH THE PROJECT APPROACH

Prior to scoping out the project, a high-level understanding of how the initiative is to unfold is essential. The project purpose/mission and objectives set the foundations for the project definition and the later detailed planning. A well-constructed plan will build on the mission and objectives, and ensure that the CSFs permeate the plan; however, it is essential that these factors are understood in terms of the approach to delivering the project.

For projects to be successful the approach must consider the changes to business processes, to systems in support of the changed processes, and people changes brought about by the project. People changes relate to both the individual acceptance of the change as well as business process impact on the way that individuals deliver work. The approach can further be illustrated using a flow chart of how the project will unfold, or it can be described via a project life-cycle diagram, identifying the major phases and phase end outputs.

Essential in the approach description is clarity on how the project outputs will be integrated into the business, and deliver stated benefits as set out in an approved proposal/business case. Methodologies are often silent on this important area of benefits realization, which is the very reason for the project's existence. Although the rationale for realizing benefits is discussed in Chapter 5 under business case, it must be translated into the project plan. The transition from project deliverables to the business benefits is referred to as the transition strategy part of the overall project life cycle.

A further consideration under the project approach is the achievement of early benefits from the project to the organization, leading to credibility and support for the project and team. Projects that take too long to deliver promised benefits run the risk of being marginalized or at worst being shut down as stakeholders lose trust in the project team's ability to deliver.

DETERMINE THE DELIVERABLES BREAKDOWN STRUCTURE

Once the purpose/mission, objectives and project approach have been determined, the initial scope of the project needs to be defined. The precursor to this is establishing the project deliverables. The essential tool used to assist in the development of the project deliverables is the deliverables breakdown structure (DBS).

The DBS identifies and displays the deliverables to be produced and/or accomplishments or results to be achieved as well as the sub-elements of the project. The number of elements in the DBS depends on the experience of the workshop group relating to the specific type of project as well as the number of objectives defined. At this early stage it is often difficult to break down the project into elements of work, but it is normally feasible to establish the deliverables or results required to achieve the project objectives.

Using the concepts of fuzzy to clear and progressive elaboration, the development of the DBS commences at a high level and progressively becomes more detailed. High-level development is normally sufficient for the project definition phase. As more information becomes available during the project planning phase (covered in Chapter 9), the DBS is modified and expanded to become the detailed work breakdown structure (WBS).

The inputs to the DBS come from the business case, purpose/mission, objectives, analysis of the issues and discussion. The development of the DBS assists the workshop group to:

● further understand and define the scope;
● develop the milestone objective chart (MOC);
● develop a cost estimate.

The DBS follows the same concepts and rules for the construction of a work breakdown structure. The WBS is explained in Appendix B. The same procedure can be used to construct a DBS. A DBS can also be developed using mind-mapping techniques. The DBS could be supported by a short description of each of the deliverables and/or results if necessary.

The second level of a breakdown structure can either be life-cycle based, or component based ('big chunks'). Life-cycle-based breakdown is mostly used where the project process is well understood and clearly defined, for example in construction/engineering/software development projects. Where the project process is not well understood and there is overlapping of life-cycle phases, a component-based second level can be useful. Irrespective of which approach is used, project management and administration must be included at the second level as it forms an essential part of the project work.

Remember this important fact: if a DBS cannot be developed for a project at this stage, then too little is known about the project to achieve it, let alone manage it!

The following deliverables breakdown structure was developed for the ITM case study. The DBS is shown here in indented list format (Appendix A also shows this in a graphical form).

01	Conference and exhibition	
	01.01	Conference
		01.01.01 Programme
		01.01.02 Speakers
		01.01.03 Handouts
		01.01.04 Facilities
	01.02	Exhibition
		01.02.01 Exhibitors
		01.02.02 Facilities
	01.03	Marketing and communications
		01.03.01 Venue and date
		01.03.02 Mailing list
		01.03.03 Brochures
		01.03.04 Registration
		01.03.05 Recruitment information packs
	01.04	Funding
		01.04.01 Go/no-go scenarios
		01.04.02 $50,000 profit
	01.05	Project management
		01.05.01 Project definition report
		01.05.02 Detail plan baseline
		01.05.03 Post implementation review report
	01.06	Web Site
		01.06.01 Appoint design and build company
		01.06.02 Design
		01.06.03 Build
		01.06.04 Hosting/maintenance
		01.06.05 Content
		01.06.06 Transfer to organization

ESTABLISH SCOPE, ASSUMPTIONS, CONSTRAINTS AND LIMITING CRITERIA

Using the DBS as input, the workshop group must develop the initial project scope, assumptions, constraints and limiting criteria (the project boundaries). These will guide and assist the group in defining the project result milestones and detail planning.

The initial project scope, assumptions, constraints and limiting criteria are developed from the business case, what has been done so far, and through further discussion and brainstorming. The stakeholders' (particularly client/upper management) support of and interaction with the workshop group is important in developing effective scope, assumptions, constraints and limiting criteria:

- The **scope** is the overall description of the project and is often described as 'what is in and what is out of the boundaries (scope) of the project' or 'what the project is and what the project is not'.
- **Assumptions** are details of the project that are not explicitly stated in any previous document or discussion but have been (or will be) used to take decisions.
- **Constraints** indicate the restraining boundaries within which the project must be achieved.
- **Limiting criteria** indicate the scope limits (quantum) of the deliverables to be produced.

The DBS and accompanying optional narrative describes what needs to be done but does not necessarily describe the constraints, limiting criteria and scope boundaries imposed on the project. These parameters need to be determined and documented.

Some typical constraints, limiting criteria and scope boundaries are:

- time (completion date, holidays, specific events);
- cost (maximum expenditure, funding method, cash flow);
- resources (source, location, quantity, availability);
- inclusions (what is included – what the project is);
- exclusions (what is to be excluded – what the project is not);
- policy, rule, or system constraints (standards to be followed);
- quantities.

The scope, assumptions, constraints and limiting criteria are usually expressed in a narrative list form. These individual components are not usually shown under separate headings (with the possible exception of assumptions) as their differentiation is often not possible. What could be a scope item could also be a limit or constraint or assumption.

For the case study (see Appendix A), the scope, assumptions, constraints and limiting criteria shown in Table 8.2 were determined.

Table 8.2   Scope, constaints and limiting criteria

Scope, constraints and limiting criteria (What is in scope)	1. Hold a conference for at least 100 delegates. 2. Create an exhibition area for at least 20 exhibitors. 3. Provide facilities for at least 2,500 visitors. 4. Develop a Web site to assist the Conference and Exhibition marketing. 5. Initial funding of $10,000 will be provided by the Institute but must be paid back. 6. A further donation of $15,000 will be provided by member organizations. 7. Project duration is 11 months. The project start date is 1 February. 8. The conference and exhibition must not take place later than the end of August. 9. Project team is to be drawn from Executive Council and ITM members only. Their time will be voluntary. 10. A recruitment pack must be developed and the ITM must be one of the exhibitors. 11. The exhibition and conference must be a three-day event. 12. The conference programme must have between 16 and 20 speakers, of whom at least one must be an international speaker. 13. The venue to be no more than an hour's travel from Capital City. 14. Catering for conference delegates and exhibition visitors must be organized. 15. Speakers' expenses will be paid, but the speakers will not receive a fee.
What is out of scope	1. The actual growth in membership will not be a deliverable from this project. 2. This project is not the complete marketing strategy. 3. This project will not be the sole contributor to greater market awareness of the ITM. 4. Continued development and maintenance of the Web site. 5. Sign-up of 20 new members is not part of the project team performance (only expected 3 months after the conference).

DETERMINE THE RESULT MILESTONES

At this point in the process, the workshop group has defined the final objectives for the project. Two definite major milestones are therefore already known: the start (the project definition workshop) and the end (the project objectives to be achieved). The final objectives or goals are defined by all that has gone before in the process but specifically the project objectives and performance measures, DBS and initial scope information. These combine to form the final goal or major milestone that the project must reach.

The workshop group now needs to develop the map, route or plan of how the project will proceed from start to end. This incorporates all that has gone before: the project purpose/mission, objectives, DBS, scope and other details. The map or plan must also illustrate how the project will unfold from start to final objective. In essence it tells a story of the project unfolding, in a simple flow of related milestones. The tool used for this is the milestone objective chart (MOC).

The milestone concept

The milestone concept is best described by using an analogy of undertaking a journey to reach some distant destination. The destination is known but is not visible from the departure point. To get to the destination, a route needs to be determined and followed. To ensure the right route is taken, milestones are identified and used to monitor the journey. These milestones could be such events as 'when city X has been reached', 'when 650 kilometres have been travelled', 'when landmark Y is visible'.

These milestones or events along the route are followed in sequence, so that when one is reached, attention is then focused on reaching the next, and so on until the destination is reached. To reach the destination, all the milestones must have occurred or been passed through. If times are attached to each milestone, progress can be monitored and it can be determined whether the project is overdue at any point. This gives an indication of the arrival time at the next milestone or ultimately at the final destination. The milestones can be considered as checkpoints throughout the route, ensuring that the journey is on course and on time.

Taking the journey analogy further, to document the route the milestones will be listed in sequence indicating the route to be followed. The actual activities carried out to reach each milestone are not planned in detail. If travelling by car, the actual activities such as driving, taking decisions to turn left or right, stopping for fuel and meals, and so on are left to the driver. The driver must do whatever is required to get to the milestone or checkpoint by the required time.

To consider a project in terms of this analogy, the same concepts apply. The objectives form the final destination, the milestones or checkpoints indicate accomplishments, results, deliverables or sub-objectives that direct the project towards its final goal. These milestones are connected to form a logical map or chart of the project.

Milestones can be viewed as gates through which the project must pass to reach its final goal. Gates open to allow the project to proceed only if the conditions required by that gate are met. If this rule were strictly applied, however, all projects would consist of a single route with sequential milestones, as illustrated in Figure 8.1.

This does not reflect the real world. In reality, a project moves towards multiple milestones at the same time. Although not a rule, these paths tend to reflect the second level of the DBS – the major deliverables. Paths can link to each other, thus reflecting the logical dependencies between deliverables. These concepts are illustrated in Figure 8.2.

Referring to Figure 8.2, an important point must be made. In every project there are points at which critical decisions are required that have a major bearing on the project results. These are referred to as critical decision points (CDPs) (milestone G in Figure 8.2), and typically are major go/no go decisions such as:

- has the financial break-even been reached at this point in time?
- are the results from the pilot acceptable to proceed with the prototype?
- considering the state of the project at this point, should the project continue or is it better to 'pull the plug'?

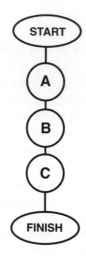

Figure 8.1 Sequential milestones

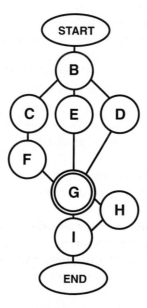

Figure 8.2 Linked paths

CDPs often appear at the end of project life-cycle phases. This may occur, for example, in research projects, where results are progressively achieved. The result of an important test may either change the focus of the research, stop the project if it is no longer feasible, or continue with the project as scoped.

CDPs also occur prior to committing large amounts of resource on projects, for example where no value is obtained until the project is completed. Construction, engineering, large software development projects and organization-wide re-engineering projects are typical examples.

Although milestones are shown as gates connected in a logical sequence, it does not necessarily mean that work towards milestone F cannot be started until milestone C is completed. Work towards milestone F can be in progress while progress is also being made towards milestone C, but the project cannot arrive at the state required by F until milestone C has been reached.

The following points and observations further define the concept of milestones as objectives. Milestones:

● describe the state the project should be in at a specific time;
● are not tasks or activities;
● do not have a duration (time);
● describe what has to be achieved and not how it must be achieved;
● describe events or states that are natural to the project and to the milestone chart users;
● can represent important decisions to be taken;
● must be measurable either quantitatively or qualitatively.

To illustrate this, the following milestone could be set for a property development project.

When a suitable property for development has been identified and approved by the client.

This milestone can be checked against the above observations:

● The milestone states what is to be achieved (the objective), being property identification and client approval. It does not describe how this is to be done (the activities needed).
● In a property development project, it is natural to select a property for development.
● It represents an important decision in terms of the project.
● It is measurable and controllable by monitoring the progress towards property location and securing.

The milestone objective chart

The graphical representation of the milestones and their logical dependencies, descriptions and timing is called the milestone objective chart (MOC). The following points and observations further define the milestone objective chart:

- The MOC must be robust, and changes to individual activities in terms of work content, timing, omissions or additions should not alter the milestone plan. The dates may change but the milestones should not. For credibility and control, it is important to have a plan that does not change in content or appearance at every reporting period.
- The MOC illustrates the project tactics or approach and not the operational plan.
- The MOC should contain relatively few milestones (maximum of 15 to 25). If more than 25 milestones are required, breaking down the project into sub-projects should be considered.
- The milestones in the MOC should be spaced at useful intervals. The intervals between milestones depend on a number of factors, such as project complexity, project duration, level of control required, information needs of project participants, decision points, and externally imposed controls and restrictions.

A well-developed MOC is easy to understand but it is not easily drafted. The workshop group's ability to consider the logical states through which the project must pass is extremely important.

Drafting the milestone objective chart

A suggested process for the workshop group to use in drafting a milestone objective chart is given below:

1. **Generate ideas for milestones.** Preferably start at the end of the project (the objectives) and work backwards as well as forward from the project start. Note ideas as they arise and display them where the entire group can see them. Use all the information derived so far in the PDW as inputs, specifically the DBS and the project approach. Some of the ideas will be activities rather than milestones, but these should also be listed. Continue until nothing new arises. This process is known as 'dumping'.
2. **Select the milestones.** From the 'dumped' list, select the milestones by discussion and workgroup consensus. Ensure that a few critical decision points are agreed. The remaining ideas or items will probably be activities that supplement the milestone objective chart.
3. **Prepare the milestone objective chart.** Vertically arrange the milestones in a logical sequence and paths. As a first draft use the second level of the DBS as paths, although paths may be grouped if a particular path has only one or two milestones on it. Connect the milestones to indicate logic, flow and paths. Draw the final chart.

The authors suggest using a flipchart and removable sticky labels (such as Post It® notes) as a simple way to prepare the MOC. The milestone descriptions are written on the labels and stuck onto the flipchart. They can then easily be rearranged into an appropriate order.

The remaining items, which were not included in the MOC, should be documented and made available during the detailed project planning phase. These will often represent some of the experiences of the workshop group in achieving similar milestones.

Initial time estimates

Target dates must be set for every milestone. These target dates must be respected, but not at any cost. They must be balanced against the project's other objectives of cost and scope. During the project definition phase, some estimate of time to achieve the project is required. Timeframes are often defined by the end-user or senior management, and the project team is expected to meet the dates set.

It is the duty of the workshop group to verify that any time targets are realistic and achievable. Research shows that unrealistic time schedules are a consistent cause of project failure and result in communication and coordination breakdowns. Certain deadlines must be met, such as contractual dates, special events with predetermined dates and dates over which the project has no control.

Time estimates during this phase are based primarily on the experience level of the workshop group, as insufficient information is available for a detailed time analysis at this point. As more information becomes available downstream, more accurate time estimates are done and the milestone objective chart is updated to reflect the changes. Difficulty in determining the initial time estimates could be due to poorly selected milestones, lack of clear milestone descriptions and illogical sequencing of milestones (dependencies).

The importance of the milestone objective chart

As the milestone objective chart is prepared and agreed to by the project participants (the workshop group) in mutual discussion, it represents the common view of how the project will unfold from start to end. Apart from being a plan of action, the drafting of the chart further commits the project participants to the project. Through the process of setting and defining the milestones, the project participants become a bonded group united through common goals and objectives. This increases their commitment and buy-in.

During the discussions and debates leading to the preparation of the chart, new issues or information might require changes to be made to the objectives and performance measures, DBS, scope, constraints and limits. This is not a problem, but is part of progressively elaborating the project definition and increasing the participants' understanding of the project.

The MOC becomes an effective communication and reporting tool. It communicates a robust plan that can be understood and followed by all project participants. As it does not reflect the detailed activities and since it consists of natural, agreed-to events, it can be used by all for monitoring and reporting.

Building CDPs into the MOC minimizes the risk to the performing organization, and also assists in managing stakeholder expectations in terms of major decision points and their expected contribution to these decisions.

The milestone objective chart and the milestone responsibility matrix (MRM), which is developed later in the process, together form an excellent basis for project communication and coordination.

The MOC excerpt shown in Table 8.3 is taken from the case study (see Appendix A) and illustrates the concepts discussed. Note the multiple routes and the naming of these (see the legend at the bottom of the chart). At this time, ignore the last three columns of the main body of the chart, as these are discussed and used during the project execution phase. Note that the descriptions start with 'When...', thus describing an event.

In practice...

The milestone – when a promise is more than just words

Laboratory Research Services (LRS) was a quasi-government organization, delivering services to large government departments and private sector clients. LRS had a major multi-year contract with an important government department to deliver research services. Of late, the client's perception of LRS was one of non-delivery of important pieces of work, poor estimation of project costs, and a lack of client focus. The LRS board had become aware of the problem, and assigned the Human Resource department the task of solving it.

A typical response was forthcoming. Training in project management should do the trick – after all, scientists are highly intelligent individuals. A two-day course in project management was delivered, with a strong focus on detail time planning and resourcing of plans. Nine months then passed, with still no improvement in the client's perception and satisfaction levels.

In frustration, the CEO of LRS called an old friend who happened to be the Dean of the Business School at a well-known university, to request assistance in solving the problem. Fortunately, at that time a well-known consultant was lecturing part-time at the university.

Following a presentation by the consultant, the LRS board agreed to the development of an integrated project process and system. This was to be followed by training in this project.

The challenge was to develop a standardized project management approach and system which would assist those scientists with a project management responsibility to deliver their projects successfully. Subsequently, a concept of planning and performance was developed whereby all estimates, budgets and performance were to be based on a well-developed result-oriented milestone approach (such as the ODPM approach). By implication, this required sound budgeting and estimating as a basis to build sustainable proposals and contracts. The nature of the projects varied in type, complexity, dollar value, size and client focus. The proposal arising from this 'first-cut' methodology had specific milestones with descriptions, quality acceptance criteria and client sign-off criteria as well as best time and cost estimates for milestone delivery. The proposal and plan were developed from a well thought-through and systematic breakdown of the work to be delivered.

Table 8.3 Milestone objective chart

Project: ITM – Conference project	**Milestone objective chart**		
Sub-project: Conference project	**Compiled by:** PM Smith		Page 1 of 2
Date initiated: 15 Jan 20xx	**Approved by:** ITM Council Chairperson		**Chart date/Rev. No:** 7 Feb 20xx – RO1

Milestone identification	Plan date	Description	Completion date	Report date	Report
10	26/02	When the date has been set and the venue located and confirmed			
20	01/05	When the speakers have been selected and confirmed			
30	06/03	When the exhibitors have been obtained and confirmed			
40	06/03	When the mailing list has been prepared and approved			
50	20/03	When the event programme has been compiled and approved			
60	05/06	When the event programme has been compiled and approved			
70	10/06	When the brochure has been mailed			
80	12/06	When speaker notes and presentation visuals have been obtained from the speakers			
90	1/07	When 50 delegates and 15 exhibitors have been registered (Go/no go decision)			

Goal routes
M C CM E

Goal routes: M = Marketing   C = Conference   CM = Council/Management   E = Exhibition   ○ Milestones   ◎ Critical decision point

Following the implementation of the above and despite the new process, further challenges arose. The scientists had to deliver multi-discipline projects using resources owned by other departments. The first round of negotiations with the client was, despite warnings, based on 'light estimates'. Estimates of resource usage were based on 'previous knowledge/experience'. Consequently, time and cost commitments were made to clients based on these 'light estimates'. As most of the scientists were subject matter experts, the specification of the work was generally well developed. As well as the problem of poor estimating, there still remained a problem of poor delivery or results. Previously, contract payments were made by the client on a monthly pro-rata system without any particular focus on the timely delivery of results. In order to address both these problems, a new client payment contract was introduced.

Most LRS client contracts are for one year. A new contract was developed which still provided for a prorata payment per month but would now be based on results as well. The new contract was still based on a monthly payment but would be retrospectively adjusted each month depending on delivery of results. In other words, one-twelfth of the contract value would be paid in month one. A further twelfth would be paid in month two but adjusted retrospectively based on the actual performance of month one. Month three's payment of one-twelfth would then be adjusted based on the performance of month two; and so on. In effect payment was now based to a certain degree on results, although still on a regular basis.

The scientists expected a minimal change to their funds flow but, with the focus now on 'payment on delivery', the funds slowed down. This process highlighted the following underlying issues:

● The scope of the milestones were being underestimated.
● Poor scoping caused a lack of understanding of what the milestone was to deliver, leading to budget and estimating problems.
● Milestones were poorly chosen and lacked sufficient definition to reflect actual achievements. Other milestones consisted of a combination of components (work elements) resulting in difficult progress monitoring and control.

As a result of the more visible impact of poor estimating and delivery, it became apparent that scientists were over-promising and under-delivering. This became a matter of extreme concern, as they did not want to be seen as letting down others in the team. It became a matter of pride and honour and long hours of work were put into achieving the milestones. The result was an unhappy work environment and burnt-out scientists, something unheard of in the past. The milestone had become a millstone around their necks.

This unhappiness was a result of the legacy of poor estimates done before the system was put into place and while the scientists were on a learning curve. The client was lenient and allowed re-estimates of milestone deliveries to be done. Once the legacy was overcome, a learning environment started to emerge.

By the following year estimating had improved considerably. Milestone estimates were carefully considered and discussed amongst the scientists before being promised. Delivery was starting to meet deadlines and the client made favourable comments on service.

LRS was beginning to mature in their approach to project management and the next step was to introduce a more advanced performance monitoring system based on earned value concepts, where the true achievement of deliverables is compared to the promised delivery. Scientists were now able to monitor their own progress, and management had early information on potential under-deliveries.

Management were now able to track monthly performance and the client was required to sign off deliverables with strict time frames. Accountability was strengthened and project performance become more visible. A training programme based around the project management system was developed and implemented for all scientists.

A culture of 'I can help if you are behind schedule' started to emerge. Some teamwork was becoming evident. Once the value of using the project management approach and system was proven, other areas of the business started to use the same concepts.

Important lessons...

1. Project management methodologies, processes and systems must be developed and owned by those who will be using them.
2. A project management system may be strong in one area and weak in another. Any system or methodology developed must be balanced.
3. When introducing project management, expect changes to occur. These changes may be unexpected and may cause pressure elsewhere.
4. A project management methodology will create a consistency of application in the organization.

DETERMINE THE RESPONSIBLE ENTITIES AND PROJECT RESPONSIBILITIES

Chapter 1 defines the concept of the core project team, and the reader is referred to that definition. During the project definition workshop the participants need to identify this team, as well as any other principals such as vendors, subcontractors, client departments or statutory organizations that could also be involved in the project. These 'responsible entities' need to be identified and their influence or involvement in the project discussed and debated by the workshop group.

At this point, the core project team and other principals are identified by functional names such as 'IT Department', 'Finance department', 'Supplier XYZ', rather than by individual names. The project may need an accountant, a programmer or an analyst but, at this point, names may not be able to be attached to the functions. What is known, however, is that the functional section or organization involved must supply the project with the people needed.

The list of identified responsible entities is required for documentation reasons and for use in the following step in the process – the development of the milestone responsibility matrix.

For the case study, the following responsible entities were identified:

- project leader;
- marketing;
- conference;
- exhibition;
- venue;
- ITM Council;
- advertising agency;
- food and beverage vendor;
- Web designer.

Now that a list of the responsible entities involved in the project is determined, their specific roles and responsibilities can be established. The milestone objective chart provides an overall view of the project. Using the list of entities and the MOC, the workshop group now needs to organize and coordinate the project.

The usual approach to organizing and coordinating a non-project organization is to construct an organization chart showing the reporting (authority) lines of functions and job positions. Job positions are defined by titles and job descriptions. Anyone joining the organization can quickly establish their role, title, responsibilities, authorities and accountability by checking their position in the organization chart. Once defined, the organization structure remains almost static unless restructuring takes place. This kind of organization structure is often referred to as hierarchical.

If the project is considered as a 'temporary' organization, in theory it could be organized and coordinated in a hierarchical manner. This, however, implies that projects are inflexible organizations, which they are not. The Project Management Body of Knowledge (PMBOK® Guide[73]) defines a project as 'a temporary endeavour undertaken to create a unique product or service'. As discussed in Chapter 1, this suggests that project team members are temporarily assigned from functional and operational departments within the performing organizations to work on the project. As project members complete their assigned tasks, they leave the project. The member's project role or position then ceases to exist – both the team member and role/position are 'temporary' to the project. Further, considering the matrix organization structures also discussed in Chapter 1, the assigned team member continues to report to a functional manager somewhere in the performing organization, while working on the project. In addition to temporary project members, a project may also involve members who are permanently part of the team.

This above situation can lead to the following problems (after Andersen, Grude, Haug and Turner[2]):

- the distribution of responsibility is not defined;
- the principles of cooperation are unclear;

- key resources are not motivated or available when required;
- functional managers and staff are not committed;
- poor communication.

A project must therefore be organized with the aim of preventing the above problems by establishing the roles, responsibilities, accountabilities and levels of authority of all participants (upper management, client and functional managers). As each project is unique, its organization must be developed to suit the needs of the project.

The following must be considered when organizing a project:

- Functional or resource managers must commit to the project, as they will be providing resources to the project at the required time. The provision of resources to a project by a functional manager is not a 'favour' but an obligation, once a project has been selected and prioritized. The role the assigned resource will fulfil on the project and when the resource is required must therefore be formally agreed as early as possible.
- Project managers have an obligation towards functional managers and team members to keep them informed of progress and changes to the agreed times when resources are required.
- Levels of authority and responsibility must be clearly defined for both permanent and temporary project participants.
- Decision-making responsibility must be clearly defined at an early stage. It is also important to ensure that the project does not take away the decision-making responsibility from those who usually hold it. Decisions on financial matters are made by the financial department, engineering decisions are made by engineers, and project management-related decisions are made by the project manager. People must not be allowed to make decisions when they do not have the necessary knowledge, skill or authority. If this is allowed, it will lead to conflict between project participants and the true owners being reluctant to accept ownership of the project's outcomes. A further problem will be that accountability for actions will not be clearly defined.
- When organizing communications between participants, it is important to ensure that interfaces are clearly defined. Informing or consulting with entities that have little or no involvement with the project is tantamount to inviting them to comment on, and possibly to politically interfere with, the project. Everybody becomes a consultant! By the same token, not communicating or consulting with the right entities could lead to ownership problems.

The project must be organized at an early stage and the organization must be agreed to by all participants through formalized discussion. This is done by the workshop group using the milestone responsibility matrix (MRM) as the tool.

Creating the milestone responsibility matrix

The milestone responsibility matrix is created by the workshop group through discussion. The parties to be committed to the project must be involved in the discussion process. This stage defines the relationship between the individual parties to the project. Potential differences in opinion or levels of expectation can be discussed, thus preventing most of the conflict that can result in the project execution phase.

The project team indicates the involvement of the responsible entities determined in the previous section in the milestones developed in the earlier section 'Determine the result milestones'. This is done by placing symbols representing the role of the responsible entities alongside the milestones. In the milestone responsibility matrix, the rows represent milestones and the columns the responsible entities.

Table 8.4 lists possible roles and responsibilities with a single identifying character.

Table 8.4   Responsibility identifiers

X	eXecutes the work (responsibility)
D	takes Decision solely or ultimately (authority)
P	manages Progress (accountability)
C	must be Consulted
I	must be Informed
a	available to advise
d	takes decision jointly or partly
p	manages function progress
Q	assures Quality
T	provides Tuition
M	provides Mentoring

The following rules apply to the use of these symbols:

● Each row must contain at least a D, P and X. Note that X refers to the major responsibility for delivering the milestone, although others may contribute to the milestone.
● There can be multiple Xs and ds on a row but only one D and one P.
● Capital P indicates who has accountability for the planning and monitors the progress, and is therefore accountable for the outcome of the milestone.
● There can be multiple symbols in a cell.

Once developed, it is essential that the project participants sign acceptance of their column on the matrix. The act of signing acceptance of the roles and responsibilities indicates the participants' commitment to the project.

The project manager has implied authority over, and responsibility and accountability for, the overall project. Based on this, DPX should appear in the project manager's column against every milestone. This of course is not reality. The project manager's implied role and responsibilities must not be indicated but must be distributed amongst the responsible entities. The easiest way of ensuring that the role of the project manager does not cause confusion is to ignore the project manager's column unless the milestone requires something specific of a project manager. If the project manager plays a dual role on the project then the roles must be shown in separate columns.

Evaluating the milestone responsibility matrix

An analysis of the completed matrix can tell much about the project. The horizontal (row) view shows the milestone as an objective (goal) to be achieved and the group and team who will achieve it. The vertical (column) view shows the role that an entity will play on the project. The number of Ds and Ps in a column is an indication of the power and influence of that entity over the project. A high number indicates a strong influence. If a column has no entries, then that entity has limited involvement on the project. If there are many Is and no Ds, Xs or Ps then the entity is probably an observer and could cause problems downstream. Too many Xs in a column could indicate a workload that needs balancing.

Besides the responsibilities associated with milestones, someone has to be responsible for performing standard functions on a project such as secretarial functions, configuration management, procurement and accounting. A function responsibility matrix can be used to specify and coordinate such functions. Charting the functions is recommended as it could identify and assist in coordinating departments outside the project.

The milestone responsibility matrix shown in Table 8.5 is an excerpt from the case study (Appendix A).

In practice...

The project heckler

A large organization, LWD, decided to replace their total management information system (MIS) as part of a programme to increase their ability to compete in a certain market. It was decided to outsource the development of the system and several proposals were evaluated before selecting ITC, a large IT consulting company. The proposal was that the system would be developed for $1.2 million over an 18-month period. Soon after the award of the contract, a competing company entered the same market. As part of a strategy to counter the competition, LWD required that the development time of the new MIS be halved.

ITC initially indicated that it was not possible to do so, but after some analysis, and an assurance that the estimated $1.2 million would still be available, they agreed to accept the challenge. To ensure every chance of success, a professional project manager (one of the authors) was appointed by LWD to manage the project.

Table 8.5 Milestone responsibility matrix

Project: ITM – Conference project	Milestone responsibility matrix	
Sub-project: N/A	Compiled by: PM Smith	Page 1 of 3
Date initiated: 15 Jan 20xx	Approved by: ITM Executive Director	Chart date/Rev. No: 7 Feb 20xx – RO1

Milestone Identification	Description	Project manager	Marketing (Andy)	Conference (Beth)	Exhibition (Peter)	Venue (Diana)	ITM Council	Graphic Designer	Advertising agency	Food & beverages
10	When project charter is signed off by the sponsor (go/no-go decision)	x	I	I	I	I	PD			
20	When the date has been set and the venue located and confirmed	d	Cd	Cd	CD	PXD	D			
30	When the keynote speakers have been selected and confirmed		I	PXd			CD			
40	When the exhibitors have been obtained and confirmed		I		PXD	C	Cd			
50	When Web organization has been appointed	D	Xd	I	I	I	C			I
60	When the mailing list has been prepared and approved		PXD	C	C		I			
70	When the event programme has been compiled and approved	Pd	C	Xd	X	I	CD		Xdp	
80	Web design and build complete	D	d				I		I	Xd
90	When the Web prototype is operating successfully	d	C	I	I	I	D		I	Xd
100	When the brochure has been designed, approved									
110	When the brochure has been mailed	P	XD	I	I					
120	When speaker notes and presentation visuals have been obtained from the speakers									

Legend: X = eXecutes the work; P = manages Progress; C = must be Consulted; p = manages function progress; D = takes Decision solely; d = takes decision jointly; I = must be Informed; a = available to advise

The approach to halving the time was, to a certain degree, risky. The approach was to replace the production of a user requirement specification, followed by various system requirements and design specifications, with a single document: the user manual. Normally a user manual is produced once a system has been developed and implemented and it usually contains example printouts and screen layouts. The idea was that if the user manual was produced first and accepted by the system users, it could then be used as the design specification. In order to produce the user manual, reports and screens would be prototyped and this would further speed up the process. Since the existing system was being reverse-engineered with improvements, the concept was feasible.

LWD's IT department had a traditional approach to systems development and were not happy with the above approach. They had also been forced to outsource the development of the new system as the LWD directors had felt that the IT department could not handle it based on their track record and existing workload. At every opportunity, the IT manager expressed his concern about the unorthodox approach and warned of pending failure. He also made it clear that neither he nor the IT department would be accountable for the failure. In order to be kept informed about the project, the IT manager assigned a systems analyst, Bruce, to act as an adviser and observer. Bruce was second-in-charge to the IT manager and had been with the company for 25 years. He was well known to the users and they respected his seniority and years of service.

A milestone objective chart, part of which is shown in Figure 8.3, was produced and

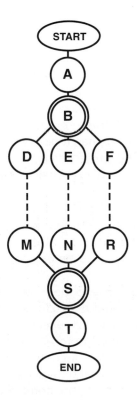

Figure 8.3 The original milestone objective chart

agreed by all during the project definition workshop. Bruce had made sure that only as and Is appeared in his column of the milestone responsibility matrix.

Milestone A's description was 'When the user manual has been developed and presented'; milestone B's description was 'When the users have accepted the user manual as representative and development can commence'.

Work began towards achieving milestone A. Some difficulties were experienced and these were raised and discussed at progress meetings. Bruce attended all of these and did not miss an opportunity to express his view that all the difficulties being experienced were due to the project's unorthodox approach. In particular, he kept insisting that all the problems could be solved by first producing the traditional user requirement and system design specifications.

His 'heckling' was beginning to have an effect on the users, who began to believe that perhaps Bruce was right. This further impeded the team's work. The situation had deteriorated to the point where the project manager had to take some quick action. The easiest approach would be to ban Bruce from any further meetings, but this would have had political repercussions and, in any case, Bruce would continue to 'heckle' outside the meetings. During one particularly harassing meeting, the solution presented itself.

Bruce had been expounding his views once again when the project manager suddenly announced to the group that he owed Bruce an apology and that perhaps Bruce was right – a traditional user requirement specification was called for. He further asked the group's permission to amend the milestone objective chart to reflect the change. This was immediately done, and the new chart now looked as shown in Figure 8.4.

Milestone Z's description was 'When a user requirement specification has been produced and accepted by all'. Taking the matter further, the project manager suggested that Bruce was the best person to carry out the work involved. Since Bruce was in fact the functional manager who would normally have the authority and be accountable for system designs and specifications, the project manager recommended that DPX be entered under Bruce's column against the new milestone on the milestone responsibility matrix. Bruce could not back down after the stance he had repeatedly taken. The group, including Bruce, accepted the recommendation. The project manager then asked Bruce to give him an initial time estimate based on his years of experience. After some humming and hawing, he gave an estimate of two months.

The project manager then pointed out to Bruce that the entire project was now dependent on him producing the specification report and would now be delayed by two months. He asked Bruce to accompany him to the project sponsor (the CEO) after the meeting to explain why the project was to be extended by two months. Bruce remained silent for the rest of the meeting.

After the meeting finished, Bruce came to the project manager and requested a few days to do some planning before they visited the CEO. He felt that with a bit of planning, he could reduce the two months to perhaps six weeks. The project manager granted him his request. Bruce was never seen or heard from again for the duration of the project! The heckling ceased, work towards milestone A continued – ignoring milestone Z – and the project was delivered on time to all the participants' satisfaction.

Some months after the end of the project, the complete IT department was outsourced to ITC. The IT manager and Bruce took early retirement packages.

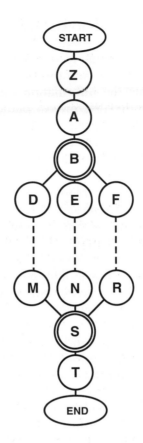

Figure 8.4 Modified milestone objective chart

Important lessons...

1. When faced with interference from unofficial project consultants, commit them to work for which they will be held accountable. Be careful, however – it may not get done!
2. Carefully select project meeting attendees, as you may end up introducing informal consultants and 'hecklers'. If they are not fully involved and committed to the project, they should not attend.
3. Be careful of 'political' appointees to a project team; they always have hidden agendas! It is easy to offer comment and criticism if you are not accountable for what is being produced.

PREPARE THE COMMUNICATIONS PLAN

Projects generate information that needs to be communicated to project participants (stakeholders) regularly and punctually, and this needs to be planned. The communications plan essentially documents the information and communication needs of the project participants. During the detailed project planning phase (Chapter 9), a more detailed communication plan is produced. That plan contains a description of the communications tools and techniques which will be used, as well as who receives what information and when. During this definition phase, an outline communications plan is developed.

The key input to a communication plan is the stakeholder analysis which was commenced during project initiation (Chapter 7). During the definition phase the stakeholder analysis is expanded and grows into a communications plan (Table 8.6). The section 'Stakeholder verification' in Chapter 7 (p 140) briefly describes the first five columns of the communications plan, as shown in Table 8.6 in the excerpt from the case study (Appendix A). Understanding stakeholder benefit and/or risks is fundamental to developing a stakeholder influencing strategy, and establishing stakeholder information required to take them along the project journey.

The plan summarizes the following.

Stakeholder category, **benefit/risk**, and **influencing strategy** are described in Chapter 7. Stakeholder information required is guided by the benefit/risk and influencing strategy. Essentially the challenge is to capture and provide relevant information to stakeholders. Often project teams report the classic information on project progress in terms of time, cost and specification/performance, but find that some key stakeholders feel frustrated or even alienated. What information do stakeholders need to develop a level of confidence that the project is on track?

Project reporting must consider the:

- business objectives the project delivers to;
- impact on stakeholders themselves;
- project process in terms of output delivery;
- improvement and learning from the project.

These four dimensions need to be considered when reporting progress to stakeholders. Clearly the project team cannot analyse the impact on every stakeholder; however, for key stakeholders such as the client/customer, the performing organization business units and key end-users, such analysis is essential. Chapter 10, The project execution phase, further discusses information required and reporting information.

Key messages, **communications medium**, **frequency** and **management responsibility** complete the plan. Key messages and communications are self-evident from the excerpt plan. The management responsibility for stakeholders varies and is often not the project manager or even the sponsor. For example, a government project that directly affects the constituents of a Parliamentary Minister requires the CEO of the performing department to manage the Minister interface.

Table 8.6 Communications plan

Project: ITM – Conference project	Communications plan	Compiled by: PM Smith Approved by: ITM Executive Director	Chart date/Rev. No: 5/5/01 v1.01

Sub-project: Date initiated: 15 Jan 20xx			

S/H category	Stakeholder (S/H)	S/H benefit / risk	S/H influencing strategy	S/H information required	Key messages	Comms medium & frequency	Mngt resp
Primary	Current members	Affiliation, support access to knowledge and prestige Low recognition of membership by industry	Keep informed – build perceived value of membership	Details of upcoming conference and other institute events and news and value of membership	Timing and content of upcoming events – how to access the Web site	Quarterly newsletter and Web site	Marketing manager
Primary	Institute Executive Council	Employment Failure of the project initiatives could be failure of the Institute	Build trust – keep informed and facilitate timely decisions where required	Progress on the project on a timely basis and whether the business objectives are still achievable	Project performance to plan	Timely project reports immediate exception reporting	Project manager
Primary	Institute staff (including project)	Employment Loss of employment, Institute fails	Keep them informed and involved – build knowledge and acceptance	Up-to-date information, clarity of what their role is and what is required of them	What is required, the importance of their contribution	Face-to-face communication E-mail (daily)	Executive director
Primary	Conference and exhibition attendees	Information Failure to meet expectations	Emphasize value of the association – keep informed	How to enrol and by when – what are the benefits of attending?	How to enrol and by when	Information packs, Web site Mail-outs	Project manager
Primary	Industry members	Opportunity to interact with others in the industry, informative Failure to meet expectations	Keep informed – encourage involvement and recognition of the industries' role	How to be involved with the conference and exhibition, how to enrol, how they can promote themselves and their business	How to enrol and by when	Information packs, Web site Mail-outs	Communications managers

Another consideration is the role that the corporate communications group have on a project. Their guidance and mentoring role is most valuable to the project sponsor and manager, as well as the provision of ongoing business resource for the various project communications required.

The communication plan does not have to be discussed in detail as part of the project definition workshop. It could be prepared after the workshop and included as part of the project definition report. However, it is important that the workshop group discuss who the communications groups are and what their information needs might be.

Should a more detailed communications plan be required, Chapter 9, 'The project planning phase', expands on the plan and approach.

PERFORM PROJECT RISK ANALYSIS

Two approaches to risk analysis and management are discussed. This section and the case study in Appendix A provide a simplified approach. Appendix B contains a more in-depth approach based on Australian/New Zealand Standard® 4360:1995.

Projects are undertaken because the projected benefits are attractive to the owners when compared to the risks of not undertaking the project. Project risks focus on future events that could prevent the project from reaching its stated business objectives. Effective management of risks will increase the probability of achieving project objectives. Managers, and more specifically project managers, need to analyse critically and manage actively risks across the project life cycle.

The concept of risk as discussed here covers the risks related to the project management process objectives of time, cost and specifications, as well as the business objectives of the project (the business results enabled by undertaking the project). Careful consideration should be given to both, rather than focusing solely on the project process. Risk management forms an integrated part of business management as well as project management. Project risk is interwoven with the project process and must be actively managed across the project life cycle.

Part I – The Essential Building Blocks referred to risk from a project type and uniqueness point of view. As discussed in Part II – Focusing Projects on the Business, organizations have portfolios of projects, derived from the strategic objectives and business imperatives. Each project is supported by individual business cases that address risks at a high level. These risks are expanded during this project definition phase and, if required, further detailed during the planning phase. Risks are managed throughout the project execution and close-out phases, as described in Chapters 10 and 11.

Project participant influence on risk

To what extent can senior management, project sponsors and managers influence and control future events by critically analysing the potential risks? Appendix C lists some of the research and surveys relevant to project failure and success. The conclusion reached is that project success or failure depends largely on project management. Accepting this argument, along with the fact that projects can be managed effectively, indicates that project participants should be able to analyse and influence future events known as risks.

What is risk?

Risk definition is elusive. While there are many definitions of risk, the following one is used for the purposes of this discussion:

Risk is an exposure to the attainment of stated objectives as a consequence of the uncertainty associated with a particular course of action.

Stated differently, project risk is anything that potentially prevents the project from achieving its stated business and process objectives.

An essential and integral part of project definition is the initial risk evaluation. From the perspective of upper management and the client, risk assessment is of the utmost importance as a decision to go ahead with the next phase of the project has to be made. From the project participants' perspective, risk assessment highlights potential problem areas, the probability of their occurrence, and the consequences/impact on the project should they occur.

When considering what can go wrong, project teams tend to focus on single risk elements or events. Although the single focus is important, there is a need to consider what combination of risk could cause project failure. For example, a software project could fail due to one of the following factors:

- technical validity: the system does not provide a technically accurate and appropriate solution to the problem;
- organizational validity: the system does not take into account organizational and behavioural considerations (culture, power and politics, comfort level with computerization, etc);
- organizational effectiveness: the new system does not contribute to the organization's ability to perform its work effectively, make its decisions more accurately, or lead to profitability (Pinto[70a]).

Although individually each factor could lead to project failure, combinations of the above factors increase the risk considerably. A further consideration is the interaction between factors, as one can trigger or influence the other.

Risks that could impact on the project must be identified and evaluated during the early phases of the project, and contingency plans developed either to avoid them or to mitigate their impact. The ability to make cost reductions and changes is easier during earlier phases of the project than during later phases.

Managing the risk areas is critical to the project, and doing so successfully will go a long way towards ensuring overall project success. Risks need to be vigorously managed in order to decrease the possibility of occurrence and their consequences/impact on the project. A tool that can be used to assist is the project risk analysis matrix shown below. This matrix can be used to assess the likelihood of the risk occurring and the consequences/impacts of the risk. The result of this analysis is the severity level analysis shown in Table 8.7.

Table 8.7 Risk analysis matrix

| | | Consequence/Impact | | |
		High (5)	Medium (3)	Low (1)
Likelihood of occurrence	High (5)	25	15	5
	Medium (3)	15	9	3
	Low(1)	5	3	1

Using Table 8.7, the selection of the expected impact and likelihood of occurrence for a particular risk results in a severity level between 25 and 1 (25 being high and 1 being low). This severity level should be recalculated and reported regularly during the execution of the project. A total risk score is determined by adding the severity rating as shown below (case study excerpt). This enables the comparison of total risk and trending overall risk across the project life cycle. Capturing this data, together with a history of risk treatment and removal, provides information that, when converted to knowledge, positions the organization to learn for future projects.

All risks need to be managed proactively and contingency plans and strategies devised to cope with the risks should they materialize. Management is applied irrespective of the risk's severity level – the severity level simply indicates the intensity of management required.

It is suggested that individuals or responsible entities be allocated risk areas to manage. This can be shown as part of the risk evaluation documentation. If the management of risks requires a team approach, a responsibility matrix can be developed along the lines of the milestone responsibility matrix.

The client should, after reviewing the risk evaluation in the PDR, develop a level of trust in the project team. The client can identify areas of the project that require inputs and attention to assist the project team. After developing the risk evaluation, the project team will have developed a better understanding of which areas are critical to the success of the project. These need to be compared with the CSFs developed above, and adjustments considered if they are different.

The project risk evaluation is prepared during the project definition phase and project planning phase of a project. During the project execution and close-out phases, this document is constantly reviewed and updated with any new risks identified during the progress of the project.

Risk is dynamic. Other than new identified risks, the profile of previously identified risks could change. A risk's likelihood of occurrence or impact on a project could change, thereby changing the severity level. Changes could occur as a result of risk management or as a result of changed circumstances. Whatever the cause, risks need to be continuously evaluated and managed to reduce the severity level or to eliminate the risk totally.

The risk identification and treatment analysis shown in Table 8.8 is taken from the case study in Appendix A.

CALCULATE THE INITIAL COST ESTIMATE

A cost estimate based on all the available information (DBS, scope, milestones, risks, responsibilities, etc) must now be prepared. The cost estimate is normally done separately from the project definition workshop and is the last step before producing the project definition report. The cost estimate is usually done by the project manager, with inputs and assistance from other project participants. A budget/estimate worksheet can be useful in creating the estimate. Appendix B contains a short discussion on the concepts of costing.

The approach is to consider primarily what it will cost to produce the deliverables given in the DBS, and defined by the scope, limits and constraints. The milestone responsibility matrix will provide some indication of the timing and resources required and these must be taken into consideration. Risk areas identified must be carefully considered and cost allowances made for the actions required to manage the risk.

The accuracy of the estimate will depend on the level of detail available up to this point. Early project estimates are made without any detailed data and could have an accuracy of approximately plus or minus 20–30 per cent, depending on the experience of the estimators. The estimated amounts are either built up from cost components (allowables) or stated as single lump sum amounts, or a combination of the two. For presentation to the client, it may be decided to show only the totals and not the individual cost component amounts.

If the project has revenue involved, this can be shown as a separate column in the estimate. Note that the estimate should not show just net figures (revenue less costs). Any assumptions made, or notes on how figures were calculated, should be kept for future reference, and for use by the planners carrying out the detailed planning work.

The estimate/budget worksheet shown in Table 8.9 was prepared for the case study (Appendix A).

Table 8.8 Risk evaluation matrix

Project: ITM – Conference project	Risk evaluation matrix				
Sub-project: N/A	Compiled by: PM Smith			Page 1 of 1	
Date initiated: 15 Jan 20xx	Approved by: ITM Council Chairperson			Chart date/Rev. No: 7 Feb 20xx – RO1	
Risk: What can go wrong?	**Occurrence H/M/L**	**Impact H/M/L**	**Severity level**	**Risk treatment**	**Management responsibility**
Quality of speakers not excellent	H(5)	H(5)	25	● Draw up job descriptions for speakers to be used for selection. ● Research which speakers the industry wants. ● Select keynote speaker carefully for maximum visibility. ● Reearch industry requirements on subject areas. ● Research other TM Institutes and Associations for current topics. ● Draw outlines for speakers.	PM & Team
Conference venue could be unsuitable	M(3)	H(5)	15	● Select venue carefully. ● Draw up a criteria list for selection.	PM
Competing conference or exhibitions				● Investigate and research what is being advertised. ● Contact TM magazines that usually carry brochures and adverts. ● Investigate whether there are any non-TM events taking place that could be of interest to the TM group.	Beth
Web site not launched on time	M(3)	H(5)	15	● Careful outsourcing of contract.	PM
Cancellation by keynote speaker	L(1)	H(5)	5	● Obtain a backup keynote speaker selected from the existing speakers. ● Brief the selected backup speaker.	Sponsor
Conference administration fails	L(1)	M(3)	3	● Discuss with ITM members and other organizations that have held similar seminars. ● Develop a list of administrative duties.	PM
Total risk score			78		

Table 8.9 Estimate/Budget worksheet

Project: ITM – Conference project	Estimate/Budget worksheet		
Sub-project: Conference project	Compiled by: PM Smith		Page 1 of 1
Date initiated: 15 Jan 20xx	Approved by: ITM Council Chairperson		Chart date/Rev. No: 7 Feb 20xx – RO1

Work element		Cost components (Allowables)						
Code	Description	Equipment	HR	Materials	Sub-contractors	Contingency	Other	Total
010101	Themes and programme						1,000	1,000
010102	Materials		9,000	8,000			1,000	18,000
010103	Speakers						12,300	12,300
010104	Prepare facility	1,500						1,500
010201	Exhibitors						300	300
010202	Prepare site				21,000			21,000
010301	Find location				2,000		450	2,450
010302	Set date						250	250
010303	Arrange food and beverages							0
010401	Brochure	1,500	550	2,000	13,500		500	18,050
010402	Registration			500			600	1,100
010501	Run proceedings		10,000	1,000	9,100		1,000	21,100
010502	End off		2,300					2,300
	Contingency					14,000		14,000
	TOTALS	3,000	21,850	11,500	45,600	14,000	17,400	113,350

PRODUCE THE PROJECT DEFINITION REPORT

The project definition report (PDR) contains all of the elements discussed in this chapter. It also includes an overview of the project, summarizing the various areas of the definition development as well as any other relevant information known about the project at this time.

The intention of the PDR is to:

- enable all participants to better understand the project in terms of the definition parameters;
- seek approval to proceed with the detailed planning phase;
- form the preliminary baseline against which the planning phase development will be measured;
- obtain commitment and buy-in from all participants through signed acceptance of the PDR.

A well-developed project definition report will normally contain at least the following:

- project purpose/mission;
- objectives, performance measures and critical success factors (CSFs);
- project approach;
- deliverables breakdown structure (DBS);
- initial scope, assumptions, constraints and limiting criteria;
- milestone objective chart (MOC);
- milestone responsibility matrix (MRM);
- communications plan;
- risk identification and treatment analysis;
- initial cost estimate.

The following can optionally be included:

- issues 'parking lot' list;
- function responsibility matrix;
- risk management responsibility matrix;
- more detailed description of the deliverables;
- contact list of all participants.

PROCEEDING TO THE NEXT PHASE

Once the project definition report has been approved, the project team can proceed with the detailed project planning phase. If all the steps in the project definition phase have been completed, the result will be an initially defined project and a team who are committed to the project's outcomes and approach.

Projects are dynamic, and in some circumstances the contents of the PDR may need to be re-evaluated and modified. This will happen as more information about the project becomes available. The components that define commitment and accountability are the milestone objective chart and the milestone responsibility matrix, and these should be changed with caution and only in consultation with those affected. Changes to the milestone responsibility matrix will probably be due to the involvement of new responsible entities on the project. The milestone objective chart should not change as long as the milestones have been well chosen and the scope does not change.

What happens if the contents of the PDR, particularly time estimates and costs, do not reflect those given in the business case or project proposal? The project manager is obliged to discuss any discrepancies with the sponsor who may, in turn, confer with the client. Ultimately the decision to proceed rests with the client, who may decide to stop the project, or accept the new dates and costs, or request that changes are made to the scope to bring the project in line. The client may of course insist that the project proceed with the business case/project proposal estimates. If this happens, the client is asserting its authority, in which case the project manager will need to clarify accountability for any date and/or cost differences with the client before proceeding.

Once any changes to the PDR have been discussed and implemented and the report is agreed to by all participants, the project can enter the detailed project planning phase.

In practice…

The 'NIPPY' project

As part of a major change programme, a new technology project was to be launched in a pharmaceutical drug company, National Pharmaceuticals (NP). The project would deliver a revolutionary hand-held computer that would radically change the way National Pharmaceuticals did business. Essentially, it would allow salespeople and other staff remote access to each other, all stores depots, all NP business areas and all essential databases for on-site transactions. This hand-held computer was affectionately known as NIPPY.

Apart from increasing service levels to their clients, NIPPY would also allow NP to be more price-competitive resulting from increased efficiency. It was possible that in future certain NP employees could work from home, further increasing cost savings.

From a technological view, vendor demonstrations proved NIPPY to be successful. Reports from similar companies in other countries where the system had been implemented, however, indicated that staff were experiencing difficulties in coming to grips with the amount of change that NIPPY was introducing throughout their operations.

Apart from NIPPY, National Pharmaceuticals had launched a number of other initiatives to redesign and change the way it did business in all its business areas. This NP change programme identified that in order to achieve sustainable results from change projects, each major area of the business must contribute to the change design and implementation process.

The NIPPY project would therefore need to interface with all other business areas. Business process re-engineering (BPR) projects led by a newly formed Strategy Group had commenced, but were not sufficiently advanced to inform the NIPPY project of the impact that NIPPY could have on the new business processes. The large IT group at NP would be responsible for developing NIPPY. The IT group currently had other IT projects that would deliver important business benefits over the next one to two years.

The NP change programme was ambitious and the benefits from the change programme had been 'sold' (promised) to the organization at a high level. However, the message flowing back from the operational departments to upper management regarding the change programme was: 'Stop telling us how wonderful it is going to be and deliver something tangible to us!'

The change programme sponsor was keenly aware that the programme had been running for a year without any significant benefits being delivered to the organization. Consequently, he would have liked some quick gains or benefits to give impetus to the change programme. The NIPPY project presented such an opportunity.

IT had done a thorough functional capability analysis of NIPPY and had verified the technical feasibility and potential operational gains. The technology had been tried and tested in other organizations internationally and could be rapidly installed, thereby creating the opportunity to deliver some tangible gains to the organization quickly. It was envisaged that the project could be operational by July 1997. The NP Sales Division would be the first recipient of NIPPY.

IT had prepared a business case indicating that a payback period of approximately six years would be needed to recover the total investment of $13 million. Since benchmarks were available from similar organizations in other countries, and since IT considered NIPPY to be a technology issue, IT did not involve the NP Sales Division much in the development of the business case.

The business case was submitted to the NP Executive Committee for approval. The case was compelling and executive approval for the NIPPY project was obtained. The change programme sponsor's strong support for the project had a major influence on the decision. The NP Sales Division was represented on the Executive Committee by the Sales and Marketing Director.

After approval, problems plagued the NIPPY project.

The project was to have been integrated across the NP Sales Division, IT and the Strategy Group and this had definitely not happened. IT accepted that it had an important research role in terms of new technologies and systems to support the business. They indicated, however, that they could not wait for the Strategy Group to complete their process redesigns and only then investigate technology to support those new processes. The Strategy Group, on the other hand, were of the opinion that IT should stall the NIPPY project until they had completed their process redesigns. NP Sales Division, who would 'own' the changes that NIPPY would bring about, felt that they should have had a larger role to play in the management of the NIPPY project.

Since IT felt that they owned the project, they took charge, with the IT Director assuming the *de facto* roles of project manager and sponsor. The IT Director's aggressive approach was to push through the project in spite of protestations from the manager of the Strategy Group and from other business area managers. IT went ahead, placed an order for the delivery of the NIPPY equipment, and commenced a development project. The Strategy Group were aggrieved about what they believed to be IT's interference in their brief and felt that the NIPPY project was premature. They now doubted the support they were receiving from the executive and began to question the authority and priority their other projects carried. The NP Sales Division felt alienated, although IT had allocated them a budget for implementation and had included them in implementation planning.

Understandably, tensions were growing between the parties involved and the conflict now threatened to overflow into other NP change initiatives. The NP change programme sponsor, who was responsible for ensuring that integration took place, now had to resolve the situation. Seeing a 'quick benefit' opportunity in jeopardy, the change sponsor reacted to the situation by appointing a project manager to the NIPPY project from within the NP Sales Division.

The project manager was a senior salesperson with many years of service with NP. He was nearing retirement and actually did not have much else to do at the time. Although he was respected because of his seniority, he knew little about information technology and even less about project management. The appointment placated the Sales Division who now felt that the project was theirs. The IT director, however, exploiting the project manager's weaknesses, was able to influence him to steer the project in ways that suited IT.

By February 1998, NIPPY had still not been implemented. The original budget of $13 million had been used up and the total cost of the project now stood at $21.5 million. A large slice of the overspend was due to a too low estimate of the cost of rollout in the Sales Division. The rollout was taking longer to execute as the Sales Division staff felt that NIPPY was being forced on them. Another major cause of the overrun was the changes required to the NIPPY system arising from the now advanced process redesign projects.

The entire NP change programme was now under threat as the cost and time overruns on the NIPPY project had reduced the executive's faith in the change programme. The slowdown in the change programme and the failure to implement NIPPY resulted in NP losing large drug supply contracts to their major competitor who, although starting later than NP, had successfully implemented a system similar to NIPPY.

NIPPY had cost National Pharmaceutical more than just time and money!

Important lessons...

1. Ensure that the project has been selected and prioritized on business value principles. The NIPPY project was launched individually in the knowledge that it should have been aligned with other initiatives.
2. Be sure that the project is being prioritized for business and not personal reasons. The change programme sponsor was more concerned with chalking up any success and not necessarily the right success.
3. Select a project manager to deliver the project based on competency in project

management and business knowledge. The NIPPY project manager was chosen on the basis of seniority and lack of current tasks. A project-competent and business-knowledgeable project manager will be able to enforce authority through respect and ability, and will be less able to be manipulated. The NIPPY project manager lacked these attributes, which allowed him to be manipulated by the IT Director.

4. Appoint the right project manager at the start of the project before it is 'hijacked' by the most dominant personality or entity. Ownership of the NIPPY project was not sorted out at an early stage, allowing the IT Director the opportunity to 'take charge' based on having had the most involvement up until that point.

5. Ensure that all stakeholder expectations and needs have been taken into consideration. The NP Sales Division was not involved in the development of the business plan or in project planning. The Strategy Group's protestations were not taken into consideration by IT.

6. The project definition phase as a method of resolving conflict and obtaining buy-in from stakeholders will prevent later issues of accountability, authority and responsibility. Definition also assists in aligning project objectives with business objectives.

9

The project planning phase

I keep six honest serving men (they taught me all I knew); their names are
What and Why and When and How and Where and Who.
                                                Rudyard Kipling, *Just-so Stories* (1902)

INTRODUCTION

Following the approval of the project definition report (PDR), the project planning phase begins in earnest. During the project planning phase we fully clarify, plan and evaluate the project. The deliverable from this phase will be the integrated project plan baseline.

Typically, detail investigations, designs and analyses, specifications, cost and price estimates, contractual documentation, and any other functional work required to fully develop the integrated project plan baseline and to specify the project deliverables are carried out in this phase. The project planning phase is often referred to as the development phase because the project plan development work is carried out.

The PDR prepared during the project definition phase provides the overall view of what needs to be planned. The integrated project plan baseline produced must operate within the scope and boundaries defined and agreed to in the PDR. If the project definition phase work has been done well, it will give a sound foundation for detailed planning.

Both project and functional managers need to manage their respective areas carefully during this phase. Incomplete or incorrect designs, documentation, specifications and contract paperwork will have major implications downstream. Poor management decisions, planning and costing will have similar effects and will compromise the position of the client, the project manager and the project team. Time and cost overruns, client dissatisfaction and project team disillusionment are the results of a poorly managed project planning phase.

Throughout this chapter, the reader is referred to the case study given in Appendix A and to the basic concepts, tools and techniques discussed in Appendix B.

CONCEPTS OF PLANNING

As this phase is concerned with planning and plans, it is important to describe these concepts in the context of projects.

The function of planning can best be described as:

● thinking ahead on how to achieve selected goals;
● creating a measurement standard against which to measure progress towards those goals;
● communicating these thoughts and the standard to others.

All of the above are very relevant to projects and planning. Planning is the most time-consuming and difficult aspect of project management, but without a project plan the chances of achieving a successful project are virtually nil. According to Kerzner[46], the four basic reasons for project planning are to:

● eliminate or reduce uncertainty;
● improve efficiency of the operation;
● obtain a better understanding of the objectives;
● provide a basis for monitoring and controlling work.

The project context

These reasons combined with the functions of planning provide us with the objectives of project planning. Neale and Neale[65] best sum up planning and plans when they state that 'Planning is the creative and demanding activity of working out what has to be done, how, by when, by whom, and with what, i.e. doing the job in the mind. Plans are not just pieces of paper. Plans represent the results of careful thought, comprehensive discussions, decisions and actions, and commitments made between people and contractual parties.'

Project planning follows a process – the output of which is the project plan. There can be only one plan for a project, although it may integrate individual plans for various aspects of the project – such as time, cost, quality, risk, human resources, procurement and communications. This concept of multiple plans forming an integrated plan is discussed later in this section, and is illustrated in the section 'Development of the integrated project plan baseline' (p 192).

There are different levels of plans relevant to projects. These can be broadly categorized as follows:

- **Strategic plans** developed by client/management with the emphasis on the change the project must bring about. These plans are discussed in Part II, specifically Chapter 4.
- **Management plans** developed by the management of the project (client, project manager and functional managers) with the emphasis on the results or deliverables the project must achieve. Such a plan is contained in the PDR described in Chapter 8.
- **Operational plans** developed by the functional departments and integrated to form the integrated project plan. This planning focuses on the activities that must be performed (the operations) to produce the project results or deliverables. This chapter focuses on operational planning.

Each type of plan leads to the next, following the sequence above. The strategic plan in the form of a business case or project proposal forms the input into the development of the management plan. The management plan in the form of the PDR is in turn the input into the development of the integrated project plan. This can be illustrated further, as follows.

The business case describes the project's objectives in terms of the business but does not chart the path towards achieving them. The milestone objective chart (MOC) contained in the PDR charts the goals, results or accomplishments needed to be attained along the path to meeting the project's objectives. The MOC does not tell us how to achieve those goals but only that they need to be achieved. At the operational level, the emphasis is on *how* to achieve these goals. At this level, the goals are broken down into work packages, which are units or packages of work activities to which specific costs, personnel, time and resources can be assigned. These activities are then arranged in the logical sequence in which they will be executed.

The above concepts are summarized by Neale and Neale[65] in their description of the project plan. They describe the project plan as 'a strategy and tactics for the execution of the project, in terms of activities, time, quantities, resources, and perhaps costs and values. The plan is expressed as charts and reports and forms the basis for communicating what has been planned.'

Integrating the plans

The project plan represents the integration and balancing of the objectives of scope, time, cost, quality and risk. In most projects, these objectives are in conflict with each other and need to be balanced without one compromising the other. This concept is discussed in Chapter 2. There are individual plans for each of these objectives as well as for the aspects of human resources, communications and procurement. All are integrated to form the project plan.

Operational plans are developed by the functional areas of the organization assigned to the project, as they are expert in the work required to produce the deliverables. Although each area develops its own plan, they are all integrated to form a single integrated project plan. This integrated project plan is often referred to as the project summary plan, the project master plan or the project master schedule. The integration is necessary because each functional area may develop its own plan with little regard for other functional areas. This could result in uncoordinated execution, inefficient use of resources, costs not being optimized and management difficulties.

Creating an integrated project plan is not a one-time, top-to-bottom process. Fleming and Koppelman[29] have this to say about the nature of project planning: 'Project planning is an iterative process. Planning becomes progressively more definitive with each cycle taken. Each iteration reinforces the viability of the plan.' What they are effectively saying is that a process is repetitively applied until a viable plan is produced.

Viability is created by applying various planning tools and techniques within the planning process. Neale and Neale[65] define planning tools and techniques as follows: 'Planning techniques form the planner's tool-kit; they assist in the analysis of the plan, organizing the information, and have a crucial effect on the way in which the plan is communicated to others'. The concept of project plan viability is discussed further in the next section, and planning tools and techniques are covered in Appendix B. The full planning process is described in the sections 'Development of the integrated project plan baseline' (p 192) through to 'An alternative approach to activity planning' (p 206).

Since the project planning process is iterative, it can continue almost indefinitely. The decision to suspend the iteration is a judgement call made by the functional area manager for their area's operational plan and the project manager for the integrated project plan. The rule of diminishing returns applies here – the value added to the project plan by an additional iteration is weighed up against the cost and time required to do it.

The integrated project plan baseline

Once the iteration is stopped, it must be understood that the integrated project plan represents the best thinking available at that time. As the project progresses against that plan, more information becomes available, which can cause changes to the integrated plan. One of the objectives of planning is to create a measurement standard for progress. It is essential therefore to 'freeze' the plan at a point in time and use that base against which to measure progress. This 'frozen' measure is called the **baseline**, and the plan or component is often referred to as having been 'baselined' – which means that a measurement standard has been set. Once a baseline has been created, it can only be altered to create a new baseline through a formal change control process.

Once the integrated project plan is 'baselined', it is referred to as the **integrated project plan baseline** and is the deliverable from this phase. The process to create the integrated project plan baseline is summarized in the section 'Development of the integrated project plan baseline' (p 192).

PROJECT PLAN MANAGEABILITY AND VIABILITY

The project plan must be physically viable – in other words, it must be workable, feasible and within the bounds of possibility. To achieve this, the project plan needs to be robust, well thought through, and capable of being managed (manageability).

To be sure that the project plan is viable (Ahuja[1] refers to this concept as project plan feasibility), the project team, client and upper management must know that the project has been evaluated from all views. Table 9.1 summarizes the areas in which the project plan must be viable and the type of questions to be addressed by any tools and techniques used to assess viability.

Table 9.1 Viability aspects of the project plan

Viability aspect	Questions addressed
Time	• What is the shortest time in which the project can be completed? • In what sequence will the activities (work) be executed? • What work can be done simultaneously? • How long will each work package take? • Which activities are critical (that is, if delayed will affect the end date)? • Can specified milestone dates be met?
Resource	• What resources will be needed? • What are the optimum levels of the required resources? • When will the resources be required? • What alternative resources can be used?
Cost	• How much will the project cost? • Are the costs within any given cost constraints? • Is the plan effective in its use of money?
Financial	• Can we afford to do the project now? • What demands will the project make on the resource of money? • What funding is required and by when? • How will money flow into and out of the project over its duration?

The following sections discuss manageability and each of the viability aspects in more detail.

Manageability of the project plan

The aspect of manageability is important in that the integrated project plan baseline needs to provide the ability for the execution of the project to be managed at all levels. It must set out responsibility for doing the work, time and cost budgets, and the expected levels of efficiency and production. There is no specific tool or analysis used to build manageability into a project plan, but it will arise out of the viability analyses done. The accuracy, completeness and quality of the integrated project plan baseline determine its manageability.

Manageability can also be specified by the practicality and applicability of the integrated project plan baseline. A brilliant project plan may be virtually impossible to execute as it may require unavailable resources or equipment, or may be out of the bounds of possibility. Such a project plan may look good on paper but cannot be executed in practice.

Time viability

In the project definition phase, dates were entered against milestones on the milestone objective chart (MOC). This was done in an attempt to verify that the time targets defined by the client, end-user or upper management were realistic and achievable. These dates were based on the limited data available at the time and on the experience of the project team – which was sufficient to obtain approval to proceed with the planning of the project. However, without a more thorough time analysis, there will be no certainty that the dates will be achieved, nor will it be known how long the project will take.

The MOC charts the goals, results or accomplishments that need to be reached along the path to meeting the project's objective. The charting of the milestones gives an indication of the road or path to be followed, but it does so at an overall level and does not indicate how the event is to be achieved. Therefore, it is important that time analysis be performed on the project's activities.

The following questions regarding time viability must be considered:

● What is the shortest viable time needed to execute a specific work package?
● What levels of efficiency and production are needed to achieve the shortest viable time for a work package?
● How long will it take to complete the project?
● Can the project be completed within the time limits set for the milestones during the project definition phase?
● Which activities are critical (that is, if delayed will affect the end date)?

The length of time (duration) an activity takes is not the only constraint on the time; the sequence of activities or precedence is another. Simply put, certain activities must run in sequence, and others can occur in parallel. To do a thorough time analysis, therefore, requires consideration of the logic and flow of the activities.

Time viability is assessed using tools and techniques that provide both logic and time analysis, such as the Gantt chart and critical path analysis. Appendix B discusses these.

Resource viability

Time is not the only restraint on a project plan. The assumption made when doing a time analysis is that resources are unlimited – which of course is not true. Under-resource and the work could take longer than planned; over-resource and costs will increase. It is important to evaluate the optimal level of resources required and any possible scarcity.

The following questions need to be considered in a resource analysis:

- What resources are needed? (allocation)
- When are they needed? (scheduling)
- How much is needed? (aggregation)
- Is their use efficient? (levelling and smoothing)

In the project definition phase, resource analysis was limited to allocating responsibility for achieving the milestones and determining the milestone dates. In estimating the dates, the team drew on their experience in assessing how much work would need to be done and what resources would be needed.

The milestone responsibility matrix (MRM) prepared during the project definition phase coordinates the project and clarifies the roles and responsibilities across functional departments, external entities, the client, upper management and members of the team. However, it does not address the questions of allocation, scheduling, aggregation, and levelling and smoothing. A detailed resource analysis is therefore needed, and the tools and techniques used are normally based on the specific time analysis tool used.

Cost viability

Cost is another restraint on a project plan. Costs are often referred to as resources sacrificed or foregone to achieve a specific objective (the project). Resources (equipment, staff time, materials, services) are consumed over the duration of the project to produce the work. A project needs to achieve the work set out in the scope as cost-effectively as possible within the restraints of time and quality. During the project planning phase, the following questions of cost viability must be addressed:

- What is the most cost-effective way of producing each work package (activities or set of activities)?
- Can the project be achieved within the cost limits set by the client/upper management?

These questions require an accurate estimate of costs, taking into consideration the time and resource analyses. During the project definition phase, there was too little information available to do a detailed estimate of the costs. During the project planning phase, more information becomes known from the viability analyses. These analyses, and the detailed design and specification work taking place in this phase, allow progressively more accurate cost estimates to be made.

Financial viability

Even if the project can be executed within the specified cost and time limits, this does not guarantee that the owner can actually afford to undertake the project. Projects are usually funded from the project owner's cash surpluses, or from funds the owner hopes to generate from normal business activities or through loans. The timing of the funds' availability is crucial. Work can be planned to be done at a certain time, but if there are no funds to pay for the resources required at that time, work stops. On certain projects, the performing organization is only paid by the project owner on achievement of an agreed milestone. Funding to achieve that milestone will have to come from the performing organization, and the level and timing of that funding needs to be known. Financial viability therefore addresses certain vital questions.

- From the performing organization's (contractor) view:
  - When the time comes, will there be sufficient funds to do the work?
  - If funding is required, where can it be obtained and how much will it cost in interest?
- For the project owner:
  - How much funding is needed and when?
  - Can financial obligations to the contractor be fulfilled?
  - If funding is needed, where can it be obtained and how much will it cost? (Interest on loans is a cost of the project and must be catered for.)

To perform a cash flow analysis, information from the time analysis, resource analysis and cost estimates is used to produce cash flow schedules and cash flow graphs. These allow the contractor and project owner to determine the financial viability of the integrated project plan baseline.

DEVELOPMENT OF THE INTEGRATED PROJECT PLAN BASELINE

As stated in the earlier section 'Concepts of planning', project planning is an iterative process. All detailed planning processes outlined in literature and contained in different project planning methodologies are fundamentally similar. They tend to follow roughly the steps of determining viability, in the sequence discussed in the previous section, in an iterative manner. The first set of analyses are done, then evaluated. Changes are made to cost, time and resources, and then the analyses are redone. This process is continued until the optimum balance between time, cost, resources and funding is achieved. This viable plan is then supplemented by, and integrated with, the quality, communication and human resources plans to form an integrated plan.

Figure 9.1 illustrates the iterative core planning process outlined above. The process is shown as a circle to symbolize the iterative nature. Although it is shown as a single full circle with 10 steps, the iteration loop can be tighter. For example, steps 2 and 3 could be

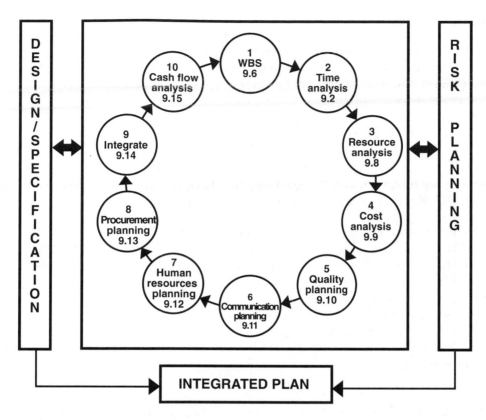

Figure 9.1 The iterative core planning process

performed repetitively until time and resources are balanced. Then move on to step 4 and iterate through steps 2, 3, 4 until time, resources and costs are balanced, and so on.

Each step is shown in sequence so that it would appear that, say, procurement planning (step 8) cannot begin before steps 1 to 7 are completed. This is not always so. In reality, procurement planning could start from step 1 and be performed in parallel to the other steps. Procurement planning, however, cannot be considered complete until steps 1 to 7 have been completed.

Two other components – design/specification and risk planning – are shown in the figure. These components interact continuously with the iterative process. Design and specification work is being performed continuously and information from this work is integrated into the planning process. Similarly, as risks are identified, their effect is taken into consideration in the iterative planning process steps.

The output of the planning process is an integrated plan, which contains all the outputs of the individual steps and components.

This core planning process can be used to perform the detail planning for project work to be done by functional departments, sub-projects and projects. Figure 9.2 shows how

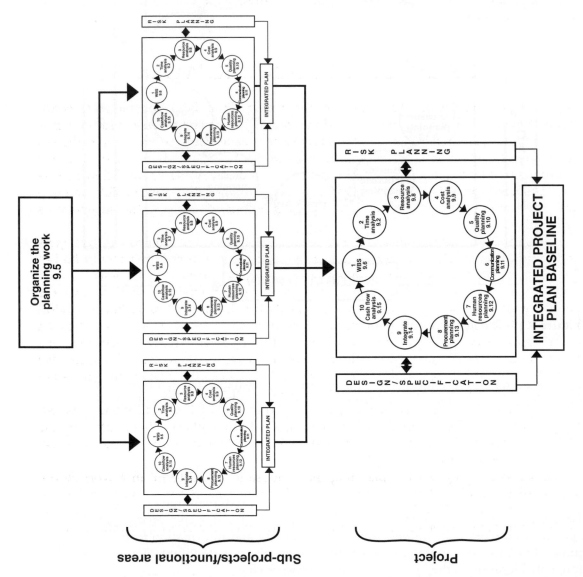

Figure 9.2   Creating the integrated project plan baseline

an integrated project plan baseline for a project is created by integrating the plans for three individual sub-projects or functional areas. The planning work is first organized, after which each sub-project is individually planned using the iterative core planning process. The resultant individual integrated plans are then integrated at the project level using the same core planning process to create the integrated project plan baseline.

The individual steps contained in Figures 9.1 and 9.2 are discussed in detail in the following sections.

ORGANIZE THE PLANNING WORK

Depending on the size and complexity of the project, a number of people and departments (functional areas) may be involved in planning. It may be necessary, for example, to brief the buying department on the procurement aspects of the project and then to allow them to get on with developing the procurement plan. Similarly, the project may be broken up into a number of sub-projects based on the deliverables breakdown structure (DBS). Sub-project leaders may then be appointed who will be responsible for planning their area of the project work and accountable for producing the sub-project's deliverables.

In this manner, responsibility and authority are delegated but department managers and individuals are still accountable and responsible to the project manager (who has overall accountability and responsibility for the project) for achieving the work.

Whoever is to be held accountable for achieving the work must also have the authority (or even the right) to plan the assigned work. If this right or authority is withheld and planning for the assigned work is done by someone else, ownership of the plan and therefore accountability for the work will not be achieved. The authors believe that if operational planning occurs at the level at which the work is to be carried out, creative and innovative thinking will flow on the project. In addition, the project manager is not expected to be a subject matter expert on every aspect of the project.

The tool used to assign responsibility for the planning work is the milestone responsibility matrix (MRM) developed during the project definition phase. When setting up the MRM, the symbol 'P' was used to indicate accountability and 'X' to indicate responsibility (who should carry out the planning work).

The teams carrying out the planning may choose to 'brainstorm' in a workshop – similar to the project definition workshop. Planning workshops do not need to be managed by an outside facilitator – members of the planning teams can take on this role. These brainstorm sessions ensure coordination and avoid overlaps and duplication.

DETERMINE THE WORK INVOLVED AT DETAIL LEVEL

During the project definition phase, the deliverables breakdown structure was produced. This can almost be regarded as an initial or high-level work breakdown structure (WBS). (See Appendix B for a detailed discussion of the DBS and WBS.) During the project planning phase more information becomes available, and it is possible to develop a detailed WBS by adding more levels to the DBS. The supplementary activity lists maintained while preparing the MOC during the project definition phase come in handy at this point.

The WBS required to further plan the project must be as detailed as possible. According to Nicholas[67]: 'During the WBS process, the questions "What else is needed?" and "What's next?" are constantly being asked. The WBS is reviewed again and again to make sure everything is there. Supplementary items are identified and added to the structure at appropriate levels.'

The authors would like to offer an additional question to those posed by Nicholas: 'What has been forgotten?'

To achieve a useful WBS, to what level is the work broken down? A rule of thumb is that the WBS is broken down to the level where time, cost and resources required for a work package can be determined with comfort. The level of detail must be balanced – too much, and little benefit to accuracy is gained with the extra effort; too little, and accuracy could suffer. It is essential, though, that all work packages are broken down to activity level. Kezsbom, Schilling and Edward[47] summarize this concept when they define work packages as 'units or packages of work activities that can be assigned specific costs, personnel, duration, etc'.

It is common, although not compulsory, to supplement a WBS with a narrative description of what has to be achieved by the work packages. This provides the production planners and personnel with input into their processes during the project execution phase. It also serves to link the WBS with the design of the product being produced and to indicate any special considerations or assumptions. The IT industry makes full use of this narrative option to support the specification of the system being developed.

If the work has been organized as discussed in the previous section, then an overall WBS for the project is first produced as a joint effort. The overall WBS is then broken down to activity level by the person or team assigned to plan those activities.

Refer to Appendix A for an example of a detailed WBS for the case study.

PERFORM THE TIME ANALYSIS

Now that the work has been defined down to activity level, a time analysis is needed in order to ensure that the plan is viable in terms of time. To do this, the activities contained in the work packages at the lowest level of the WBS must be scheduled – in other words, determine when an activity will take place and how long it will take to do. This means estimating the duration of each activity and sequencing the activities in a logical order of execution or precedence. To illustrate this, consider the task of building a house. Some activities could be: build walls, lay foundations, put up roof, plaster walls. But imagine trying to execute the construction in that sequence. The logical order would be: lay foundations, build walls, put up roof, plaster walls.

There are a number of tools used to perform a time analysis, the most common of which is **critical path analysis** (CPA). If the project has few activities and is not complex, a simple Gantt chart can suffice. Both tools are described in Appendix B. Irrespective of which tool is used, the time each work package will take must be estimated and its precedence determined.

An alternative method of activity planning that is more suited to projects where there is insufficient detail available to plan the entire project at activity level is given later in this chapter, in the section 'An alternative approach to activity planning (p 206)'. This method can be used to either replace or supplement the time and resource analyses presented in this section and the following section. The authors have found this method more suited to projects such as IT systems development, research marketing and culture change projects.

When performing the time analysis, the milestones and dates set on the milestone objective chart during the project definition phase need to be assessed. If the time analysis indicates that they cannot be achieved, they need to be renegotiated with the client/upper management. Other dates too may need to be regarded as milestones, such as contractual delivery dates and dates where another contractor requires 'access' to completed project work so that they can fulfil their obligations. Holidays and industry shutdowns must also be taken into consideration.

The time analysis is repeated until the most realistic set of dates is obtained within the time constraints – either those determined during the project definition phase, or those renegotiated in this phase. Ultimately, the MOC dates may need to be changed as a result of the time analysis.

Refer to Appendix A for an example of a network diagram for the case study.

PERFORM THE RESOURCE ANALYSIS

The time analysis provides a clearer picture of how long the project will take, how long each activity will take, and when each activity should start and end. This analysis only superficially considered production rates and the resources required to do the work. The assumption made while doing the time analysis is that unlimited resources are available. It is now time to formalize the resource requirements of the project and ensure that the project plan is viable in terms of resources. The resource analysis is always performed on the results of the time analysis irrespective of the time analysis tool used.

The resource analysis involves determining the resource requirements for each activity. There are two reasons for analysing the resource requirements: 1) to determine the effect of the resources required on the project time schedule; 2) to provide a basis for the price/cost estimating process.

Resources can be people, materials, equipment and services. Money (expenditure and revenue) can also be regarded as a resource, and it is an important consideration, as discussed in the following section on cost analysis.

Resource analysis consists of two steps: 1) allocating and scheduling; 2) levelling or smoothing.

ALLOCATING AND SCHEDULING

This involves examining each activity included in the time analysis to determine what resources are required to do the work and how those resources are spread over the duration of the activity. The following are the most common spread rules.

Straight line or variable demand

The resource level is divided by the number of time periods required, and an equal resource is allocated to each period. It is used when a set amount of work must be done (or resource consumed) on an activity irrespective of the estimated time. Then, if the time is shortened, the resource demand per time period will increase. If the time is lengthened, the resource demand per time period will decrease. For example, a 600-page manual is to be produced. If a typist can produce 100 pages per day, then one typist will be needed for six days – the resource demand will be for one typist per time period. If the time to do the typing is reduced to three days, the effort remains the same (600 pages) so the resource demand will increase to two typists per day.

Fixed per period or fixed demand

This method is used when a resource is consumed for as long as the activity continues. The same level of resource is allocated to each time period. Whether the time is shortened or lengthened, the resource demand per time period stays the same. Using the typing example, there will be work for a typist every day. Irrespective of whether work is produced or not, a typist must be available each day.

Profile

The level of resource varies by time period; for example, two typists will be needed for the first three days and then one for the remainder. A profile is sometimes expressed in percentages, such as 60 per cent of the resource is needed over the first 20 per cent of the time, and the remaining 40 per cent over the last 80 per cent of the time. The level is then split into the percentages and divided equally ('straight-lined') over the corresponding split periods.

Start/end

All the resource is taken up or used in the first or last time period of the duration. Up-front expenditures, payments, and payment for work done are normally allocated in this manner.

All assumptions made (such as production rates) should be recorded for reference at a later stage.

Since the activities have been scheduled in time by means of the time analysis, the resources attached to the activities are also now scheduled in time. By now adding up each type of resource required in each time period, the total resource demand for that period can be determined. This demand is normally shown in the form of a resource histogram per resource type. This is needed for the next step. Scheduling is made easier with the use of a Gantt chart.

Levelling or smoothing

The availability of some resources is fixed at a certain level, meaning that this level per time period cannot be exceeded. This level is known as the 'clipping' level and is particularly relevant if the resource is scarce. A resource histogram will usually show 'peaks' (periods during which the resource level is higher than the clipping level) and 'valleys' (when the resource levels are lower than the clipping level). Figure 9.3 illustrates this.

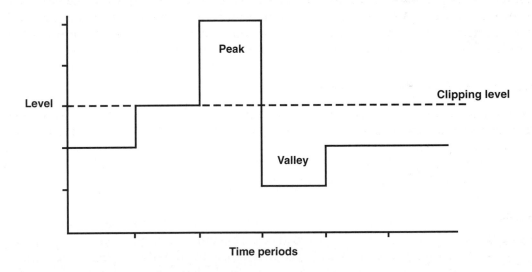

Figure 9.3   Resource histogram or resource demand profile

If the availability of a resource is limited (scarce), then the aim of levelling or smoothing is to eliminate the peaks and fill the valleys to keep it on or below the clipping level. In doing this, the time schedule may be affected. If the resource is readily available (theoretically unlimited) then the object of levelling and smoothing is to find the most economical level of resource without affecting the time schedule.

There are a number of methods for levelling and smoothing, the more common of which are as follows:

● Shift the activities around by rescheduling them (time analysis). Activities with the most float are rescheduled first within their float. The last activities to be shifted will be the critical activities.

- Eliminate certain activities.
- Substitute activities with less resource-consuming activities.
- Change production rates.
- Use alternative resources.
- Split activities (stopping an activity and then restarting it at a later point). This could cause learning curve problems and should only be tried as a last resort.

If any changes are made that could affect the time schedule, the time analysis must be repeated, followed by another resource analysis to gauge the effect of the changes. The time and resource analyses continue until an optimum balance of time and resources within the limits of the project is reached.

Resource levelling is an iterative and time-consuming process and is a task well suited to the use of a computer. A common problem with levelling is that no sooner has one resource been balanced then another that was balanced now becomes unbalanced. Because of this, resource analysis tends not to be done, or is done superficially, leading to incomplete or inaccurate estimating and project plans. Virtually all the project planning software packages available on the market today perform some time and resource analysis. In the authors' opinion, it is well worth investing in such a planning package for performing time and resource analyses alone.

Readers needing a more in-depth discussion on the subject of resourcing will find texts by the following authors useful: Moder, Phillips and Davis[64], Meredith and Mantel[60], Nicholas[67], Badiru[7], Ahuja[1], Lewis[53] and Lockyer[57].

PERFORM THE COST ANALYSIS

Now that the level and timing of resources are known, the cost estimate produced in the project definition phase can be improved. The cost estimate is developed using the cost breakdown structure (CBS). The CBS is produced from the detailed WBS by adding cost elements that are not necessarily related to work. Such elements could be provisions for risk (contingencies), interest on loans, licence fees and royalties, and certain administration overheads. This concept and the CBS are discussed in detail under 'Cost management' in Appendix B.

In practice, the CBS is created and the estimating process is started as soon as the detailed WBS is defined. Cost information is fed into the CBS as and when it becomes available. While the project planning is being done, detailed design of the project's products is also being developed. Material lists (bills of quantities) are now becoming available, decisions are being made as to the use of subcontractors, and the procurement department is already pricing necessary items. As this information becomes available, the cost estimate becomes more accurate until the best and final estimate is reached. Essentially, the estimating process is similar to that done to create the earlier estimate during the project definition phase. The differences are that there is now a more detailed framework within which to estimate and more information available to support it.

The information produced by the resource analysis substantiates and supplements the cost estimate as well as acting as a control. The resource information can be readily converted to money by applying a standard, average, or exact rate per resource unit. If the resource analysis was comprehensive, there should be a clear relationship with the cost estimate. For example, the resource analysis shows that a total of 500 consulting hours are required, which translates into money at an average rate of $100 per hour, equalling $50,000. If the best estimate done in the cost analysis reaches a figure of $10,000, then there is obviously something wrong – either in the estimate or with the resource analysis. The numbers should be a lot closer.

If a reduced resource analysis were performed, modelling only certain resources, the results of that as well as the time analysis would still be valuable for preparing estimates. Questions such as, 'When and for how long will we need that overseas specialist? What is the provision needed for travelling and accommodation expenses?' can be addressed. The cost of the specialist will be determined by the length of time they are required. The provision for travelling will be made in the time period that the specialist starts and accommodation expenses will be allocated for the time the specialist is on site.

The cost analysis will indicate whether the project can be achieved within the cost limits set. If it cannot, the estimates will have to be reconsidered to find ways to reduce cost. This is an ongoing process even if the estimate is within limits. There are many ways to reduce cost, such as cutting time, increasing production rates, reducing the use of resources, alternative resources, more comprehensive resource levelling and smoothing, alternative approaches to doing work, and use of subcontractors. All these options must be investigated and applied if beneficial. This could result in changes to the time and resource estimates. The time and resource analyses will then have to be redone. At all times, the impact of any cost reductions on the parameters of time, quality, scope and other trade-offs must be considered.

Refer to Appendix A for an example of a detailed cost estimate for the case study.

PREPARE THE QUALITY PLAN

The quality plan adds the dimension of quality to those of cost and time. The quality plan is needed to ensure that the project's products or outcomes meet the specifications or requirements as contained in the scope of the project. The detailed quality plan usually reflects the type of industry the project is being carried out in, and contains at least the quality criteria the project outputs must meet and the testing and validation activities to be adopted. Most important, quality review procedures must be established, and review activities must be defined and resourced. The activities defined to conduct quality inspections, and other functions related to quality, must be integrated into the plan being developed.

At a high level, the quality plan sets the overall quality strategy for the entire project. It defines the standards to be followed and the quality criteria for the products or outcomes. It also needs to identify any external constraints such as the use of specific configuration management or change control methods.

At the production level, the quality plan identifies the quality criteria, test and validation methods, and review guidelines for each product or deliverable. Activities are defined for quality reviews and for approval of test specifications and results down to the level of specifying quality review inspectors.

Quality assurance is normally defined or regulated by generic standards such as the ISO9000/ISO10006 series, the BS5750 standard, and TickIt (aimed at software). The quality plan must ensure that the project adheres to whatever standard is being used. This could involve additional administrative procedures or processes.

Quality activities take time, consume resources and have costs attached, and this all needs to be taken into consideration. The quality plan could therefore affect the time, resource and cost analyses, and these may need to be redone.

PREPARE THE COMMUNICATIONS PLAN

Projects generate information that needs to be communicated to all participants in a timely manner. Channels of communication must be established between all involved. The communications plan essentially documents the information and communication needs of the stakeholders, such as who needs what information, when they will need it, how it will be presented, and in what form or media.

An outline communications plan was developed during the project definition phase, and this now needs to be expanded. Communication activities such as report preparation and meetings need to be identified. Systems to process the project information, staff to prepare the reports, distribution systems (faxes, e-mail, computers), graphics artists and editors to produce newsletters and posters may need to be acquired. Communication strategies may need to be formulated.

All this needs to be documented in the detailed communications plan, which must then be costed and resourced against the activities scheduled. Once again these elements could affect the time, resource and cost analyses and these may need to be redone.

PREPARE THE HUMAN RESOURCES PLAN

During earlier processes, human resources required for tasks and activities were determined. At this point, there should be a good understanding of the type of person required and the level of skills they should have. The following tasks are necessary to prepare the human resources plan:

- Determine and document how the human resources will be brought into and out of the project team.
- Create role or job descriptions and people profiles.
- Identify specific people with the correct profiles to fill the roles. This may involve negotiations with functional managers, individuals and other project managers. If

the resource is not available within the organization, recruitment agencies or individuals outside the organization may have to be approached. This may require interfacing with the human resources and procurement functional departments.

- Develop and document reward and incentive schemes as well as team-building activities.
- Plan and schedule any specific training required for the project.
- Take into account leave and any other reasons assigned staff may be unavailable.

All the above aspects are documented in the human resource plan. Some factors such as staff availability, training, and incentive and reward schemes will affect the time, cost and resource analyses.

PREPARE THE PROCUREMENT PLAN

The procurement plan indicates which project needs can best be met by obtaining products or services outside the organization. It involves consideration of whether to procure, how to procure, what and how much to procure, and when to procure it.

If the organization does not have a procurement 'facility' (buying department), such a function may need to be established for the project or outsourced. Even if a procurement facility does exist, the project may require that specialists be approached to assist in contractual, specification or quality assurance aspects.

Procurement has an impact on timing. Certain materials may need to be imported or may have long lead times that could affect project schedules. The concept of 'just-in-time' procurement could have an effect on the cash flow and funding.

Procurement invariably involves some form of contract, and such contracts need to be drafted if they do not exist, or evaluated if they do. Conditions contained in contracts may mean that the time, cost and resource analyses need to be considered and redone if necessary.

It is essential, therefore, that a procurement strategy and plan be developed to address all of the above issues.

INTEGRATE THE PROJECT PLAN

Although different people, departments and teams may be working on different parts of the project plan, the project manager still has the overall responsibility and accountability for it. The project manager must ensure that all components fit together to produce an integrated plan.

It is the project manager's responsibility to ensure that:

- the planning is complete and thorough;
- all the planning work done is reflected in integrated project plans, particularly the

planning work done by individual departments (the integrated plans are created by consolidating the plans from the individual departments);

- all risks identified previously and during the planning have been taken into consideration and the necessary risk responses have been developed;
- all adjustments to cater for risk have been made to the time and cost schedules;
- the right people have been selected for the project roles;
- the developed project plan is sufficient to fulfil the project objectives;
- all details in the specifications and designs (where applicable) have been taken into consideration and are as complete as required at this stage;
- all cost analyses correctly reflect the economics and finance aspects of the plan;
- all components and aspects of the plan have been integrated.

Through the process of ensuring the above, the project manager develops confidence in the plan and takes ownership for it. The project manager will be accountable and responsible for executing the plan and therefore must be completely satisfied that it is robust, viable and manageable. If the project manager has any doubts they must be voiced now, so that the plan can be strengthened before it is too late.

Where the planning process is being used to plan a sub-project or where the planning is being done by a specific department, the integration step serves a similar function. The difference is that the step must ensure that the components of the plan (scope, cost, time, quality, risk, communications, human resources and procurement) are integrated.

DO THE CASH FLOW ANALYSIS

This analysis is only carried out once an accurate and stable plan has been developed. It entails taking the money estimate and phasing it over the duration of the project in a similar way to the resource analysis (that is, money is regarded as a resource). For the cash flow analysis, expenditure (outflows) must be separated from income (inflows). The result must be a graph or schedule showing the cumulative outflow and inflow of funds for each time period in the project. Appendix B contains a discussion on cash flow as part of the section on cost management.

The prepared graph is an indication of the funding requirements of the project, as discussed in the earlier section of this chapter on financial viability. The project manager needs to analyse this graph in consultation with the organization's finance manager to determine whether the organization can afford to implement the project. The project manager cannot make this decision alone, as the project manager has no authority over the allocation of the organization's funds.

Acting on the advice of the finance manager, the project manager and the project team may need to 'smooth' and 'optimize' the project cash flow in a similar way as for scarce resources. The strategies for optimizing cash flow are similar to those for reducing cost and levelling resources. The process of optimizing the cash flow may require changes to the cost, resource and time components.

Cash flow optimization, like resource levelling, is an iterative and time-consuming process and is well suited to the use of a computer. Virtually all the planning software packages available on the market perform some form of cash flow analysis, normally as a result of the resource analysis.

Projects in certain industries behave in a consistent manner and produce cash flow curves that have a similar shape. Set formulae exist in certain industries that will produce the graphs based on certain global parameters. If a formula exists in your industry and your organization has confidence in it, then there is no reason why it should not be used.

The cash flow graph is normally supplemented with a description of how the project will be funded. This is often prepared by the finance manager.

PRODUCE THE INTEGRATED PROJECT PLAN BASELINE

The integrated project plan baseline contains all of the elements discussed in this chapter. The project definition report produced at the end of the project definition phase is added to provide a complete overview of the project.

The intention of the integrated project plan baseline is to:

- obtain authorization to proceed with the project execution phase (if required);
- form the only baseline (scope, time, quality and cost) against which the success of the project execution will be measured;
- fully define and set the parameters for the management of the project execution.

The integrated project plan baseline consists of at least the following:

- fully developed project scope, which includes the specifications for the work to be done;
- time schedules;
- cost breakdown structure and cost budgets;
- project funding details;
- human resources plan;
- quality plan;
- communications plan;
- procurement plan;
- the required project management information system (PMIS) and key performance indicators (KPIs).

The baseline is further supported by at least the following:

- detailed WBS;
- the results of a time analysis;
- the specifications of what has to be done;

- the results of a resource analysis;
- the results of a cost analysis;
- the results of a cash flow analysis.

The above components should be regarded as the minimum contents. Any additional information and documentation that can provide more clarity and background to the project should also be included.

CONTROL MECHANISMS, THE PMIS AND KPIs

An important part of manageability is the methods or mechanisms that will be used to manage the project during the project execution and close-out phases. It is essential at this point to consider how the project will be managed and what controls are necessary. Aspects such as reporting standards, progress measurement methods, costing procedures, purchasing procedures, change control and configuration management procedures and progress meetings need to be addressed, clarified and documented. Some of these aspects would have been considered when preparing the communication and procurement plans and will now have to be documented here as part of the overall control mechanisms.

Many organizations have standards for most of the above already in place. If they exist, they need to be referred to in the planning documentation. If they do not exist, they will need to be developed or acquired before the start of the project execution phase. The project team must not be allowed to begin implementing the plan without the necessary control mechanisms in place.

Chapter 10, The project execution phase, discusses the concepts and principles of project monitoring and control. It covers key performance indicators (KPIs) that may be required to monitor and control the project. The necessary project management information system (PMIS) must be formulated and acquired if necessary to capture, process and report on project information. This needs to be done before beginning the project execution phase.

AN ALTERNATIVE APPROACH TO ACTIVITY PLANNING

This approach to planning activities is appropriate for planning 'fuzzy' projects. On 'fuzzy' projects, the desired results are usually known, even though the work required to achieve them may not be known. This planning approach thus concentrates on the results to be achieved. These results were set during the project definition phase and documented on the milestone objective chart (MOC) as event milestones. This approach expands on the MOC by concentrating on the activities needed to achieve a milestone. Activity planning encompasses the definition of the work required to attain the milestones (the results) within the constraints of time, cost and quality.

The essential concept of the method of planning given here is to adopt a moving window approach to planning activities.

The moving window approach

Essentially the moving window approach means that the project is viewed through a window that can only 'see' part of the project at any time. As a particular part of the project comes into view, it is planned in detail. Planning thus follows a 'just-in-time' approach – being left as late as possible. This means that the results of previous steps in the plan could provide information and details to generate activities for the next step. If the milestones on the MOC are regarded as the steps, it means that the project is executed one or two milestones at a time.

In reality, what is being done is to regard the work required to reach each milestone as a 'project' in itself. As such, we can take each milestone through the phases of definition, planning, execution and, to a certain degree, close-out.

On fuzzy projects where there is little experience of the work to be done, any attempt to plan detailed activities several months or years into the future is invariably wasted effort. The only certainty about a plan for a fuzzy project that details work a year hence is that it is wrong. Before work is due to start, a multitude of factors both internal and external to a fuzzy project will render the plan useless. There will rarely be enough information available to plan accurately that far in advance.

Planning the activities

To plan the activities required to reach a specific milestone, steps similar to those for defining milestones in the project definition phase are followed:

- *Identify the activities.* The activities required to achieve the milestone are identified and listed. The supplementary activity list drawn up during the milestone planning could be useful here. To be manageable, there should not be more than about 20 activities to reach a milestone.
- *Define the people involved.* This step is similar to determining the responsible entities and developing the milestone responsibility matrix, as described in the sections 'Determine the responsible entities' and 'Determine the project responsibilities' in Chapter 8. The difference here is that, instead of milestones and responsible entities, the activities and specific people's names and/or roles are used.
- *Estimate the work content.* Estimate the amount of work and duration for each activity.
- *Schedule the activities.* The activities must be scheduled in time. If there are few activities, the activity list may suffice. If needed, the activities can be scheduled using a Gantt chart. A critical path analysis can be used if the activity dependencies are complex.

Refer to Appendix A for an example of an activity schedule for a milestone defined for the case study.

Advantages of this approach

The advantage of this approach is that the results required during the project definition phase can be defined using the MOC. By considering each milestone as a decision point, decisions can be made regarding:

● the work done to reach the milestone – is it of sufficient quality to continue?
● the cost to date – does it justify continuing?
● time – has it taken too long getting here; is it viable to continue?

Since the steps are small and incremental, the team can proceed down a path without losing control too far down the project. This provides a margin of safety and the project owner has control over a fuzzy project. The opportunity exists to abandon the project at any point if a defined critical result is not achieved.

The approach allows planning for results on a project with limited detail – possibly even projects that otherwise would not have been contemplated because of the uncertainty surrounding the work to be done.

Disadvantages of this approach

Because of the fuzziness and because there is insufficient detail, it is sometimes difficult to determine an accurate total cost and duration for the project.

PROCEEDING TO THE NEXT PHASE

The project manager takes the ultimate decision on the viability, manageability and accuracy of the integrated project plan baseline. If the project manager is satisfied that the plan is sound, authorization is sought from the client/upper management to continue with the project execution phase. This request for authority to continue is often dispensed with and the decision is left to the project manager. This can happen if the demarcation between the project planning phase and the execution phase is not distinct. In many cases, some of the project work would have already started before the detailed planning is completed. Obtaining permission to proceed under these circumstances is almost meaningless.

However, if there are large discrepancies between the budgets and dates determined during this phase and those of the project definition phase, the project manager is obligated to discuss these with the client/upper management. The decisions that could be made as a result of these discussions are similar to those discussed in the corresponding section of the previous chapter.

If the project manager is satisfied with the integrated project plan baseline and the necessary authority has been obtained, the project can officially enter the project execution phase.

In practice...

Philip's perfectionist planning

Philip had taken to his role as project planner with great enthusiasm. Focusing on detail gave him great satisfaction – you could almost say he was the ultimate Mr Detail. Meticulous and fastidious by nature, detailed project planning suited him perfectly.

A month into the planning of a project to merge and relocate two major production facilities, Philip had developed a 2,000-activity network diagram. To Philip this was solid planning and the project director, Rod, felt confident that with this very detailed plan they would certainly succeed in delivering this mission-critical project.

Rod had, however, recently read an interesting article in a project management publication. The article stated that detailed planning up-front in the absence of clear strategies and objectives greatly increases the risk of project failure. The article further stated that the lack of an appropriate supporting project management system and methodology also contributes to the increased risk of project failure. Rod, who prided himself on his thoroughness and lateral thinking ability, reflected on the article and wondered if he had in fact approached the planning correctly.

Rod asked his personal assistant Jenny to 'Get hold of this consultant who wrote this article. I want to talk to him.' Jenny contacted Kelvin Cowry, the author, and arranged a meeting. A week later, the meeting took place in Rod's office.

Rod studied the consultant for a moment, and said: 'Kelvin, as you know, we are at the early stages of planning an important project. Take a look at this planning and tell me what you think of it.' Rod handed Kelvin the 2,000-activity Gantt chart and the results of a critical path analysis.

Kelvin immediately recognized that the *Gantt chart guru* (see Chapter 2) had struck. 'How am I going to tell him that the only thing certain about his planning is that it is wrong? How can anyone plan to a detailed level up to two years ahead, especially when detail designs have not yet been produced? A tall order!', Kelvin thought.

Kelvin voiced his thoughts to Rod, who immediately took offence. Kelvin used his tact and disarming style to steer the discussion diplomatically. Eventually, Rod came round to Kelvin's way of thinking. He realized that he would have to elaborate the planning progressively, and he conceded that perhaps they had gone too far and had been too detailed too early.

The 2,000-activity plan would be scrapped and a structured project management approach would be taken. The project would initially be described by carefully considered strategies and objectives, supported by a solid deliverables breakdown structure, scoping, and result milestones. A sound implementation approach would also be developed.

As the designs progressed, the information was fed to the project planner. Detailed project time, cost and quality plans emerged. A project management information system was designed and implemented. Philip flourished – he was on top of his planning, and the structured and systematic approach based on result milestones suited his perfectionist style. The project manager's wealth of operational experience and his strong delivery focus ensured that Rod was getting his project delivered, while production volumes and quality remained within acceptable limits.

The two-year project delivered the required results. Philip had initially felt embarrassed, wary and even fearful of the consultant. Over time, as trust grew, he finally came round, and a mutually beneficial relationship was built.

Important lessons...

1. Beware of attempting to create detailed activity plans based on insufficient information too early in a project's life.
2. The absence of strategic business thinking creates a tendency to delve down to detailed planning when faced with a difficult project.
3. Irrespective of how much is known about a project, progressively elaborating the planning is still the less risky way to proceed.
4. The availability of easy-to-use computer planning software packages encourages the construction of over-detailed activity plans.
5. A structured project management methodology increases the probability of project success.

10

The project execution phase

INTRODUCTION

At the end of the project planning phase, the integrated project plan baseline was produced and agreed, and authority given to proceed with the project execution phase. During this phase and the following phase (close-out), the planned project objectives must be achieved. The integrated project plan baseline provides the strategies, tactics and approaches to get there. A poorly developed plan will result in a poorly executed project with accompanying loss of time, cost and quality.

The project execution phase has to do with monitoring and control, and applying corrective responses as necessary. This is done through a continuous and consistent loop of review, reporting, control feedback and revision; until the project is fully implemented. This chapter discusses these processes in more detail.

THE PROJECT EXECUTION PHASE PROCESSES

A project must be implemented with the aim of achieving the project's objectives. This is done by:

- monitoring project progress and performance;
- comparing and evaluating against the planned objectives;
- taking corrective action where required.

The essential functions here are explained below:

● **Monitoring** is the collecting, recording and reporting of information concerning all aspects of project performance that the project manager and others wish to know.
● **Evaluation** is judging the quality and effectiveness of project performance.
● **Controlling** is using the gathered information to bring actual performance in line with planned performance.

The project execution phase consists primarily of the following steps:

1. 'Kick-off' the project.
2. Establish the monitoring and control tools.
3. Monitor and evaluate project performance and progress.
4. Produce progress status and performance reports.
5. Apply control feedback and problem solving.
6. Revise the integrated project plan baseline if required.

The next sections of this chapter explain these steps one by one.

In parallel to and integrated with these steps, any changes to any aspect of the integrated project plan baseline must be monitored, recorded, evaluated and communicated to affected parties. It is imperative that a formal change control process be in place and that all changes are made through that process. Such a process is discussed later in this chapter, in the section 'Revise the project plan baseline' (p 230).

PROJECT EXECUTION KICK-OFF MEETING

It is essential to 'kick off' the project execution phase with a get-together of everyone involved in the project. Depending on the size of the project, this could be a round-table meeting or a seminar/workshop or videoconference depending on the geographical spread of the participants. The purpose of the meeting is to ensure that:

● all the essential elements are in place;
● the team understands what is to be achieved;
● all participants are motivated and committed to achieving project success.

The meeting also provides a forum for the project sponsor to address the team to show support for the project, and confidence in the team and the project plan.

All problems and queries must be addressed and responded to in an open manner by the project manager and project sponsor.

At this meeting, the integrated project plan baseline should be presented in a summarized form. It is also important to consider the project organization and responsibility matrices to ensure that roles, authorities, accountabilities and responsibilities are clear and accepted.

The meeting should end by formally 'kicking-off' the first activities in the plan.

ESTABLISH MONITORING AND CONTROL SYSTEMS AND INFRASTRUCTURE

The monitoring and control systems and the project infrastructure must be established. During the project planning phase, the project manager would have already considered reporting standards, progress measurement methods, costing procedures, purchasing procedures, change control and configuration management procedures, and progress meetings. The systems and infrastructure required to implement all this now need to be put into place.

Project information needs to be measured through meaningful control systems in an economical manner. Systems need to be appropriate for the size and complexity of the project. Efficient monitoring and control systems will enable project participants to receive relevant and accurate information in a consistent and timely manner.

The following should then be considered when implementing project control systems (after Kezsbom, Schilling, and Edward[47]):

- It is not necessary to collect data the project team does not intend to analyse. The effectiveness of a control system is not dependent on sophisticated computer systems and large amounts of data. The control system must be appropriate to satisfy the needs of it users.
- Trivia should not be measured. The effort of measuring things that have no effect on overall project performance and results will be wasted. If the data does not contribute to efficient and effective control, it should not be measured.
- Measure only what can be collected in a consistent manner. If the collection of certain data is inconsistent and difficult, then that data must be used with caution.
- Report on those elements that can be compared to predetermined standards, such as a baseline plan against which the collected data can be compared and deviations reported.
- Measurement systems should be as accurate as their use demands. Progress percentages reported to three decimal places are no more useful than rounded figures – 54.643 per cent is no more meaningful than 55 per cent. The additional effort to obtain precision may not be worth it. It is better to be reasonably right than to be accurately wrong!
- Reports must be generated from timely and accurate data. Late data is as inaccurate as incorrect data. Finding out today that the budget was overspent three months ago is useless information.
- Give all team members access to the control systems. Information should not be hidden or difficult to obtain. Tailor the systems to meet the information needs of all

team members. Encourage team members to access the information and use it to manage more effectively.

● Control systems should be robust, organized and simple to use; in other words, useful and usable.

Project control systems are contained in the project management information system or PMIS as it is commonly called. Typically, a PMIS will be a collection of processes, procedures and systems that facilitate the collection (monitoring) of data, the processing of that data and the reporting of the project information. Most modern PMISs are computerized, but need not be.

An effective PMIS should include:

● **scheduling and network planning**: software used to perform critical path analysis and produce reports such as Gantt charts, activity lists and network diagrams;
● **cost budgeting**: systems that allow cost budgets to be determined and recorded against a cost breakdown structure (CBS);
● **cost control**: systems that capture actual costs and other cost information and produce reports comparing it against the CBS budgets, and calculate trends, variances and cash flow information;
● **performance analysis**: systems that compute and report on project performance indices, earned value and other aspects of project performance;
● **resource management**: software functions that perform resource allocation, scheduling and levelling;
● **reporting and graphics**: report writers and graphics tools to generate ad hoc user reports, performance and other graphs such as cash flow graphs and resource histograms;
● **word processing**: to create and print documents such as progress reports;
● **spreadsheets**: to capture, process and report numerical and other data;
● **various**: software and systems used to perform functions of a more specific nature such as materials management, records management, equipment management, change control, human resource management and subcontractor management.

Care should be taken not to over-emphasize the importance of the PMIS. Meredith and Mantel[60] state that one of the most common errors of project management is to manage the project control systems rather then the project itself. They go on to quote Thambain who describes other such errors, as summarized below:

● **Computer paralysis**: Excessive computer involvement can lead to computer activity replacing project management, and losing touch with project realities.
● **PMIS verification:** PMIS reports mask real project problems, are massaged to look good, or simply verify that real problems exist yet are not acted on.
● **Information overload**: Too many reports, too detailed reports, or distributing PMIS information to too many people overwhelms managers and effectively hides problems.

- **Project isolation**: The PMIS reports replace useful and frequent communication between the project manager and top management, or even between the project manager and the project team.
- **Computer dependence**: The project manager or top management wait for the computer reports before reacting to problems rather than being proactive and avoiding problems in the first place.
- **PMIS misdirection**: Due to the unequal coverage of the PMIS, certain project sub-areas are over-managed and other areas receive inadequate attention. Symptoms of problems (budget overruns, schedule slippages) are monitored and managed, rather than the problems themselves.

MONITOR AND EVALUATE PROJECT PERFORMANCE AND PROGRESS

Monitoring is the collecting, recording and reporting of information concerning all aspects of project performance that the project manager and others wish to know. Control and monitoring are not the same. Monitoring is measuring and reporting against progress; control includes monitoring, but it also includes taking timely, corrective action to meet project objectives or goals.

Monitoring, therefore, is an essential part of control. Monitoring is the activity that determines whether the project is proceeding according to plan, and reports any variances.

It must be stressed that the purpose of monitoring is not to provide a basis for penalizing or rewarding project members. The intention is to highlight deviations from the plan, identify the need for possible corrective action, and establish a basis for taking corrective action before the situation becomes irrecoverable or uncontrollable.

Monitoring is a function of the PMIS. Data is obtained from project transactions such as timesheets, orders, deliveries, invoices, payments, milestones and activity progress sheets. The PMIS collects, records, processes and reports on this data.

Monitoring reports must be prepared at regular, predetermined intervals otherwise control will be neglected. The frequency of reports is dependent on the level of control desired and where the project is in terms of its life. Reports can be prepared less often for clients/upper management, but more frequently at project management and operational level. Reporting frequency can change over the life of the project, as some projects require more reporting earlier and others more reporting later in their life cycle.

Progress monitoring

Essentially, monitoring reports indicate progress and performance information. Performance information can generally be derived from data recorded in the PMIS through consistent and verifiable transactions. Progress information, on the other hand, is generally more difficult to obtain accurately and is often subjective rather than objective.

Progress completion is usually expressed as a percentage. There are numerous techniques for determining the progress completion of a project, such as the following:

- Milestones achieved and percentage complete (or preferably the percentage still to complete) towards the next milestones.
- Elapsed time is compared to the estimated time on activities.
- Actual resource usage (such as human resource) is compared against planned requirements.
- 'Experienced' people estimate the percentage complete on individual activities or work packages.
- The quantity of work units in place is physically surveyed and compared to those shown on drawings, in a bill of quantities, or in other specifications.

Each method has its advantages and disadvantages. It is usual to use a combination of methods to determine progress on a project. In many instances, several methods are used to arrive at progress estimates for a specific element. These different estimates are then cross-checked to determine the best estimate.

It is important to note that the determination of progress is not a scientific process. It relies heavily on observation and experience. There is always an element of guesswork involved and care should be taken to prevent undue optimism or pessimism. The most important point is that progress monitoring must be consistent. Once the best method of measuring is decided on, it must be consistently applied.

In contrast to progress completion monitoring, cost and revenue progress monitoring is quite straightforward. As costs are incurred and revenues earned, they are accumulated against the relevant cost codes defined in the PMIS.

As part of the monitoring process, the project manager must continuously estimate the amount of money or work still required to complete the project. This is known as the estimate to complete or ETC. Adding this to the moneys already committed or time already spent gives an estimate at completion or EAC. These figures allow detailed planning for future time and cost requirements, and also identify any need to prevent budget overruns by replanning, changing production rates, or changes in methods.

As well as progress, costs and revenue, the quantity of resources used and the quantity of work units produced should be monitored and recorded wherever applicable. These figures are used to control project performance.

Reports and tools

Some typical monitoring and control reports and tools are explained below.

Cost report

This report should show at least the following against each cost code or work package:

- budgeted cost;
- committed cost;
- actual cost;
- budget variance;
- estimate to complete (ETC);
- estimate at completion (EAC).

Milestone charts

A schedule listing the milestone objectives, their dates and comments on the progress towards meeting them.

Marked-up Gantt charts

The project Gantt chart marked up to show the actual progress as at the date of reporting.

Project performance schedule or chart (earned value analysis)

This will show the budgeted cost for work scheduled, budgeted cost for work performed, actual cost for work performed, schedule variance and cost variance against each cost code or work package, either in schedule form or in chart form. Earned value (EV) is discussed later.

Key performance indicators (KPIs)

This will show various statistics and ratios, such as milestones and tasks planned against completed milestones and tasks, and schedule and cost performance indicators. These KPIs are discussed in more detail later.

'S-curves'

These show actual expenditure or revenue versus budgeted cumulatively over time. This could be supplemented with schedules showing the project's cash flow, both actual and projected.

Activity charts

Schedules listing the activities, dates and comments on the progress towards completing them.

All the above are in addition to any narrative reports and minutes. It is not imperative to use all the suggested tools and reports shown. Each organization normally builds its own standards for project reporting.

OVERALL PROJECT PERFORMANCE

Monitoring the actual progress and costs individually against the schedule and budget does not ensure performance is proceeding to plan. The project may be ahead of schedule but running over budget, resulting in an overall below-par performance. It is necessary to monitor project performance by integrating time and cost monitoring. This can be accomplished by determining the following figures at project and work package level.

Budgeted cost of work scheduled (BCWS)

This is a record of the costs originally budgeted to be spent in order to carry out the work scheduled in a particular time period. Simply stated, this is the 'promise' of what the project should achieve at a point in time.

Budgeted cost of work performed (BCWP)

This is the budgeted cost to do the work actually completed in a given time period. It is sometimes referred to as earned value (EV). It is what the project has 'actually achieved' or 'earned' at the point in time.

Actual cost of work performed (ACWP)

This is the cost actually expended to do the work completed in the given time period. It is simply the 'cost of what has been achieved' at the point in time.

These figures are normally cumulative. Cumulative figures rather than periodic or incremental figures will tend to smooth out any periodic variations caused by placing good data into the wrong time frame (period). The BCWS, BCWP and ACWP can be evaluated to assess the performance status of the project. Table 10.1 shows how this can be done.

The variables BCWS, BCWP and ACWP can be used to calculate variances that provide more insight into the status of the project. Essentially the variances answer the same questions as Table 10.1 except that values are arrived at which can be used for further analysis.

Three variances can be calculated:

Schedule variance   SV = BCWP – BCWS (Achievement – Promise)
Cost variance   CV = BCWP – ACWP (Achievement – Cost)
Accounting variance   AV = BCWS – ACWP (Promise – Cost)

Accounting variance is the accountant's view of the project, as it measures the difference between budgeted costs (promised) and expended funds (cost). However, it ignores the

Table 10.1 Assessing performance status

BCWS	BCWP	ACWP	Schedule status	Cost status
$1,000	$1,000	$1,000	On time	On cost
$2,000	$2,000	$1,000	On time	Under cost
$1,000	$1,000	$2,000	On time	Over cost
$1,000	$2,000	$2,000	Ahead	On cost
$1,000	$2,000	$1,000	Ahead	Under cost
$1,000	$2,000	$3,000	Ahead	Over cost
$2,000	$1,000	$1,000	Behind	On cost
$3,000	$2,000	$1,000	Behind	Under cost
$2,000	$1,000	$3,000	Behind	Over cost

achievement dimension. For example, a project may have expended more funds than promised at a point in time, thus signalling an overrun to the accountants, whereas the achievement could be ahead of both promise and cost, indicating that the project is ahead of schedule and under cost.

Project teams must appreciate the financial obligation to manage the organization's cash flow. As projects are important users of the organization's cash, and thus influence the flow of funds, the promise must be continually replanned and compared to the cost for cash flow management purposes.

Using the values in Table 10.1, the variances are calculated as shown in Table 10.2. CV should not be taken alone, as it could be misleading. SV must also be considered. If SV is positive and CV is negative, the project could be ahead of schedule and a cost overrun could easily be justified. If both SV and CV are positive, the project is both ahead of schedule and below cost.

Table 10.2 Calculating variances

BCWS	BCWP	ACWP	SV	CV	AV	Schedule status	Cost status
$1,000	$1,000	$1,000	0	0	0	On time	On cost
$2,000	$2,000	$1,000	0	1,000	1,000	On time	Under cost
$1,000	$1,000	$2,000	0	−1,000	−1,000	On time	Over cost
$1,000	$2,000	$2,000	1,000	0	−1,000	Ahead	On cost
$1,000	$2,000	$1,000	1,000	1,000	0	Ahead	Under cost
$1,000	$2,000	$3,000	1,000	−1,000	−2,000	Ahead	Over cost
$2,000	$1,000	$1,000	−1,000	0	1,000	Behind	On cost
$3,000	$2,000	$1,000	−1,000	1,000	2,000	Behind	Under cost
$2,000	$1,000	$3,000	−1,000	−2,000	−1,000	Behind	Over cost

By graphing the cumulative BCWS, BCWP and ACWP over time, a project performance chart (sometimes referred to as an earned value chart) can be produced. This is an excellent, compact way of visually indicating project performance. Such a graph is shown in Figure 10.1.

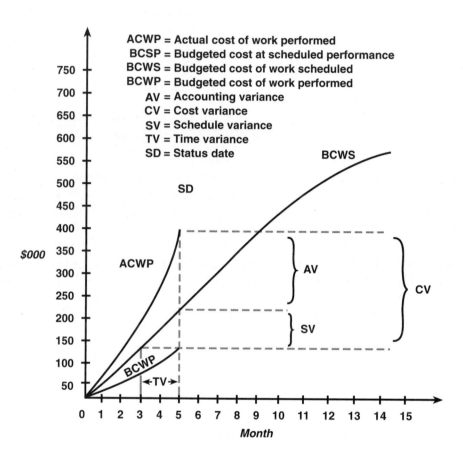

Figure 10.1 Project performance chart/earned value chart

From the data contained in Tables 10.1 and 10.2, two performance indices can be calculated that are used to assess the schedule and cost performance of the project and work packages and the relative size of the variances. These indices provide quick performance indicators that summarize the earned value graphs.

Schedule performance index $SPI = BCWP \div BCWS$
Cost performance index $CPI = BCWP \div ACWP$

If SPI > 1.0 then work is ahead of schedule.
If CPI > 1.0 work is under cost budget.
A value <1.0 means the opposite – behind schedule or over budget, and a value of exactly 1.0 indicates on schedule or on budget.

Table 10.3   Performance indices

BCWS	BCWP	ACWP	SPI	CPI	Schedule status	Cost status
$1,000	$1,000	$1,000	1.0	1.0	On time	On cost
$2,000	$2,000	$1,000	1.0	2.0	On time	Under cost
$1,000	$1,000	$2,000	1.0	0.5	On time	Over cost
$1,000	$2,000	$2,000	2.0	1.0	Ahead	On cost
$1,000	$2,000	$1,000	2.0	2.0	Ahead	Under cost
$1,000	$2,000	$3,000	2.0	0.67	Ahead	Over cost
$2,000	$1,000	$1,000	0.5	1.0	Behind	On cost
$3,000	$2,000	$1,000	0.67	2.0	Behind	Under cost
$2,000	$1,000	$3,000	0.5	0.33	Behind	Over cost

If the indices are graphically plotted over time they can provide an indication of the changing performance (trend) of the project and work packages. An even more useful graph is to plot the SPI against CPI. This provides a more visual representation of the project performance. Figure 10.2 is an example of such a graph based on the data for a fictitious project given in the Table 10.4.

Table 10.4   Examples of project performances indices

Month	SPI	CPI
1	1.1	1.2
2	1.2	1.3
3	1.1	1.0
4	1.0	0.9
5	0.9	0.7
6	0.8	1.1
7	0.75	1.2
8	0.95	1.3
9	1.05	1.1
10	1.15	1.2

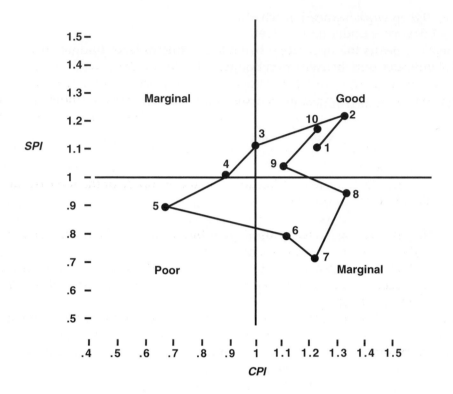

Figure 10.2 Performance indices for months 1 to 10

Looking at the graph in Figure 10.2, the performance of the fictitious project started off well for the first two months and then declined, going from marginal to poor then back to marginal again before recovering in months 8, 9 and 10.

To know the status of the project, information on the performance of all work packages is needed. Similar calculations and graphs to those above can be prepared for all work packages, although they are normally prepared at the total project level or at subproject level.

It is important to focus on both the project level and work package level. Focusing only on the project level could overshadow the good performance of some activities and hide the poor performance of others. Focusing only on individual work packages could conceal the cumulative effect of slightly poor performance in many activities. Even small cost overruns on many individual work packages can add up to large overruns for the project.

Thus, all the monitoring tools available must be continuously checked to ascertain the project progress and performance. Focusing on one area only could lead to incorrect assumptions on project status and performance.

Forecasting 'at completion'

As the project moves along, it is necessary to review what has been achieved so far, but more importantly to determine 'what remains to be done'. Depending on the status and performance trend of the project, the expected final cost and completion date might often have to be revised. Significant schedule and cost overruns or under-runs early on in a project indicate that the planned completion date and final cost estimate will have to be revised.

Monthly 'at completion' forecasts should therefore be prepared. These are forecasts of the time and cost as they will be at the end of the project. According to Fleming and Koppelman29, three factors have an influence on the accuracy of the forecasts and these need to be taken into consideration:

1. **The quality of the integrated project plan baseline** – the better the quality of the planning, the more accurate the forecasts will be.
2. **Actual performance against the baseline plan** – how realistic have the measures of the actuals been? Have the measurements of BCWS, BCWP and ACWP been consistent and accurate?
3. **Management's determination to control (change) the final results** – to what degree is management prepared to take aggressive actions on the remaining work to alter the final outcome?

Cost at completion

There are fundamentally two methods for forecasting the estimated cost at completion (ECAC).

The first method entails re-estimating the cost of the remaining work in the manner originally used to estimate the total project cost. This estimated cost to complete is then added to the actual costs to date to arrive at the ECAC.

The second method involves the use of the performance indices CPI and SPI to calculate the forecasts statistically. The following formulae are used to estimate the cost at completion (ECAC):

Estimated cost at completion:
$$ECAC = (BCAC - BCWP) \div CPI + ACWP$$
or
$$ECAC = (BCAC - BCWP) \div (CPI \times SPI) + ACWP$$

In these formulae, BCAC is the original budgeted cost at completion.

Although both formulae calculate the ECAC, they will produce different results. The first considers only the cost performance, whereas the second considers both cost and time performance. According to Fleming and Koppelman[29], both formulae are widely used, although the first is considered to be the 'most likely' model and the second as the

Table 10.5 Calculating estimated cost at completion

BCWS	BCWP	ACWP	ECAC (1)	ECAC (2)	Schedule status	Cost status
$1,000	$1,000	$1,000	$10,000	$10,000	On time	On cost
$2,000	$2,000	$1,000	$5,000	$5,000	On time	Under cost
$1,000	$1,000	$2,000	$20,000	$20,000	On time	Over cost
$1,000	$2,000	$2,000	$10,000	$6,000	Ahead	On cost
$1,000	$2,000	$1,000	$5,000	$3,000	Ahead	Under cost
$1,000	$2,000	$3,000	$150,000	$9,000	Ahead	Over cost
$2,000	$1,000	$1,000	$10,000	$19,000	Behind	On cost
$3,000	$2,000	$1,000	$5,000	$7,000	Behind	Under cost
$2,000	$1,000	$3,000	$30,000	$57,000	Behind	Over cost

'worst case' model. It is a matter of choice as to which one is used, but whichever is chosen, it must be consistently applied throughout the duration of the project.

Assuming a BCAC of $10,000 and the data contained in the previous tables, Table 10.5 illustrates the calculations using the above formulae.

The estimated cost at completion (ECAC) less the current actual cost status of the project (ACWP) provides a revised estimated cost to complete (ECTC) the project, as follows.

Estimated cost to complete $ECTC = ECAC - ACWP$

Time at completion

There are two commonly used methods for forecasting the estimated time at completion (ETAC). The first method entails re-estimating the durations of the remaining work in the manner originally used to estimate the total project time and by recalculating the critical path (refer to Chapter 9).

The second method involves the use of the earned value chart discussed earlier. With reference to the earned value chart (Figure 10.1), an additional variance can be produced that gives an indication of how far behind or ahead the project is. This time variance is calculated as follows.

Time variance $TV = SD - T_{BCWS=BCWP}$

In this formula:

SD = Status date (time period now)
$T_{BCWS=BCWP}$ = Budgeted cost at scheduled performance. It is the time period where BCWS = BCWP (promise = achievement)

This variance (TV) added to the original budgeted time at completion (BTAC) gives a revised estimate of the time at completion (ETAC), as follows:

Estimated time at completion   ETAC = TV + BTAC

Calculating the ETAC for a project gives a 'snapshot' at a point in time, and it must be recognized that ETAC is based on several assumptions:

● that the current time status of a project will remain constant for the remainder of the project;
● that any delays will not be recovered;
● that work will unfold exactly as planned.

Figure 10.3 further illustrates the forecasting of the completion time using the above calculations.

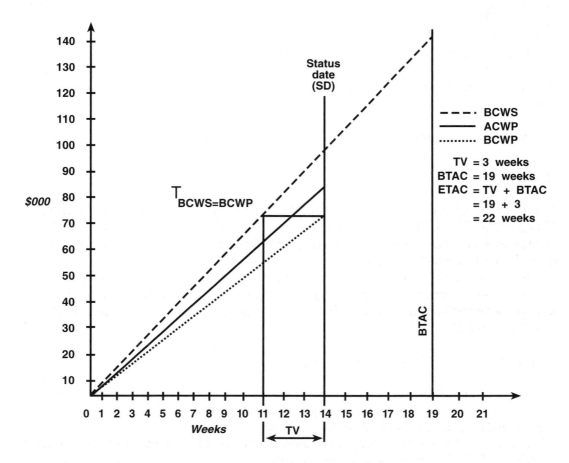

Figure 10.3   Estimating time at completion

Irrespective of which method is used, the revised completion date must be verified against an evaluation of the activities on the critical path.

Other performance measures

Many projects have one or more repetitive activities that are critical to the timely completion of the project, such as cubic metres of concrete placed or lines of computer programming code produced. A cumulative plot of actual production versus planned gives a quick but fairly reliable indication of whether or not the project will finish on time.

A healthy production rate in fact may have an overrun in the resource budget (human resource hours). This can be detected if production is divided by the human resource hours expended for each item of work, to determine current productivity. A forecast of productivity can then be made. When determining productivity the learning curve effect must be considered. This is best explained by the fact that at the start of a repetitive activity, the production rate tends to be low as the task is learnt, and increases as the activity is performed more often. Stopping such an activity and restarting it at a later stage will cause a drop in the production rate as the process is relearnt, but not to the extent of the initial learning level.

Other monitoring required

The above discussions have focused on the cost, time and work progress issues to be monitored and evaluated. Other aspects of the project also need to be monitored and evaluated, such as those listed below:

- **quality issues**: the number of non-conformance reports, the amount of rework etc;
- **project risks**: new risks, changed risk profiles, risks occurred etc (Appendix B discusses risk and describes the management of risk throughout the life of the project);
- **procurement**: orders outstanding, late deliveries, changed lead times, procurement issues etc;
- **project issues**: personnel, political, morale, infrastructure, organizational issues;
- **scope changes**: any changes to any aspect of the project scope.

Monitoring activities towards a milestone

Whichever method is used to manage the project's activities, progress towards the agreed milestones on the milestone objective chart must be reported on. Team members tasked with achieving the milestones must report on the progress towards achieving them. If use was made of the activity schedule introduced in the section 'An alternative approach to activity planning' in the previous chapter (p 206), then the same template could be used to report on activities. Refer to Appendix A for an example of a progressed activity schedule for a milestone.

The method of reporting outlined above consists of answering a few simple questions. Most can be answered yes or no; the remaining few by entering a number. Once work has started, the actual time used and time still to go columns should always be completed. The remaining columns only need to be used if there is a deviation from the plan. If there are deviations, a space to expand on them is provided. There are columns to report on whether a quality check has been passed, whether the responsibility matrix has been adhered to, and a column to indicate if a problem is being experienced and, if so, what type.

There is also space to indicate whether the deviations will affect the milestone plan, and to suggest text for the milestone report. The consequence for the milestone plan can again be indicated with 'yes' or 'no', but other words may be used. Even if there are deviations in an activity schedule, it may be that those deviations can be contained within that schedule, so the effect on the milestone plan will be indicated as 'no', or 'unlikely'. Even if there is no likely consequence for the milestone plan, it may still be worth suggesting a text for the milestone report. This could be to inform other project members not connected with this milestone about progress, in case it affects their work.

Finally, there is space for the manager to comment. He or she should comment, and return a copy to the person submitting the report, to reinforce the feedback loop and to show the person that the reports are valued.

PRODUCE PROGRESS STATUS AND PERFORMANCE REPORTS

If a project is to be successfully completed, all relevant project participants must be kept informed about the status of the project. If everyone is aware of the objectives and how well they are being achieved, they will also know what needs to be done and will be motivated to work towards remaining goals. There are no set standards for communicating project status – various schedules, graphs and reports can be used. Enough information must be reported to indicate status and allow decision making, without causing an 'information overload'.

The information in the reports is summarized from the various monitoring and controlling schedules and reports. The content of the report depends on its destination – upper management, client or project team. The communications plan developed from the stakeholder analysis during the definition and planning phases must be taken into consideration in this and the next step.

A typical project progress report could contain the following:

● project status overview;
● schedules such as cost reports, Gantt charts, activity schedules, performance reports (earned value calculations);

- progressed milestone objective chart;
- quality report;
- issue lists;
- performance, cash flow and production graphs;
- problems and possible solutions;
- risk evaluation;
- decisions required.

For business-focused projects a concise summary report containing the following may be sufficient:

- project status: determined by milestone delivery; time status now and at completion; cost variance now and at completion;
- project objectives; are they still achievable at time of report?
- stakeholder satisfaction at reporting time (primary stakeholders mainly considered);
- risks: an indication of the high-risk areas that require careful management;
- issues: critical issues that require management intervention; the number of open and closed issues, together with ageing information;
- resources: available resources compared with resources required to complete.

A one-A4-page report containing the above information is, in the experience of the authors, well received by most key stakeholders who do not have time to wade through reams of paper to ascertain project status. This type of report is easy to communicate electronically, and is more often than not actually read and responded to.

Milestone reporting

The milestone objective chart (MOC) developed during the project definition phase is the client/upper management view of the project. It is the project manager's responsibility to control progress in relation to the MOC. The project manager prepares the progressed MOC by referencing and collating information and data from other project monitoring reports and particularly activity progress information. The progressed MOC is then sent to the relevant parties (client/upper management).

Milestone status is reported directly onto the MOC. Appendix A contains an example of a progressed MOC.

Each line of the MOC has space for three entries. These are explained below:

- The date of the report: a report is being made against that milestone on this date. It will be the same date as the last activity progress report received.
- The report itself: comments on the status of the milestone are given here. This information is usually gathered from the activity schedules.
- The date completed: if the milestone has been reached, the date it was reached is entered here and 'completed' is entered in the report area.

The MOC is the tactical (or administrative) plan for the project and will have been developed to remain current throughout the duration of the project. Circumstances may arise, however, that require a change to the MOC by adding, changing or deleting milestones, or by changing the logical connection between them. The need to make such changes must be reported, and the changes controlled as part of any change control process.

Report distribution

The progress reports are circulated to all relevant parties. The various responsibility matrices developed during the project definition and planning phases as well as the communications plan must be taken into consideration. Meetings to discuss the report could be held – either formally or informally. Whether meetings are held or not, the report content must be acted on. Monitoring, evaluating and reporting without any action being taken invalidates the whole monitoring purpose and process. Effective reporting is ineffective control if it is not followed up by corrective action.

APPLY CONTROL, FEEDBACK AND PROBLEM-SOLVING

Control is management, not paperwork. Control is about:

● analysing the situation reflected in the reports;
● deciding what course of action is necessary to recover the plan;
● proceeding with the recovery actions.

Day-to-day problems are addressed as they arise. Problems arising that can be dealt with rapidly should not wait to be reported on first at a regular meeting. Others that cannot be resolved are escalated via the issues management system. Managers at all levels, but particularly the project manager, must be resolute in taking action. They must act for the sake of the project, even when that means making tough decisions. They must also be seen to be taking action by the project team, to reinforce the need for control and to motivate the team.

The project manager must hold formal and regular review meetings individually with the project team, management and the client, to discuss the status of the project, resolve problems and decide on action. These meetings can be co-located or virtual via videoconferencing. Although all address similar aspects, the level of detail will vary depending on the meeting participants. These meetings normally occur in the following sequence.

The project team meets first, as regularly as required but at least weekly. Prior to the meeting the project manager receives reports from task group leaders. Either the project manager personally or support staff collate the information, and prepare the progress report for discussion. Following the discussion a summary report for management and/or the client is created along the lines discussed in the previous section of this chapter. This summary is discussed at a client/management meeting.

Having reviewed and analysed the reports, the relevant project participants must take corrective action to overcome any problems identified. The course of action obviously depends on the problem, but will generally be one of the following:

● rearranging the workload;
● putting in more resource or effort;
● moving milestone dates;
● lowering the level of quality/expectation.

These options are presented in order of decreasing acceptability. The top one should be tried first, the bottom one last.

The analysis of the reports should reveal which course of action is appropriate. Only the first two are truly available to the group controlling the activity level. If either of the last two is more appropriate, that information must be given to the project manager controlling the milestone level for a decision to be made in consultation with the client/management and other interested stakeholders.

The option of rescheduling the current and subsequent milestones may be acceptable if the date of the current milestone does not affect the duration of the project. Delaying a project is usually not readily accepted by the team. In many projects, however, the goals of cost and quality are more important than time. By considering only time, the project manager may be tempted to increase resources simply to finish the project on time. This must be guarded against, as increasing resources could remedy the time delay but could also dramatically increase the costs and make quality management less effective.

Where the goals of quality are the most important, the least acceptable option is to reduce the scope (expectations) of the project. The specification will usually have been drawn up to reflect the optimum project. However, if during project execution it becomes obvious that the required performance cannot be achieved, except at excessive cost, the level of quality or expectations may have to be lowered.

The above discussion assumes that the project objectives are still intact. As the project positions the organization to achieve its business outcomes, there may be instances where the objectives have changed for a variety of reasons and that the time, cost and quality dimensions may have to change to achieve the revised objectives.

It is important to note that two unacceptable attitudes must be avoided: 1) waiting to see if there really is a problem; 2) hoping the problem will sort itself out.

The project manager and team must be willing to acknowledge problems, and to take necessary measures to overcome them.

REVISE THE PROJECT PLAN BASELINE

During the project execution phase many changes will be made to project plans, budgets and specifications. These changes can arise from changes in the method of work, client changes, corrective action, external factors and so on. All changes to the project need to be evaluated in terms of the baseline, and the baseline amended to reflect the change. Failure to do so will result in a distorted baseline against which to measure the performance of the project.

Change control

Changes have an adverse effect on project performance and should be kept to a minimum. Changes to scope are a common source of conflict between project participants. To reduce the negative impact of changes and to make them more manageable, a formal method for change review and control must be introduced. This is often referred to as the change control process. According to Harrison[38], such a process should:

- continually identify changes as they occur;
- reveal their consequences in terms of impact on project costs, project duration and other tasks;
- permit managerial analysis, investigation of alternative courses of action, and acceptance or rejection;
- communicate changes to all parties concerned;
- specify a policy for minimizing conflicts and resolving disputes;
- ensure that changes are implemented;
- report a monthly summary of all changes to date and their impact on the project.

PROCEEDING TO THE NEXT PHASE

The project execution phase consists of an iterative process, steadily moving the project towards completion. At some point, however, progress begins to slow and it seems that the project will never end. The project team begins to shrink and the motivation of the remaining members appears to have dissipated. When this starts to happen, it can be assumed that the project is entering its final phase: the project close-out phase.

In practice...

The predetermined progress report

Peter Stonewall was the project director of a large internal redevelopment project, as well as the technical director of the company that owned the project. The project manager and project administrator reporting to him also reported to him in the course of the company's normal operational work. This was to be Stonewall's first project but, as he himself put it, he was strong in the technical field and had always performed as a manager by meeting his targets, so why should managing a project be different?

Stonewall was an extreme autocrat who ruled his division and the project with an iron fist. His approach to people motivation was to threaten his staff with dismissal if things were not done his way or to his satisfaction. Needless to say, his staff lived in absolute terror of him.

Stonewall would rarely visit the project site as he strongly believed in a method of progress reporting that involved volumes of paper, most of which would be supporting schedules proving the progress numbers given in the summary sheets. Stonewall had got away with his management style and reporting requirements for many years, and believed that nothing should change because of the project.

A progress meeting would be held every Friday morning at which the project manager and project administrator would be grilled for hours on the veracity of the reported progress and, needless to say, admonished and threatened if things were not to Stonewall's liking.

Mrs Robinson, Stonewall's long-suffering personal assistant, was the informal communication conduit between Stonewall and the rest of the staff. She would issue a daily 'grapevine bulletin' on Stonewall's mood, needs, wants and expectations. The staff would then react to this by ensuring that the unofficial expectation list would be satisfied should Stonewall call for something.

With the advent of the project, a further titbit of information was added to the 'bulletin': the expected project progress. After most Friday sessions, Stonewall would comment to Mrs Robinson about how dissatisfied he was with the progress. He would make comments such as 'If the project is not 45 per cent complete by next Friday, they might be out of a job!' or 'The project had better not be over its cost budget – or else!'.

This valuable information would be communicated on the next Monday morning, and for the remainder of the week the project manager and the project administrator would work feverishly to massage the numbers and tweak the reports, so that Stonewall's desired progress would be reported on the Friday. As there were copious reports and computer systems, this took up a lot of the project manager's and administrator's time – which meant that the real project work was neglected. Come the Friday meeting, Stonewall would be presented with a set of progress reports that reflected his expectations precisely and, since he did not visit the site, he accepted them as an accurate reflection of the status. Stonewall in turn dutifully reported this progress upwards, earning him praise for being on target.

The project manager honestly believed that he could catch up by accelerating so that the project would be on target as it entered its second half. To his credit, this was beginning to happen, and it looked like he would be able to pull it off. He actually kept a second set of numbers to reflect the reality of the situation, which he used to manage the project. Unfortunately though, the project manager ran out of time.

Disaster struck when Stonewall decided to appoint a quantity surveyor to audit the work completed. The quantity surveyor's report indicated that the actual progress was at 35 per cent complete rather than the reported 55 per cent, and that the project was actually overspent in terms of the 35 per cent progress by some 25 per cent.

Stonewall fired both the project manager and the project administrator, and appointed replacements. The damage, however, was already done, and Stonewall himself was asked to take early retirement two months later.

Important lessons...

1. Honesty is the best policy! Always be honest in reporting progress – the truth has a habit of catching up.
2. A project cannot be managed in the same way as a production facility. Projects are unique and one-time and offer little opportunity to do it right next week (or in the second half of the project). With production, on the other hand, staff can keep at it until the required level is reached.
3. All project participants must 'walk' the project rather than 'read and talk' the project! Peter Stonewall succumbed to the computer paralysis or project management information system verification syndrome. Excessive involvement with computers, reports and schedules rather than the realities of the project leads to losing touch with the project and the masking of the real issues by numbers, facts and figures.
4. The unofficial office grapevine can be a dangerous method of communication on a project. It is far better to be up-front with issues and risk confrontation than rely on hearsay and rumour.
5. Project management by progress statistics is misleading. Managing by results achieved is tangible and realistic.

In practice...

The PMIS conflict

It was late Friday afternoon. Jeannette sat quietly preparing her project progress report, which she had to present to upper management on the coming Wednesday. It had been a difficult week and she was looking forward to a relaxing weekend with her family.

Jeannette had been a project manager for the past 10 years and had successfully managed many projects, both large and small. She had the advantage of working with a good team that had also been with her on a number of other projects.

On completing her report using costings, progress reports and other information prepared by her team, Jeannette leant back, once again thankful that they had designed a project management information system (PMIS) that had stood the test of time and provided her with all she needed. Although it consisted of a number of self-developed spreadsheets, it was sufficiently accurate, consistent and easily understood by all levels. In fact, all the project managers in the company had adopted, and in some cases adapted, the system for their own projects. After placing the report and supporting information on her secretary's desk with instructions to distribute it on Monday, she switched off the lights and walked to her car.

As she drove out of the car park, she saw Jack, the new director of projects, getting into his car. Jeannette cast her thoughts to next Wednesday's project meeting, which would be the first involving Jack since he had joined the company. Jack had spent the past five years as a project manager with a large consulting firm. He was widely regarded as an aggressive, 'high-tech' manager who had reportedly been brought in to blow some new life into the company and to overhaul the existing management information systems.

Jeannette knew it was necessary as some of the company's projects had recently faltered. Again, Jeannette was grateful that her trusted PMIS was functional and had successfully carried this project almost two-thirds of the way. She was actually looking forward to Wednesday's meeting.

Wednesday arrived and the project meeting was over. Jeannette sat fuming at her desk. She had been hauled over the coals for producing inadequate reporting and schedules that, according to Jack, incorrectly reflected the status of the project. She had also been accused of using outdated methods, not using the latest technology, and not performing a critical path analysis on her project. According to Jack, the fact that the project was on time and within budget was 'just lucky' or Jeannette was probably massaging the reports to look good. He had told her that from now on she was to use an earned-value approach to reporting progress. Jack had ended the meeting by informing Jeannette that her project was to be audited – by Richard, Jack's assistant, who had also joined from Jack's previous company.

The audit was duly done and, as predicted, reported exactly what Jack wanted to hear. Within weeks, a sophisticated, fully integrated computerized PMIS was installed on Jeannette's project and Jeannette's elementary system was totally discarded. Jeannette's secretary was trained to input data and produce reports 'at the touch of a button'.

All the cost codes had been changed to reflect what Jack wished to see. Their structure was a complete mystery to Jeannette, as were many other aspects of the system. Jeannette felt lost and, for the first time as a project manager, felt out of touch with her project. Her protests were ignored, and she was forced to accept the system.

Within two months, Jeannette's project began to slip. Jack repeatedly told her that the new system had proved that she had been incorrectly reporting the project status in the past and was now forced to 'tell the truth'. Jeannette's argument was that trying to understand the new system and cope with it was taking up too much of her time, preventing her from effectively managing the project. Jack's answer was that Jeannette should become more computer-literate as soon as possible.

Three months later, the project was totally out of control and Richard replaced Jeannette as the project manager. Jeannette decided to leave the project management field, resigned, and returned to working as a consulting engineer.

Despite Richard's claims that he would quickly turn the project around, the project ended over-time and over-budget. He blamed this on Jeannette's old systems and the fact that the management team he had 'inherited' refused to accept the output produced by the new PMIS and continued to use their old system. Richard could not understand this, as the new system had been in use at his previous company for three years and had proved highly effective and widely used.

Despite numerous training sessions, the new system proved to be only mildly successful on other projects and particularly on those where the systems in place had previously been weak. After two years of disillusionment, Jack and Richard resigned and returned to their previous company where they again enjoyed respect and success.

Within months, the new PMIS system was abandoned as being too complicated, and Jeannette was invited to consult in the creation of a 'standard' PMIS for the company along the lines of her old system.

Important lessons...

1. Because a PMIS works well for one organization it will not automatically suit another. Jack's previous company could have been operating in a totally different environment or industry. The fact that Jeannette was asked to develop a system along the lines of her old one is an indication that the organization was comfortable with what they previously had.
2. Project management is about managing projects and not about sophisticated systems. Project managers do not require sophisticated state-of-the-art systems to be successful. They need systems that provide them with adequate management information to do the job at hand.
3. The best PMISs are those that project managers trust and feel comfortable about using. PMISs are not about producing volumes of complex reports for everyone else's use but rather about producing adequate information to enable the project manager and major stakeholders to manage their relevant areas of the project.
4. Change for change's sake causes confusion and disruption. If the PMIS system had to be changed, then the change transition should have been well planned and executed. Abrupt change places any project at risk. Jeannette's system was abruptly changed, and then she was abruptly replaced by Richard.
5. Beware of forcing a particular analysis method as a standard to be applied on all projects as part of a methodology or system. Some projects may not require a critical path analysis to be done or may require a different time planning technique to be applied.

11

The project close-out phase

Dream creative dreams.
Set high and worthwhile goals.
Take the first decisive step toward your goal.
And then what?
Then take another step, and another, and another until the goal is reached, the ambition realized, the mission accomplished. No matter what it takes, *persist*. No matter how discouraged you might get, *persevere*. No matter how much you want to quit, *hang in there*.

> Norman Vincent Peale, US theologian and author,
> *The Plus Factor* (1987)

INTRODUCTION

In Chapter 1, a project was defined as a temporary endeavour undertaken to create a unique product, service or outcome. Being temporary, a project by definition has a limited life – which means that it must end at some point. The fact that a project produces some product, service or outcome means that there is some event that makes the project end recognizable. A project must be formally terminated. If not, it will limp on, turning an otherwise successful project into a financial failure. Formal project closure is performed during the project close-out phase.

After the excitement of new discovery at the start of the project, followed by the challenge of planning and the hectic pace of execution, approaching the end is almost anticlimactic. Yet, of all the project phases, the close-out phase is the most crucial in the life of a project. Nicholas[67] says this about project closure: 'The process of terminating a project is so critical that it can determine whether, ultimately, the project is a success or failure.'

This all-important phase, which should ensure effective and timely completion of the project, is often poorly managed as described below in 'Project close-out issues'. The way this phase is managed can affect how a project is remembered – as Turner[89] realistically states: 'No one remembers an effective start-up, but everyone remembers an ineffective close-out; the consequences are felt for a long time.'

The manner in which the closure of the project is planned, monitored and controlled will determine how the project will reach conclusion. Meredith and Mantel[60] describe the closure of a project philosophically, as follows:

> As it must to all things, termination comes to every project. At times, project death is quick and clean, but more often it is a long process; and there are times when it is practically impossible to establish that death has occurred. The skill with which termination, or a condition we might call 'near termination', is managed has a great deal to do with the quality of life after the project.

Nicholas[67] makes similar observations: 'Termination occurs in a variety of ways; the best way is by a planned, systematic procedure; the worst is by an abrupt cancellation of work, slow attrition of effort, or higher priority projects siphoning off resources. In the latter cases the project goes sour; it is either terminated before goals are reached, or allowed to "limp along" and just fizzle out before completion.'

The way a project closes out is also influenced by the reason for its termination. According to Nicholas[67] some reasons for termination are as follows:

- Project objectives have been achieved.
- It is no longer feasible to achieve the project objectives (changing market conditions, skyrocketing costs, depleted critical resources, lost opportunities, changes in need, no longer feasible, change in priorities).
- Simply by default, perhaps due to unsatisfactory project performance, poor quality or workmanship, violation of contract, poor planning and control, bad management, or customer dissatisfaction with the contractor.

Irrespective of the reason for, and manner of, the closure, the project manager is responsible for the closure of the project and must carry out this task diligently.

PROJECT CLOSE-OUT ISSUES

There can be no progress if people have no faith in tomorrow.
John F Kennedy, 35th President of the United States of America

The project close-out phase is a stressful time for all involved for the following reasons:

- The client is taking ownership of the major project deliverables, and is being called on to take final decisions of quality and acceptance.
- Resources are being diverted from the project to new projects just starting.
- There is a shift in client/management attention to new projects, with a resultant lack of interest in the project nearing completion.
- The project team is being reassigned to other projects.
- Closing tasks are not always clear cut.
- The team may lack the motivation to complete the work.

Of these, the last is of most concern, as without the support of a motivated team, the project manager will have difficulty managing the project to a successful completion. A lack of motivation can be caused by a number of factors, such as the following:

- The project team is experiencing a sense of loss, as they realize that the project is coming to an end, and with it the end of the team and the relationships built.
- Most major achievements and breakthroughs have been achieved by this stage, and there is little left to challenge the team.
- Team members are concerned about what their next assignments will be, or even if there will be a next assignment.

This problem of morale occurs at the worst possible time – when the project is almost over and the project manager's emphasis is on completing the work. Also during this phase, the client's interest is peaking as the project's products or services are transferred to them. Acceptance and validation performance testing, knowledge transfer to operations, manuals and final documentation, contractual sign-off and final accounting are all-important areas that the project manager must deal with. To this list of administrative, technical and contractual closure tasks, the project manager must also add 'emotional' closure.

With the project rapidly running out of time and resources, the project manager has to be more vigilant. Tighter control is needed, with more frequent progress meetings, which can lead to increased pressure on the project team and management.

THE PROJECT CLOSE-OUT PROCESS

Once the decision is made to terminate the project, the closure must be planned and scheduled, monitored and controlled – as if it is a project in its own right. This administrative closure work is carried out in addition to the activities already planned to complete the production of project deliverables. Both these plans need to be monitored and controlled to ensure timely and effective completion of the project – using the processes explained in Chapter 10.

Certain primary steps or duties that form the basis for the close-out plan must be performed during close-out, and these form a process starting with planning the completion, through to terminating and archiving the project. Later sections of this chapter, from 'Verification of the deliverables' to 'Terminate and archive the project' discuss these steps in detail.

To allow the project manager to focus on the client's needs and on the outstanding deliverables, a specialist in close-out is often appointed to oversee the close-out reporting to the project manager.

PLAN THE COMPLETION OF THE WORK

> After climbing a great hill, one only finds that there are many more hills to climb … I dare not linger, for my long walk is not yet ended.
> Nelson Mandela, South African leader, President of the Republic of South Africa 1994–99, *The Long Walk to Freedom* (1994)

All technical and administrative work to complete the project must be planned in detail. Implementing the closure of a project is a complex operation with a myriad of small tasks to be done.

Standard checklists can assist in the development of the close-out plan. One possible checklist is shown below. This is derived from a comprehensive checklist provided by Meredith and Mantel[60]:

A. Project office and project team organization
   ● Conduct project close-out meeting.
   ● Carry out necessary personnel actions.
   ● Personnel performance evaluations.
   ● Reassign/release staff.
B. Instructions and procedures
   ● Terminate project office.
   ● Terminate reporting procedures.
   ● Complete and store project files.
C. Financial
   ● Finalize financial documents and records.
   ● Audit final charges and costs.
   ● Prepare final project financial reports.
   ● Collect outstanding claims and revenue.
D. Project definition
   ● Document final 'as built' project scope.
   ● Prepare final project WBS and file.
E. Plans, budgets and schedules
   ● Document actual delivery dates of all contractual deliverables.
   ● Document actual completion dates of all other contractual obligations.
   ● Prepare final project and task status reports.

F. Work authorization and control
- Close out all work orders and contracts.

G. Project evaluation and control
- Ensure completion of all work.
- Prepare final evaluation reports.
- Conduct final review meeting.
- Terminate financial, personnel and progress reporting procedures.

H. Management and client reporting
- Submit final report to client.
- Submit final report to management.

I. Marketing and contract administration
- Compile all final contract documents with revision, waivers and related documents.
- Verify and document compliance with contractual terms.
- Compile client acceptance documents.
- Officially notify client of project completion.
- Initiate and pursue any claims against client.
- Prepare and conduct defence against claims by client.
- Initiate publicity about project completion.
- Prepare final project status report.

J. Extension – new business
- Document possibilities for project extension or other related new business.
- Obtain commitment for extension.

K. Project records control
- Complete project files.
- Dispose of other project records as required.

L. Purchasing and subcontracting
- Document compliance and completion for each contract, subcontract and purchase order.
- Verify final payments for each contract, subcontract and purchase order.
- Notify all vendors/contractors of final project completion.

M. Technical documentation
- Compile and store all technical documentation.
- Prepare final technical report.

N. Acceptance and handover
- Final delivery instructions.
- Final client acceptance and handover.
- Ownership transition plan.

O. Site operations
- Close down site operations.
- Dispose of equipment and material.
- Release accommodation.

Another aid to developing a close-out plan can be to consider the close-out using the project objectives of scope, time, cost, quality, risk, procurement, human resources, communication and integration (as defined and discussed in Chapter 2). The question asked about each area is, 'What needs to be done to ensure that this objective is met?'

Once all the close-out activities have been identified, an integrated project close-out plan must be developed. The planning processes and techniques introduced in Chapter 9 can be used to develop the close-out plan.

VERIFICATION OF THE DELIVERABLES

The client's final approval of all the project's deliverables signals the project's completion. It is essential therefore to ensure that all deliverables have been formally accepted and signed off by the client.

This has probably been taking place throughout the project execution phase and will continue throughout the close-out phase. The project manager must ensure that there is a signed acceptance certificate for each contractually agreed deliverable. It is imperative that the acceptance be in writing and signed by an authorized person. Verbal acceptance, or tacit acceptance, documented in progress reports and minutes is best avoided.

Acceptance certificates form an essential part of the project's contractual and legal documentation, and must be accorded the same status. Acceptance certificates must be signed and obtained, even for internal projects.

REVIEW PERFORMANCE CRITERIA

Project closure is when the project team's success is measured. One of the measures of project success is whether the project has achieved what it set out to do – in other words, did the project deliver the benefits it should have? A further measure is whether the project's performance criteria (cost, time, scope, quality, etc) were met.

The project's objectives, benefits and performance criteria are contained in the initial business case and project proposal, and in the project definition report (PDR) produced in the project definition phase. It is important to differentiate between the benefits of the project's outputs and the project's performance criteria. The fundamental difference is that the project manager is only accountable for the completion (performance) of the project and not for what happens after the project is completed (project benefits). It is for this reason that the following caveat was given in Chapter 8, in the section 'Determine the objectives and performance measures': 'It is important to note that the objectives and performance measures are related specifically to the project deliverables. They do not measure the success of business outcomes that will be derived from the products and services produced by the project.' The criteria against which the project team's success will be measured are those contained in the PDR.

Should the project manager or the project sponsor (champion) be responsible for the success or failure of the project to deliver the benefits? According to Turner[89], 'Whether this final step is the responsibility of the project manager or project champion will depend on the circumstances, but it should be agreed as part of the project strategy at the start. It will probably be the champion who will be held accountable if the owner does not receive adequate return on the investment, and so the onus rests on the champion to ensure that it happens.' The authors agree with this view.

The project's actual performance is evaluated against agreed performance criteria and the final project performance evaluation report is produced. This will be used during the post implementation review (see p 244).

RELEASE RESOURCES

All resources, equipment, materials, and particularly personnel must be released from the project. In addition, all resource managers must be informed that they are relieved of their commitments to the project.

Equipment and materials can simply be returned to stores or suppliers, but people require special attention. Equipment and materials cannot have any further influence on current or future projects. People, however, can have a profound influence on the success of future projects. Turner[89] puts it succinctly as follows: 'Project team members may have made significant contributions, or even sacrifices, to the success of the project. If it is not recognized, the project will at best end on an anti-climax, at worst it will leave lasting resentment that will roll over into the next project.' If the releasing of people is not handled with tact and fairness, a feeling of resentment will form.

People need to be reassigned when released, and if this can be organized at an early stage, it will go a long way to removing some of the uncertainty and lack of motivation discussed earlier in this chapter. People may be returned to their functional areas or assigned new projects, or both, or may have to be let go. What happens to released personnel can be summed up as one of the following (after Baker and Baker[8]):

- **Inclusion** – team members are absorbed as part of the project's outcomes into the client organization.
- **Integration** – team members are reintegrated into the organizations and departments from which they were 'borrowed'.
- **Extinction** – once the project is closed down, the team members' jobs simply end.

The project manager is responsible for releasing the resources off the project, and is therefore morally obligated to ensure that personnel are released in a fair and proper manner.

CONTRACTUAL ASPECTS AND FINAL ACCOUNTING

The project manager must ensure that all the contractual aspects are settled and that the final project accounting is done. All contractual commitments to clients, vendors and suppliers must be scrutinized and finalized. This may require reports to be exchanged and final payments to be made and received.

The final accounting of the project must be completed. This will include totalling the costs and revenues, producing the final cost evaluations and reports, paying all accounts, and closing the project's books. Once this is done, no further costs can be incurred against the project, and this is why the closing of the books is done after the resources have been released and contractual commitments settled.

The contractual documentation and final cost and accounting reports are used during the post implementation review (covered later in this chapter).

COMPLETE THE DOCUMENTATION

Projects generate substantial volumes of documentation and it is essential that these are collated and filed for future reference. Certain documents, such as the final cost reports, contracts and claims documents, only become available during the close-out and this step in the process ensures that these documents are completed and collated.

The project documentation is necessary, as it serves as a basis for settling any future questions or disputes that may arise from the project. It can also serve as a training guide for other project managers and is a source of information for future projects of a similar nature.

The project documentation could include (but is not limited to) the following:

- originating documentation (business case, project proposal);
- definition and planning schedules and documents (PDR, integrated project plan baseline);
- performance and status documents (cost reports, performance evaluation reports, audits, minutes of meetings);
- contractual documents;
- general correspondence (memos, letters, electronic communications, faxes);
- accounting and cost information;
- change control documents (variation orders, change control registers);
- technical documentation (specifications, drawings);
- procurement documents (purchase orders, quotations, brochures).

Where relevant, both the original plans and documents as well as the final 'as built' plans must be kept. The documentation can be stored on various media (video, photographic, electronic, paper).

The authors have been called on to be expert witnesses in disputes arising from projects completed in the engineering and construction industries, and invariably the party with the most complete documentation was the winner. The golden rule is that it should be possible to 'reconstruct' the progress and events of the project from the available documentation.

CONDUCT A POST IMPLEMENTATION REVIEW

Those who cannot remember the past are condemned to repeat it.
George Santayana, Spanish-born US philosopher, poet and humorist

Good project management requires that some form of post implementation review or audit be performed to establish what went well, what did not, and what lessons can be learnt from the project experience. In addition, the review (often called a 'post-mortem') can determine whether the proposed benefits of the project were indeed realized (refer to the discussion in the section 'Review performance criteria' on p 241). A further benefit of conducting a review is that the results can be used to help the performing organization develop better project management practices. The post implementation review (PIR) is a unique opportunity to learn from experience; therefore it is vital that senior management read the resulting report.

Post implementation reviews can be conducted as a formal audit or as a workshop involving the project participants. Whichever method is used, a written report must be produced. This report could form the basis or part of the project final report (see the section 'Write the project final report' on p 245).

Whoever conducts the review needs to understand what influences success or failure of projects (this is discussed fully in Appendix C). This understanding will ensure they ask the right questions and analyse the right aspects of the project. It is important to remember that, although the PIR is a candid look at the project, the aim is not to find fault or apportion blame. Finger pointing and reprimanding serve no purpose – rather they encourage the cover-up of mistakes, which defeats the purpose of the PIR.

The following topics (not an exhaustive list) are offered as suggestions of what could be reviewed. The suggested contents for the project final report can also be used as a guide. Generally, the following aspects of each topic should be considered: what went right, what went wrong, what could have been done better, and what lessons can be learnt:

- acceptance and handover;
- administration procedures;
- change control;
- claims (payment) management;
- communications;
- decision making;
- documentation quality and standards;
- financial and costing management;
- human resources;

- management and client reporting;
- plans, budgets and schedules;
- pre-project issues (feasibility studies, business case/proposal);
- procurement management (suppliers, vendors, subcontractors);
- project definition and planning;
- project evaluation and control;
- project management processes;
- project performance;
- project records control;
- public relations;
- quality management;
- reporting procedures;
- risk management.

WRITE THE PROJECT FINAL REPORT

There is one last administrative task the project manager must perform before terminating the project – to write the project final report summarizing the history of the project and evaluation of the performance. This is one task that cannot be delegated. It is the project manager and the project manager alone who must write this final report.

Most of the information about the project is already contained in the project documentation (covered earlier in this chapter), or has resulted from earlier steps in the close-out process. Most of the remaining content of the report will be reflective, giving the project manager's honest and candid view of the completed project. It should be written as soon as possible after the project has been completed.

Meredith and Mantel[60] provide us with a description of the intent of the project final report:

> Good project management systems have a memory. The embodiment of this memory is the Project Final Report. The final report is not another evaluation; rather it is the history of the project. It is a chronicle of the life and times of the project, a compendium of what went right and what went wrong, of who served the project in what capacity, of what was done to create the substance of the project, of how it was managed.

The format of the report is not important but the content is. The following is a summary of suggested contents, derived from Nicholas[67]:

1. Review:
    - the initial project objectives in terms of technical performance, time and cost;
    - the soundness of the initial objectives in hindsight;
    - the evolution of the objectives up to the final objectives, and how well the project team performed against them;
    - the reasons for changes to the objectives, noting which were avoidable and which were not;

- the activities and relationships of the project team throughout the project life cycle;
- the interfaces, performance and effectiveness of project management;
- the relationships among top management, the project team, the functional organization and the client;
- the cause and the process of termination;
- customer reactions and satisfaction;
- expenditures, sources of costs and profitability.
2. Identify:
   - areas where performance was good and note the reasons, organizational benefits, project extensions and marketable innovations;
   - problems, mistakes, oversights and areas of poor performance, and determine the causes.
3. Comment on:
   - recommendations for changes to existing policies and procedures;
   - the need for new policies and procedures to incorporate the lessons learnt.

The project final report should be made available to senior management and aspiring project managers, to give them the opportunity to apply the experience to future projects.

TERMINATE AND ARCHIVE THE PROJECT

The project is declared ended and all the documentation is archived. Advice of the termination must be communicated to all who were involved in the project. The project is now officially closed.

Any further work requested to be done on the project must be rejected and the project manager must resist the temptation to do 'just this last small thing'. The objectives of the project have been met, the scope has been delivered, the project terminated. Any further requests must become part of a new project or directed to those responsible for integrating the project's deliverables into the owner's operations.

The completed project has no funds, no purpose and no resources – all that is now out the door. The project manager is the last out through the door, and the last one out switches off the lights...

> For when the One Great Scorer comes to write against your name,
> He marks – not that you won or lost – but how you played the game.
>
> Grantland Rice (1880–1954), US sportsman and author

In practice...

The unhappy client of a 'successful' project

National Paper Industries (NPI) was one of the largest paper manufacturers in the country. Buoyant market conditions, together with the prospect of continued growth, led to the decision to create a new 250,000-square-metre, high-bay warehouse facility. A high-bay facility is a series of high shelves on which items are stacked using forklift trucks. This facility would be using electronically guided forklifts capable of lifting up to a maximum of 15 metres high.

It's Friday evening and Stuart, the NPI project manager, is sitting in his new office overlooking the now completed facility. He feels both relieved and disappointed but, for some reason, not proud of what has been achieved. How was it possible, he thought to himself, that in spite of appointing experienced architects and engineers, a competent main contractor and capable subcontractors, the final result was less than satisfactory?

The problem had occurred late in the project. He recalled how well the project had been progressing. Deliveries of important milestones were on time, costs were slightly over budget and generally quality was acceptable – but then it had all suddenly changed.

A critical part of the construction was the concrete floor of the warehouse. It was constructed to the engineer's specification of 6 mm variance over a 3-metre straightedge. This meant that there could not be more than 6 mm of variance off straight and level over a 3-metre surface. This variance was an industry-accepted standard for concrete floors, and had been specified in the engineering documents and drawings. Since NPI had wanted to negotiate and appoint the forklift subcontractor themselves, neither the engineer nor the architect were at an early stage aware of any specific floor tolerances required by the forklifts.

Stuart pondered on why NPI had taken over the responsibility of purchasing the forklifts from the main contractor. He had thought it was strange at the time, but the purchasing manager had insisted on dealing with the supplier as it was in 'his area of the business'. When Stuart had queried the situation with the CEO of NPI, he had been told that NPI wished to do the purchasing, as they had more leverage than the main contractor and could therefore negotiate a better price. The difficult and uncompromising attitude of the purchasing manager was well known at NPI, and being a personal friend of the CEO gave him a certain amount of influence. Since the purchasing manager had handled the entire transaction, Stuart was unaware of any special requirements. The purchasing manager, not being a technical person, had not addressed any special requirements. His main concerns were how much it would cost and how long it would take to deliver. The result was that by the time the forklift supplier was appointed, the floor construction had been complete for some time.

Stuart clearly remembered the first meeting held on-site between the forklift supplier, NPI, architect, engineer, and the main contractor. During that meeting, the forklift supplier had requested a guarantee that the floor variance was 3 mm over 3 metres, as that was the maximum the forklifts could tolerate. A greater variance would cause the forklifts to sway when fully extended. This could cause them to crash into the top racking at maximum extension, causing damage and placing lives at risk.

Everyone looked at each other, at first confused, and then with anger, fear and horror as they all realized that 250,000 square metres of floor had been constructed to the incorrect variance.

NPI blamed the engineer, who ought to have known that normal high-bay floor variances were different to those for forklifts. The engineer was angry with NPI for excluding him from negotiations with the supplier until the last minute when it was all too late. The main contractor pointed out that it was not their fault, as they had built the floor to specification. The architect shuffled around looking uncomfortable and Stuart remembered that, at the time, the architect was often seen with the purchasing manager. Was it possible that he had not conveyed the requirement to the engineers? The forklift supplier pointed out that the variances had been included in their proposals, which had been given to both the purchasing manager and the architect. The forklift supplier was disgruntled, as she would have to delay installing the electronic guide floor strips until remedial work was complete on the floor.

Three months and $2,500,000 later, the floor had been rectified with a self-levelling epoxy resin. This carried a 5-year guarantee as opposed to the 20-year guarantee for a hardened polished concrete floor as had been originally specified.

All parties believed another was to blame, and each (except NPI) believed the project had been delivered on time, at the original cost (excluding the floor repair), and to an acceptable quality standard. Stuart felt that the post implementation review due next month would highlight some interesting issues.

Stuart watched the forklifts operating quietly and efficiently. The roof lighting reflected off the wheel marks left by the forklifts as they shifted their heavy loads. He thought to himself that the floor would need repairs a lot sooner than the guaranteed period of five years.

He finally concluded that taking over the main contractor's purchasing responsibility in order to save money could lead to an expensive experience in quality and performance. He also vaguely remembered a saying he had heard a long time ago: 'The pleasure of a cheap price is often replaced by the pain of poor-quality product.' The project was successful – but he was not happy.

Important lessons...

1. Communication between all parties on a project is vital and is the project manager's responsibility. Stuart should have had responsibility for communications between the purchasing department, forklift supplier, engineer and architect, but that had been taken out of his hands by the CEO.
2. Beware of functional departments protecting their 'turf' by usurping the authority of the project manager. This almost always leads to a communication breakdown somewhere on the project, which can in turn cause a number of other problems.
3. The project manager should delegate tasks and authority to the purchasing manager, so that information flowing back can be disseminated to other parties.
4. The results of the project live on after the project has been completed. In this case, the project was a 'success', but the long-term effects would be less than successful.

Appendix A – The conference project

Conference and exhibition to be held by the Institute of Technology Management

BACKGROUND

The Institute of Technology Management (ITM) is a non-profit organization in the business of furthering the aims and objectives of technology management and increasing the professionalism of technology managers through ongoing education and training. It is affiliated to the International Institute of Technology Management (IITM). The Institute is managed by an Executive Council consisting of eight elected voluntary members and a full-time Executive Director. The Institute maintains contact with its members through regular meetings, newsletters and the publication of a bimonthly journal. Financing is obtained through membership subscriptions and payments for training.

In the first three years of its five-year existence, membership of the Institute grew rapidly to 325 members. Over the past two years, however, the Institute has attracted only 10 new members. Of more concern to the Executive Council is the loss of 17 members in the past year. In the light of the above, a survey was conducted amongst existing members and through other professional bodies and institutes. This survey revealed: 1) a general lack of awareness of the ITM in industry; 2) that members of the ITM felt the lack of an annual conference lessened the visibility of the Institute, and lowered the value of membership.

With the growing need for technology management in business and government, and from the survey data, it was apparent to the Council that the opportunity existed to increase membership by 10–15 per cent each year. It was obvious, therefore, that action was needed to raise awareness of the ITM as a professional body and publicize the benefits of membership. The Council now faced the challenge of developing a short-term focus on survival and growth while simultaneously ensuring that medium- to long-term goals were achieved.

The Council decided to review the Institute's business strategies. They began by engaging a consultant who was experienced in helping organizations move from strategies to programmes to business outcomes. The consultant facilitated an executive one-day workshop, where the Institute's overall strategies (the Strategic Wrapper) were elaborated into business objectives (the Business Wrapper). This is shown in Table A.1.

Following the workshop the Executive Director reviewed the list of programmes and projects identified, and reflected on whether they were in danger of launching too many or the incorrect projects up-front. Facing the dilemma of limited resources for many competing projects, a further planning workshop was held focusing on prioritization and selection, resulting in a prioritized list of projects as shown in Table A.2. This analysis confirmed that a marketing strategy was an important stepping stone to achieving future goals.

After the prioritization and selection workshop, the Council decided to launch a marketing campaign. To kick off the campaign, the first Technology Management Conference and Exhibition is to be held over three days, which will generate funds to initiate the marketing campaign. As the conference will only deliver benefits downstream, the Executive Director recommended that a Web site should run in parallel with the conference and exhibition.

The conference and exhibition will also increase awareness of the Institute, and provide a forum for the exchange of ideas and developments. This should enhance the image of the ITM amongst its members and other interested parties. As the very existence of the ITM is at stake, the Council decided to minimize its risk and appoint a professional project manager to manage the conference and exhibition.

THE PROJECT BRIEF

The ITM contracted the project manager to manage the national conference and exhibition. Specifically, the project manager will be responsible for planning, organizing, coordinating and controlling the project.

The Institute has allocated an amount of $10,000 for initial expenditure, but this has to be paid back out of the conference and exhibition proceeds. Technology management companies have been approached for sponsorship and $15,000 has been raised. Funding over and above these amounts is to be generated through the conference and exhibition fees.

The Institute expects the conference and exhibition to realize a net profit of at least $50,000. To achieve this target, at least 100 conference delegates and 20 exhibitors are

Table A.1 The Institute of Technology Management Strategy

Vision	
To achieve excellence in technology management	
Mission	
To further the aims and objectives and increase the professionalism of technology management	

Goals/Outcomes	**Risks**
● Increase professionalism of members ● Increase stakeholder support and confidence in the ITM ● Enhance ITM image ● Increase and retain membership ● Affiliation with similar management institutes/bodies	● ITM members will not be valued in industry ● Lack of support and confidence in ITM and consequential membership loss ● Resulting drop-off in membership and lowering of industry ● Continued existence of ITM threatened ● National and international knowledge and credibility will be lost

Strategies	Business objectives	Programmes/Projects
Marketing strategy	● Increase awareness of ITM ● Profile booklet produced by 1 July xxxx ● Maintain membership growth equal to market growth	● Publicity campaign ● Conferences/meetings ● Electronic communications programme
Build professionalism	● Obtain ITM accreditation for ITM professional development programme ● Implement accreditation programmes by 1 Jan xxxx ● Certify 50 Professional Technology Managers (PTM) by 1 Jan yyyy	● Pre-accreditation programmes ● Accreditation development programme
Increase value of membership	● Reduce cost of membership by 5% by 1 Jan xxxx ● Internal membership communications	● Cost-saving programme ● Establish Web site by 1 July zzzz
Engage stakeholders (members and industry)	● Member input to the vision, mission and strategies ● Industry involvement	● Communication and feedback to members ● Sponsorship programme ● Establish affiliation programme
Position ITM nationally and internationally with other professional management bodies	● Develop five national and two international associations by 1 Jan xxxx	● Institute association programme

Table A.2 Prioritized list of projects

Factor	Publicity campaign	Conference	Web site	Cost-saving programme	Weight	Publicity campaign	Conference	Web site	Cost-saving programme
Strategy									
Increased profile	5	4	5	1	5	25	20	25	5
Successful conference	4	5	5	1	4	16	20	20	4
Membership growth	3	5	3	1	5	15	25	15	5
Accreditation programme	3	3	3	1	2	6	6	6	2
Risk	-3	-4	-5	-1	5	-15	-20	-25	-5
Value to membership	4	5	4	3	5	20	25	20	15
Urgency	5	4	5	1	4	20	16	20	4
Total weighted score						87	93	81	30

needed. A minimum of 20 new members are expected to enrol as a result of the proceedings. Over the three-day period, approximately 2,500 visitors are expected to visit the exhibition.

To attract both members and non-members, a quality professional programme highlighting nationally known technology management experts as well as an international keynote speaker is planned.

The project start date is 1 February and it is estimated to take 11 months.

The project manager draws up a project charter capturing the above parameters, and the Executive Director, acting as sponsor, approves it.

PROJECT STAFFING

The project has just been initiated and the project manager and sponsor have assessed the high-level staffing requirements in terms of skills and time required. Four members have been seconded from project-based organizations on the basis that their time is donated in return for advertising space in the conference brochure. The four team members (Andy, Beth, Peter and Diana) are assigned part-time to the project due to existing workloads.

EXTRACT FROM THE MINUTES OF THE FIRST PROJECT TEAM MEETING

The project team held its first meeting, chaired by the sponsor and facilitated by the project manager. There is recognition that the team consists of technology professionals in the field of projects and that the executive is placing considerable trust in their ability to deliver successfully.

The project manager presented a proposal arguing the need for a project definition workshop that would scope out the project, define the deliverables and determine the success criteria. A further aim of the workshop would be to obtain key stakeholders' support during definition, leading to ownership of the project definition report. This ownership was discussed as being critical to the successful outcome of the conference. Following the presentation by the project manager, the sponsor (Executive Director) and team agreed to hold the workshop. They also agreed that the workshop would be the start of their own team building that would be further strengthened by committing to dedicating their time and enthusiasm to the project. The team also concurred that a clear and unwavering focus on the project process and business results was paramount to a successful conference.

The project team then drew up the following implementation guidelines:

1. A suitable venue has to be selected. This must be within one hour's travelling distance from Capital City.

2. A promotional brochure will be required. This will be mailed to prospective conference attendees.
3. All conference materials need to be of high quality.
4. The conference programme will require between 16 and 20 speakers.
5. A full set of conference notes must be provided to conference delegates.
6. There will be no entrance fee to attend the exhibition.
7. Potential exhibitors will be contacted personally and through the Institute's normal communication channels.
8. Facilities will need to be provided to the exhibitors for their exhibition stands.
9. Catering for conference delegates and exhibitors will be required.

Later that afternoon the project manager reflected on the meeting. The team members' keenness to begin working out details so early in the project confirmed that the decision to hold the project definition workshop was correct. An essential input to the workshop would be the strategies, objectives and programmes document developed at the executive workshop. The workshop would also serve to verify the skills and team composition required for the project.

Prior to the definition workshop, the Executive Director decided to include the Web site in the conference and exhibition project. A Web design organization, managed by the conference project manager, is to be appointed to develop and deliver the Web site. Initially the Web site will be used to market the conference and exhibition, and then be handed over to the organization for further development and maintenance. As the site would benefit the ITM as a whole, the sponsor agreed to fund this work from ITM's central fund.

PROJECT DEFINITION WORKSHOP OUTPUTS

These are shown in Tables A.3–A.10.

Table A.3 Project definition report

Project: ITM Conference project		
		Project purpose and objectives

Sub-project: Conference project	Compiled by: PM Smith	Date initiated:
	Approved by: ITM Council Chairperson	Chart date/Rev. No: 7 Feb 20xx – RO1

Project purpose mission

In order to contribute to the future growth of the ITM, the ITM Executive council has decided that a publicity campaign is required. A conference and exhibition is to be held which will generate funds for the campaign.

This will also create awareness and contribute to membership building, which is aligned with the marketing strategy of the ITM.

Objectives	Performance measures	Critical success factors (CSFs)
● Hold a successful conference	● 80% or more delegate satisfaction level measured off evaluations ● Realize a net profit of $50,000 ● Attract at least 100 conference delegates	● Internationally acclaimed keynote speaker ● Excellent programme
● Hold a successful exhibition	● 80% or more delegate satisfaction level measured by exit survey ● 20 exhibitors ● 2500 exhibition visitors	● Careful screening and selection of industry-representative exhibitors
● Increase membership numbers	● 20 new members within 3 months of the proceedings	● Add value to members both in run-up and at the conference ● ITM follows up potential new members prior to and after the conference
● Create a Web site in support of the conference and hand over to the organization	● Number of hits on Web site ● Length of stay at the site	● Design a user-friendly, highly advertised Web site ● Research and appoint a professional and successful Web designer

Table A.4 Deliverables breakdown structure

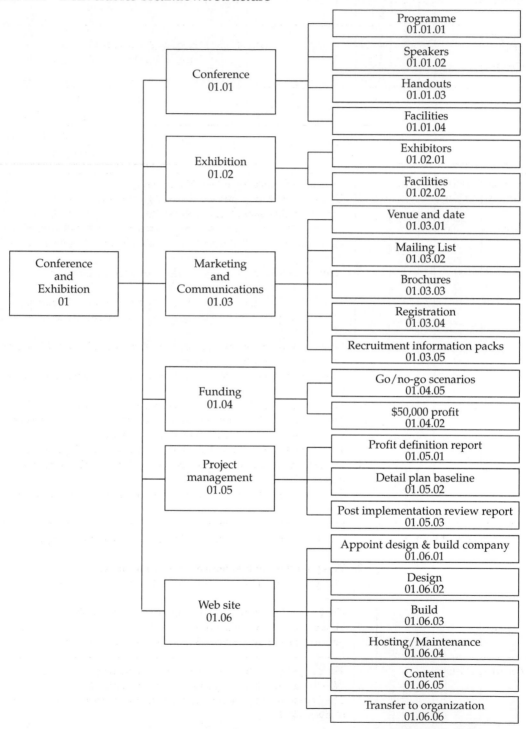

Table A.5   Initial scope, constraints and limiting criteria

Project: ITM Conference project	Initial scope, constraints and limiting criteria	
Sub-project N/A	Compiled by: PM Smith	Date initiated: 15 Jan 20xx
	Approved by: ITM Executive Director	Chart date/Rev. No: 7 Feb 20xx – RO1
Scope, constraints and limiting criteria (What is in scope)	1. Hold a conference for at least 100 delegates. 2. Create an exhibition area for at least 20 exhibitors. 3. Provide facilities for at least 2,500 visitors 4. Develop a Web site to assist the Conference and Exhibition marketing. 5. Initial funding of $10,000 will be provided by the Institute but must be paid back. 6. A further donation of $15,000 will be provided by member organizations. 7. Project duration is 11 months. The project start date is 1 February. 8. The conference and exhibition must not take place later than the end of August. 9. Project team is to be drawn from Executive Council and ITM members only. Their time will be voluntary. 10. A recruitment pack must be developed and the ITM must be one of the exhibitors. 11. The exhibition and conference must be a three-day event. 12. The conference programme must have between 16 and 20 speakers, of which at least one must be an international speaker. 13. The venue to be no more than an hour's travel from Capital City. 14. Catering for conference delegates and exhibition visitors must be organized. 15. Speakers' expenses will be paid, but the speakers will not receive a fee.	
What is out of scope	1. The actual growth in membership will not be a deliverable from this project. 2. This project is not the complete marketing strategy. 3. This project will not be the sole contributor to greater market awareness of the ITM. 4. Continued development and maintenance of the Web site. 5. Sign-up of 20 new members is not part of the project team performance (only expected 3 months after the conference).	
Assumptions	1. The budget and other resources are available when required. 2. Web design and build expertise will be outsourced. 3. The four staff and project manager will be available for the duration of the project.	

Table A.6   Milestone objective chart

Project: ITM – Conference project	Milestone objective chart		
Sub-project: N/A	Compiled by: PM Smith		Page 1 of 2
Date initiated: 15 Jan 20xx	Approved by: ITM Executive Director		Chart date/Rev. No: 7 Feb 20xx – RO1

Goal routes M C CM E	Milestone identification	Plan date	Description	Completion date	Report date	Report
	10	07/02	When project charter is signed off by the Sponsor (go/no-go decision)			
	20	26/02	When the date has been set and the venue located and confirmed			
	30	01/03	When the key note speakers have been selected and confirmed			
	40	06/03	When the exhibitors have been obtained and confirmed			
	50	10/03	When Web organization has been appointed			
	60	14/03	When the mailing list has been prepared and approved			
	70	20/03	When the event programme has been compiled and approved			
	80	30/04	Web design and build complete			
	90	21/05	When Web prototype is operating successfully			
	100	05/06	When the brochure has been designed, approved and printed			
	110	10/06	When the brochure has been mailed			
	120	10/06	When speaker notes and presentation visuals have been obtained from the speakers			
	130	01/07	When 50 delegates and 15 exhibitors have been registered (Go/no-go decision)			

Goal routes: M = Marketing   C = Conference   CM = Council/Management   E = Exhibition   ○ Milestones   ◎ Critical decision point

Table A.6 Milestone objective chart (continued)

Project: ITM – Conference project	**Milestone objective chart**		
Sub-project: N/A	**Compiled by:** PM Smith		**Page 2 of 2**
Date initiated: 15 Jan 20xx	**Approved by:** ITM Executive Director		**Chart date/Rev. No:** 7 Feb 20xx – RO1

Goal routes M C CM E	Milestone identification	Plan date	Description	Completion date	Report date	Report
	140	10/07	When the presentation visuals and signage have been completed			
	150	19/08	When arrangements for speakers, exhibitors, venue, facilities and catering are complete and confirmed			
	160	27/08	When the conference and exhibition site has been prepared			
	170	27/08	When the conference handouts have been prepared			
	180	28/08	When the conference and exhibition has started			
	190	31/08	When the conference and exhibition has ended			
	200	31/08	When Web site has been handed over to ITM for ongoing support			
	210	06/09	When evaluations of satisfaction levels, profits and volumes have been done			
	220	30/11	When at least 20 new applications have been received by ITM			
	230	15/12	When the project review report has been presented to the ITM Council			
	240	20/12	When all the project's objectives have been achieved and the project archived			

Goal routes: M = Marketing   C = Conference   CM = Council/Management   E = Exhibition   ◯ Milestones   ◎ Critical decision point

Table A.7 Milestone responsibility matrix

Project: ITM – Conference project	Milestone responsibility matrix	
Sub-project: N/A	Compiled by: PM Smith	Page 1 of 3
Date initiated: 15 Jan 20xx	Approved by: ITM Executive Director	Chart date/Rev. No: 7 Feb 20xx – RO1

Milestone Identification	Description	Project manager	Marketing (Andy)	Conference (Beth)	Exhibition (Peter)	Venue (Diana)	ITM Council	Graphic Designer	Advertising agency	Food & beverages
10	When project charter is signed off by the sponsor (go/no-go decision)	x	I	I	I	I	PD			
20	When the date has been set and the venue located and confirmed	d	Cd	Cd	CD	PXD	D			
30	When the keynote speakers have been selected and confirmed		I	PXd			CD			
40	When the exhibitors have been obtained and confirmed		I		PXD	C	Cd			
50	When Web organization has been appointed	D	Xd	I	I	I	C			I
60	When the mailing list has been prepared and approved		PXD	C	C	I	I			
70	When the event programme has been compiled and approved	Pd	C	Xd	X	I	CD		Xdp	
80	Web design and build complete	D	d				I		I	Xd
90	When the Web prototype is operating successfully	d	C	I	I	I	D		I	Xd
100	When the brochure has been designed, approved									
110	When the brochure has been mailed	P	XD	I	I					
120	When speaker notes and presentation visuals have been obtained from the speakers									

Legend: X = eXecutes the work; P = manages Progress; C = must be Consulted; p = manages function progress; D = takes Decision solely; d = takes decision jointly; I = must be Informed; a = available to advise

Table A.7 Milestone responsibility matrix (continued)

Project: ITM – Conference project	Milestone responsibility matrix		
Sub-project: N/A	Compiled by: PM Smith		Page 2 of 3
Date initiated: 15 Jan 20xx	Approved by: ITM Executive Director		Chart date/Rev. No: 7 Feb 20xx – RO1

Milestone Identification	Description	Project manager	Marketing (Andy)	Conference (Beth)	Exhibition (Peter)	Venue (Diana)	ITM Council	Graphic Designer	Advertising agency	Food & beverages
130	When 50 delegates and 15 exhibitors have been registered (go/no-go decision)	Pd	C	Xd	Cd	Xd	D			I
140	When the presentation visuals and signage have been completed	d	Xd	Cd	PXd	C	D	Xdp		
150	When arrangements for speakers, exhibitors, venue, facilities and catering are complete and confirmed	D	I	Xd	Xd	Xd	I	Xd		Xd
160	When the conference and exhibition site has been prepared	D	I	Xd	Xd	Xd	I	Xd		Xd
170	When the conference handouts have been prepared	d	C	PXD	C	I				
180	When the conference and exhibition has started	PXD	I	X	X	X	I			
190	When the conference and exhibition has ended	PXD	C	X	X	X	I			
200	When Web site has been handed over to ITM for ongoing support	Pd	CXd				D			
210	When evaluations of satisfaction levels, profits and volumes have been done	PX	I	I	I	I	D			I

Legend: X = eXecutes the work; P = manages Progress; C = must be Consulted; p = manages function progress; D = takes Decision solely; d = takes decision jointly; I = must be Informed; a = available to advise

Table A.7 Milestone responsibility matrix (continued)

Project: ITM – Conference project	Milestone responsibility matrix		
Sub-project: Conference project	**Compiled by:** PM Smith		Page 3 of 3
Date initiated: 15 Jan 20xx	**Approved by:** ITM Executive Director		**Chart date/Rev. No:** 7 Feb 20xx – RO1

Milestone Identification	Description	Project manager	Marketing (Andy)	Conference (Beth)	Exhibition (Peter)	Venue (Diana)	ITM Council	Graphic Designer	Advertising agency	Food & beverages
220	When at least 20 new applications have been received by the ITM	PXd	I	I	I	I	I			
230	When the project review report has been presented to the ITM Council	pX	I	I	I	I	PD			
240	When all the project's objectives have been achieved and the project archived	pX	I	I	I	I	PD		I	

Legend: X = eXecutes the work; P = manages Progress; C = must be Consulted; p = manages function progress; D = takes Decision solely; d = takes decision jointly; I = must be Informed; a = available to advise

UPDATE

The project definition workshop was successful – resulting in enthusiastic stakeholder support and a clear direction for the conference. The project definition report was signed off by the executive and communicated to members in user-friendly language. The team is starting to work well together and the early deliverables have been achieved. As the project is elaborated, decisions are made, and the following further information is now available to the team:

1. A potentially suitable venue for the conference and exhibition has been identified. A deposit is required to secure a firm booking. Venue staff will prepare the facility for the conference.
2. To ensure quality, a freelance graphics designer will be used to produce all conference and exhibition signs, notices and speaker visuals.
3. A professional agency will be contracted to design and print the promotional brochure. The brochure will contain details of the conference programme and speakers, the names of exhibitors and a brief overview of what they will be exhibiting. The Institute will mail the brochure, using mailing lists obtained free of charge from other institutions.
4. The agency will also design and print an exhibition guide for distribution at the exhibition itself.
5. Speakers will be paid travel expenses and one night's accommodation.
6. Speakers will provide their notes in a predetermined format, thus requiring only copying. The conference notes will be provided to delegates in a binder.
7. Some speakers will require an overhead projection facility connected to a computer. This equipment must be supplied.
8. A professional catering company will arrange and provide food and beverages, and will pay a one-off fee to the Institute for the right.
9. Exhibition stands will require power points, lighting, partitioning and telephone/fax facilities.
10. Conference delegate and exhibitor fees have been agreed. There is no fee for attending the exhibition.

COSTING INFORMATION

The team member responsible for finances has prepared the following costing information necessary for costing out the project in detail:

1. Personnel costs:
   - graphics artist @ $300 per day;
   - casual labour @ $35 per day;
   - a typist @ $150 per day.

Table A.8 Communications plan

Project: ITM – Conference project		Communications plan					
Sub-project: Date initiated: 15 Jan 20xx		Compiled by: PM Smith Approved by: ITM Executive Director				Chart date/Rev. No: 5/5/01 v1.01	

S/H category	Stakeholder (S/H)	S/H benefit /risk	S/H influencing strategy	S/H information required	Key messages	Comms medium & frequency	Mngt resp
Primary	Current members	Affiliation, support access to knowledge and prestige Low recognition of membership by industry	Keep informed – build perceived value of membership	Details of upcoming conference and other institute events and news and value of membership	Timing and content of upcoming events – how to access the Web site	Quarterly newsletter and Web site	Marketing manager
Primary	Institute Executive Council	Employment Failure of the project initiatives could be failure of the Institute	Build trust – keep informed and facilitate timely decisions where required	Progress on the project on a timely basis and whether the business objectives are still achievable	Project performance to plan	Timely project reports immediate exception reporting	Project manager
Primary	Institute staff (including project)	Employment Loss of employment, Institute fails	Keep them informed and involved – build knowledge and acceptance	Up-to-date information, clarity of what their role is and what is required of them	What is required, the importance of their contribution	Face-to-face communication E-mail (daily)	Executive director
Primary	Conference and exhibition attendees	Information Failure to meet expectations	Emphasize value of the association – keep informed	How to enrol and by when – what are the benefits of attending?	How to enrol and by when	Information packs, Web site Mail-outs	Project manager
Primary	Industry members	Opportunity to interact with others in the industry, informative Failure to meet expectations	Keep informed – encourage involvement and recognition of the industries' role	How to be involved with the conference and exhibition, how to enrol, how they can promote themselves and their business	How to enrol and by when	Information packs, Web site Mail-outs	Communications managers

Secondary	Consultants on Web and brochure design	Cash flow, exposure Negative association	Clarity on roles and achieving targets	A clear contractual arrangement of what is expected of them and by when	What is required	Contract, letters, direct communication	Project manager
Primary	Speakers at the conference and exhibitors	Increased profile, prestige, industry recognition being associated with an unsuccesful/ unprofessional event	Keep informed – recognize contribution	What is required of them and by when, what arrangements have been made for them	What is required and thanks for their involvement	Information packs, Web site Mail-outs	Project manager
Primary	International Institute of Technology Management	Publicity, increase in affiliated members, increase in awareness of the industry and institute roles May be portrayed in a unsatisfactory way	Build/retain reputation as serious affiliated Institute	The way the local Institute is being promoted and the impact on membership	We are an active part of the international technology management Institutes	Web site Regular membership reports	Executive director
Secondary	Potential members	Learn more about the Institute Meet and interact with existing members	Focus on the value of membership and attending the conference/exhibition	Benefits of membership	The benefits of membership and how to enrol	Information packs, Web site Mail-outs	Marketing manager
Secondary	Community	Increased business in the local community from attendees, prestige of professional body in the neighbourhood Increased noise, vehicles in immediate conference arena	Focus on expected income opportunities for local business	Benefits for the community	This is good for the local area	Local newspapers and other media such as radio	Executive director

Table A.9 Risk evaluation matrix

Project: ITM – Conference project	Risk Evaluation Matrix		
Sub-project: N/A **Date initiated:** 15 Jan 20xx	**Compiled by:** PM Smith **Approved by:** ITM Executive Director	Page 1 of 1 **Chart date/Rev. No:** 7 Feb 20xx – RO1	

Risk: What can go wrong?	Occurrence H/M/L	Impact H/M/L	Severity level	Risk treatment	Management responsibility
Quality of speakers not excellent	H	H	25	• Draw up job descriptions for speakers to be used for selection. • Research which speakers the industry wants. • Select keynote speaker carefully for maximum visibility. • Research industry requirements on subject areas. • Research other TM Institutes and Associations for current topics. • Draw outlines for speakers.	PM & Team
Conference venue could be unsuitable	M	H	15	• Select venue carefully. • Draw up a criteria list for selection.	PM
Competing conference or exhibitions	M	H	15	• Investigate and research what is being advertised. • Contact TM magazines that usually carry brochures and adverts. • Investigate whether there are any non-TM events taking place that could be of interest to the TM group.	Beth
Web site not launched on time	M	H	15	• Careful outsourcing of contract.	PM
Cancellation by keynote speaker	L	H	5	• Obtain a backup keynote speaker selected from the existing speakers. • Brief the selected backup speaker.	Sponsor
Conference administration fails	L	M	3	• Discuss with ITM members and other organizations that have held similar seminars. • Develop a list of administrative duties.	PM

Total risk score	78

Table A.10 Estimate/Budget worksheet

Project: ITM – Conference project	Estimate/Budget worksheet			
Sub-project: N/A	Compiled by: PM Smith		Page 1 of 1	
Date initiated: 15 Jan 20xx	Approved by: ITM Executive Director		Chart date/Rev. No: 7 Feb 20xx – RO1	

Work element		Cost components (Allowables)						
Code	Description	Equipment	HR	Materials	Sub contractors	Contingency	Other	Total
010101	Themes and programme						1,000	1,000
010102	Materials		9,000	8,000			1,000	18,000
010103	Speakers						12,300	12,300
010104	Prepare facility	1,500						1,500
010201	Exhibitors						300	300
010202	Prepare site				21,000			21,000
010301	Find location				2,000		450	2,450
010302	Set date						250	250
010303	Arrange food and beverages							0
010401	Brochure	1,500	550	2,000	13,500		500	18,050
010402	Registration			500			600	1,100
010501	Run proceedings		10,000	1,000	9,100		1,000	21,100
010502	End off		2,300					2,300
	Contingency					14,000		14,000
	TOTALS	3,000	21,850	11,500	45,600	14,000	17,400	113,350

2. Speakers' costs:
   - there will be no speaker's fee;
   - travel and accommodation expenses @ $750 per speaker.
3. Printing costs:
   - brochure printing $7,500;
   - conference notes (binders and photocopying) $200 per copy;
   - exhibition guide $6,000.
4. Mailing expenses (stamps, labels and envelopes) $2,000.
5. Conference site:
   - conference facility @ $2,200 per day with a deposit of $1,000;
   - exhibition centre @ $1,500 per day with a deposit of $1,000;
   - hire of computer and overhead projection system $350 per day.
6. Other miscellaneous expenses:
   - telephones and faxes for the three days $1,000;
   - hire of partitioning $15,000;
   - electrical work $5,000;
   - stationery and other materials $1,000.
7. Revenue estimates:
   - delegate fees @ $1,500 per delegate payable on registration;
   - exhibitor fee @ $2,500 per stand;
   - food and beverage rights $3,000.

PREPARING THE PROJECT PLANS

The output from the work done in the project definition workshop (PDW) is a project definition report (PDR), as set out on the previous pages. This serves as input to the project planning phase, where detailed plans are developed. The deliverables breakdown schedule (DBS) is elaborated into a work breakdown schedule (WBS), and the milestone objective chart (MOC) acts as input to the activity schedule. The detailed budget/estimate is developed from the PDR budget/estimate. Tables A.11–A.13 and Figure A.1 show some of the detail plans.

MONITORING AND CONTROL

As the project progresses, the work must be monitored and corrective action taken to ensure that the deliverables remain on track. Examples of a progressed activity schedule and milestone objective chart (MOC) are shown in Tables A.14 and A.15. Note that the project team monitors more than just these two components – they must also monitor issues and risks, costs, resources, procurement contracts and scope control. Most importantly, the project manager and sponsor should continually review if the project objectives are still achievable.

Table A.11 Detailed work breakdown structure (WBS)

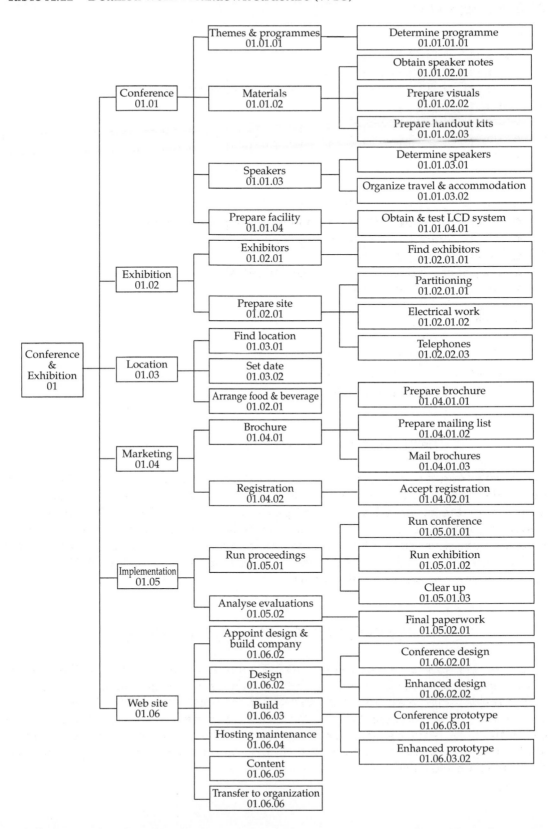

Table A.12 Activity schedule

Project:	Activity schedule		Page 1 of 1
ITM – Conference project			
Sub-project: Start to Milestone Id 20	**Compiled by:** Diana		
Date initiated: 15 Jan 200xx	**Approved by:** Project leader		**Chart date/Rev. No:** 7 Feb 20xx – RO1

Consequence to milestone:

Text for milestone report:

Activity ID	Activity description	Estimated duration	Actual time	Time to go	Quality Y/N	Responsibility Y/N	Problem	Comments/consequence/ action
010	Investigate date clashes	3d						
020	Decide on provisional data	1d						
030	Investigate and compile list	2d						
040	Contact venue suppliers	2d						
050	Prepare short-lists of possible venues	1d						
060	Visit locations	5d						
070	Select location	1d						
080	Confirm date	1d						
090	Confirm location	1d						
100	Arrange food and beverages	5d						

Further comments

Manager's comments:

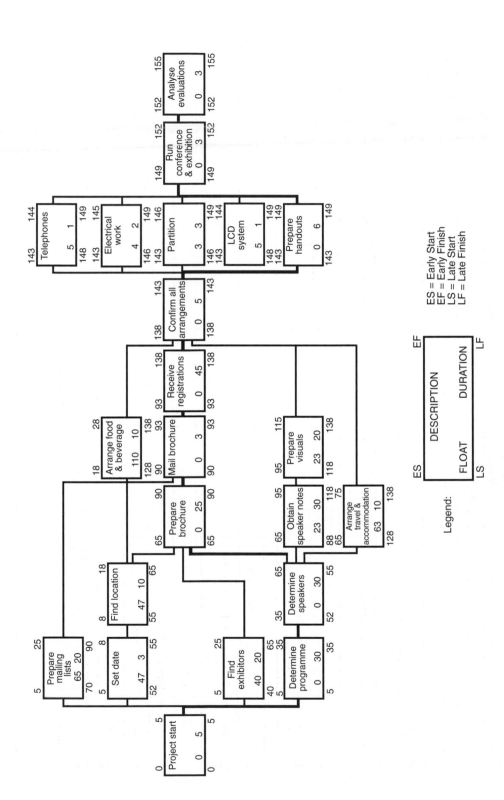

Figure A.1 The network diagram

Table A.13 Estimate/Budget worksheet

Project: ITM – Conference project	Estimate/Budget worksheet	
Sub-project: N/A	Compiled by: PM Smith	Page 1 of 5
Date initiated: 15 Jan 200x	Approved by: ITM Executive Director	Chart date/Rev. No: 7 Feb 20xx – RO1

Work element:		Cost components (allowables)								
Code	Description	Equipment	Human resources	Materials	Sub-contractors	Contingency	Other	Total cost	Revenue	P/L
0101	CONFERENCE									
010101	Themes and programme									
01010101	Determine programme						1,000	1,000		
	Total for themes and programme						1,000	1,000		
010102	Materials									
01010201	Obtain speaker notes						1,000	1,000		
01010202	Prepare visuals		7,500	3,000				105,00		
01010203	Prepare handout kits		1,500	5,000				6,500		
	Total for materials		9,000	8,000			1,000	18,000		
010303	Speakers									
01010301	Determine speakers						300	300		
01010302	Organize travel and accommodation						12,000	12,000		
	Total for speakers						12,300	12,300		
010104	Prepare facility									
01010401	Get/test LCD system	1,500						1,500		
	Total for prepare facility	1,500						1,500		
	TOTAL FOR CONFERENCE	1,500	9,000	8,000			14,300	32,800		

Table A.13 Estimate/Budget worksheet (continued)

Project: ITM – Conference project	Estimate/Budget worksheet		Page 2 of 5
Sub-project: N/A	Compiled by: PM Smith		
Date initiated: 15 Jan 200x	Approved by: ITM Executive Director		Chart date/Rev. No: 7 Feb 20xx – RO1

Work element: Cost components (allowables)

Code	Description	Equipment	Human resources	Materials	Sub-contractors	Contingency	Other	Total cost	Revenue	P/L
0102	EXHIBITION									
010201	Exhibitors									
01020101	Find exhibitors						300	300		
	Total for exhibitors						300	300		
010202	Prepare site									
01020201	Partitioning				15,000			15,000		
01020202	Electrical				5,000			5,000		
01020203	Telephones				1,000			1,000		
	Total for prepare site				21,000			21,000		
	TOTAL FOR EXHIBITION				21,000		300	21,300		
0103	LOCATION									
010301	Find location				2,000		450	2,450		
010302	Set date						250	250		
010303	Arrange food & beverage							0		
	TOTAL FOR LOCATION				2,000		700	2,700		

Table A.13 Estimate/Budget worksheet (continued)

Project: ITM – Conference project	Estimate/Budget worksheet	
Sub-project: N/A	Compiled by: PM Smith	Page 3 of 5
Date initiated: 15 Jan 200x	Approved by: ITM Executive Director	Chart date/Rev. No: 7 Feb 20xx – RO1

Work element:

					Cost components (allowables)					
Code	Description	Equipment	Human resources	Materials	Sub-contractors	Contingency	Other	Total cost	Revenue	P/L
0104	MARKETING									
010401	Exhibitors									
01040101	Prepare brochure				13,500			13,500		
01040102	Prepare mailing list	1,500	400				500	2,400		
01040103	Mail brochure		150	2,000				2,150		
	Total for brochure	1,500	550	2,000	13,500		500	18,050		
010402	Registration									
01040201	Accept registrations			500			600	1,100		
	Total for registration			500			600	1,100		
	TOTAL FOR MARKETING	1,500	550	2,500	13,500		1,100	19,150		
0105	IMPLEMENTATION									
010501	Run proceedings									
01050101	Run conference		10,000	1,000	9,100			20,100		
01050102	Run exhibition						1,000	1,000		
	TOTAL FOR IMPLE'TATION		10,000	1,000	9,100		1,000	21,100		

Table A.13 Estimate/Budget worksheet (continued)

Project: ITM – Conference project	Estimate/Budget worksheet
Sub-project: N/A	Compiled by: PM Smith
Date initiated: 15 Jan 200x	Approved by: ITM Executive Director
	Chart date/Rev. No: 7 Feb 20xx – RO1

Work element:

Code	Description	Cost components (allowables)							Revenue	P/L
		Equipment	Human resources	Materials	Sub-contractors	Contingency	Other	Total cost		
010502	End-off									
01050201	Clear up		1,500					1,500		
01050202	Final paperwork		800					800		
	Total for end-off		2,300					2,300		
	TOTAL FOR IMPLEMENTATION		12,300	1,000	9,100		1,000	23,400		
0106	REVENUE									
010601	Revenue from proceedings2								104,500	
01060101	Revenue from conference								50,000	
01060102	Revenue from exhibition								3,000	
01060103	Revenue from food and beverages concession									
	Total for revenue from proceedings2								157,500	
010602	Revenue from sponsorship									
01060201	From Institute								10,000	
01060202	From commercial sponsors								15,000	
	Total revenue from sponsorship								25,000	
	TOTAL REVENUE								182,500	

2: Revenue from 100 delegates @ $1,500 = $150,000. Deducted from the $150,000 revenue is $40,000 for the Project Manager fees, and $5,500 cost for the facility.

Table A.13 Estimate/Budget worksheet (continued)

Project: ITM – Conference project	Estimate/Budget worksheet	
Sub-project: N/A	Compiled by: PM Smith	Page 5 of 5
Date initiated: 15 Jan 200xx	Approved by: ITM Executive Director	Chart date/Rev. No: 7 Feb 20xx – RO1

Work element:

Code	Description	Cost components (allowables)							Revenue	P/L
		Equipment	Human resources	Materials	Sub-contractors	Contingency	Other	Total cost		
	SUMMARY									
	TOTAL FOR CONFERENCE	1,500	9,000	8,000			14,300	32,800		
	TOTAL FOR EXHIBITION				21,000		300	21,300		
	TOTAL FOR LOCATION				2,000		700	2,700		
	TOTAL FOR MARKETING	1,500	550	2,500	13,500		1,100	19,150		
	TOTAL FOR IMPLEMENTATION		12,300	1,000	9,100		1,000	23,400		
	CONTINGENCY					14,000		14,000		
	TOTAL REVENUE								182,500	
	TOTAL FOR CONFERENCE AND EXHIBITION	3,000	21,850	11,500	45,600	14,000	17,400	113,350	182,500	69,150

Table A.14 Activity schedule

Project:		
ITM – Conference project	Activity schedule	

Sub-project: Start to Milestone Id 20	Compiled by: Diana	Page 1 of 1
Date initiated: 15 Jan 20xx	Approved by: Project leader	Chart date/Rev. No: 7 Feb 20xx – RO1

Consequence to milestone:
Based on present situation, milestone completion may be delayed by three days.

Text for milestone report:
Difficulty in coordinating suitable meeting dates with team. Diana will consult with each member individually. Will take longer. Knock-on impact will be three days.

Activity ID	Activity description	Estimated duration	Actual time	Time to go	Quality Y/N	Responsibility Y/N	Problem	Comments/consequence/ action
010	Investigate date clashes	3d	2d					Completed
020	Decide on provisional data	1d		3d			Decision	Difficult to convene joint meetings – three-day delay. Can we change authorities?
030	Investigate and compile list	2d						
040	Contact venue suppliers	2d						
050	Prepare short-lists of possible venues	1d						
060	Visit locations	5d						
070	Select location	1d						
080	Confirm date	1d						
090	Confirm location	1d						
100	Arrange food and beverages	5d						

Further comments:
The problem being experienced at this early stage is going to occur whenever meetings and joint decisions will be required. We have to address. Project leader to take up issue with Executive Council. We may need to give more authority to individuals.

Manager's comments:
This milestone leg is critical and I am concerned that the delay could get worse. February seems to be a year-end/budgeting time for all members of the team. Should we consider date changes?

Table A.15 Milestone objective chart

Project: ITM – Conference project	Milestone objective chart		
Sub-project: N/A	Compiled by: ITM Executive Director		Page 1 of 2
Date initiated: 15 Jan 20xx	Approved by: ITM Executive Director		Chart date/Rev. No: 7 Feb 20xx – RO1

Goal routes M C CM E	Milestone identification	Plan date	Description	Completion date	Report date	Report
	10	07/02	When project charter is signed off by the Sponsor (go/no-go decision)	07/02	10/02	Project launched and all resources engaged.
	20	26/02	When the date has been set and the venue located and confirmed		10/02	Difficulty in coordinating suitable meeting dates with team. Diana will consult with each member individually. Will take longer. Knock-on impact will be 3 days.
	30	01/03	When the keynote speakers/have been selected and confirmed			
	40	06/03	When the exhibitors have been obtained and confirmed			
	50	10/03	When Web organization has been appointed			
	60	14/03	When the mailing list has been prepared and approved			
	70	20/03	When the event programme has been compiled and approved			
	80	30/04	Web design and build complete			
	90	21/05	When Web prototype is operating successfully			
	100	05/06	When the brochure has been designed, approved and printed			
	110	10/06	When the brochure has been mailed			
	120	10/06	When speaker notes and presentation visuals have been obtained from the speakers			
	130	01/07	When 50 delegates and 15 exhibitors have been registered (Go/no-go decision)			

Goal routes: M = Marketing   C = Conference   CM = Council/Management   E = Exhibition   ◯ Milestones   ◎ Critical decision point

Appendix B – Basic concepts, tools and techniques

DELIVERABLES BREAKDOWN STRUCTURE (DBS) AND WORK BREAKDOWN STRUCTURE (WBS)

Introduction

The essential tool used to assist in the development of the project deliverables is the deliverables breakdown structure (DBS).

The DBS identifies and displays the deliverables to be produced and/or accomplishments or results to be achieved as well as the sub-elements of the project. At the early stage, it is often difficult to break down the project into elements of work, but it is normally feasible to establish the deliverables or results required to achieve the project purpose/mission.

In developing a project plan or estimate, the planner starts with limited information and then gathers increasingly more detail. The project is broken down into its various components, which are in turn divided ('cascaded') into sub-components. Following the concepts of fuzzy to clear and progressive elaboration, the development of the DBS begins at a high level and progressively becomes more detailed. As more information becomes available during the project planning phase (covered in Chapter 9), the DBS is modified and expanded to become the detailed work breakdown structure (WBS).

For the sake of clarity, further reference will be made to the DBS only when it is explicitly required to explain a key concept. The WBS is referred to as the elaborated DBS.

The WBS definition from the PMI Standards Committee's *A Guide to the Project Management Body of Knowledge*[73] reads: 'The WBS is a deliverable-oriented grouping of project elements which organizes and defines the total scope of the project. Each descending level represents an increasingly detailed definition of a project component. Project components may be products or services.'

As more detailed information becomes available during the various design stages, more levels can be added to the cascaded structure. This process creates a tree-like structure called the WBS and is the means of dividing a large project into components or elements called work packages. The lowest level is always the detailed task to be performed. Using the WBS, the planner can tackle one clearly defined part of a project at a time instead of trying to grapple with the whole.

The WBS is a tool that can be used to plan scope. Kerzner[46] has the following to say about the WBS:

> The WBS is the single most important element, because it provides a common framework from which:
>
> - the total program can be described as a summation of subdivided elements;
> - planning can be performed;
> - costs and budgets can be established;
> - time, cost, and performance can be tracked;
> - objectives can be linked to company resources in a logical manner;
> - schedules and status-reporting procedures can be established;
> - network construction and control planning can be initiated;
> - the responsibility assignments for each element can be established.

What does a WBS look like?

The WBS is typically a chart that looks similar to an organization chart – as illustrated in the WBS chart in Figure B.1. For readers who prefer a more flexible approach, a WBS can also be developed using mind-mapping techniques, where level 1 forms the central theme, the first set of branches becomes level 2, and so forth.

Note that Figure B.1 shows the full branches of only the pickling plant buildings structure. A full WBS would show the branches and work packages flowing from each component at each level. In an IT system, the WBS is often used to show the components of a system, such as software modules.

Coding the WBS

This visual representation of a WBS shown in Figure B.1 is excellent for providing an overall view of the project and its structure. However, in this format it is not suitable as a framework around which to build any further systems. For example, it is difficult to deal with a block 'on the third level, two blocks from the right'. The solution is to give each block a code.

LEVEL

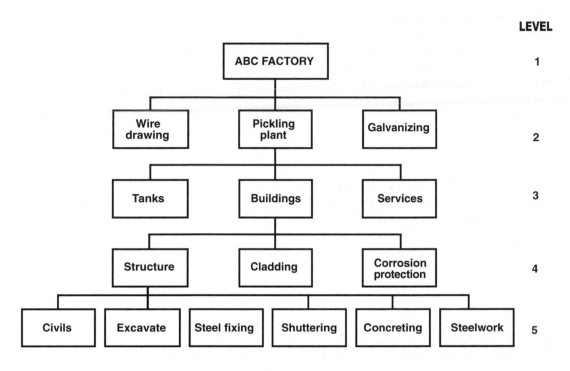

Figure B.1   Work breakdown structure (WBS) example

Codification is the basic framework upon which any system using the WBS is built. It provides a common 'language' of identification to facilitate the use of computers and for ease of communication for all concerned with project costing. Table B.1 gives the codes for the chart in Figure B.1. It is now easy to allocate costs, quantities, progress, etc to a code such as 1.1.1.1.2 (Excavation of the civils for the structure of the pickling plant buildings). Note the use of an indented table as a non-graphic method of presenting a WBS.

The size of the WBS and the number of levels depend on the size and complexity of the project. The most common structure consists of five levels, as shown below:

1. total project;
2. sub-project (deliverables or accomplishments);
3. work package;
4. tasks;
5. activities.

The WBS levels can take on a variety of names depending on industry type, established organization methodologies and individual project managers' preference. Programme level is usually designated level 0. The development of the WBS is a continuous process that follows the phases and progress of design and implementation.

Table B.1　Coding the WBS

1.	Project ABC Factory				
	1.1	Pickling Plant			
		1.1.1	Buildings		
			1.1.1.1	Structure	
				1.1.1.1.1	Civils
				1.1.1.1.2	Excavate
				1.1.1.1.3	Steel fixing
				1.1.1.1.4	Shuttering
				1.1.1.1.5	Concreting
				1.1.1.1.6	Steelwork
			1.1.1.2	Cladding	
			1.1.1.3	Corrosion protection	
		1.1.2	Tanks		
		1.1.3	Services		
	1.2	Wire Drawing			
	1.3	Galvanizing			

A WBS can, at level 2, be broken down either on a product basis or on a life-cycle basis. A well-developed product-based WBS should have the following characteristics:

● Level 2 defines the major products that the project will deliver, irrespective of which life-cycle phase they are in.
● WBS elements are not listed in any specific sequence. Task and activity schedules, and budgets may be prepared after the work elements have been defined.
● It must cover all the known deliverables/work required to accomplish the project.
● The WBS must cover all effort, including project management and administration.
● The tasks should be mutually exclusive and, as a rule, not overlap.
● When a deliverable/task or activity repeats in various parts of the WBS, it is useful to group them together at a higher level. This guideline does not apply to the phased approach.
● The elements of a developed WBS always look obvious after the fact.

In addition, the WBS:

● must not be people-orientated – it must not indicate who will do the work;
● is not the project time plan, as it ignores time;
● does not indicate the sequence in which the activities or work packages are executed, except for the phased approach.

The life-cycle-based WBS has the following characteristics that are different to the above product based structure: 1) it defines level 2 of the WBS in terms of the project life cycle; 2) the deliverables/tasks and activities can repeat in various phases.

Either WBS approach can be used and should yield the same result if correctly developed. Different WBSs convey different views of the project work contents, reflecting the structure of the performing organization, the managerial style of the project manager and other factors. Projects that have well-developed life cycles and established processes tend to follow the life-cycle WBS. A project where there is a different project manager for each phase would also tend towards a life-cycle approach.

Remember, if a WBS cannot be developed for a project, then too little is known about it to plan it – let alone to try to manage it!

For Fog-type projects that require a large amount of 'fuzzy to clear' elaboration, the DBS development proceeds as the information becomes available. The conversion of the DBS takes place downstream, once sufficient clarity is developed.

RISK MANAGEMENT

Introduction

Note: This section draws on the Australian/New Zealand Standard for Risk Management(r) AS/NZS 4360:1995. The authors have integrated the philosophy and process outline of the AS/NZS into the book and the ODPM™ process.

The main elements of a risk management process are as follows (extracted from the Australian/New Zealand Standard for Risk Management® AS/NZS 4360:1995):

(a) **Establish the context.** This step establishes the strategic, organizational and risk management context in which the rest of the process will take place. Criteria against which risk will be evaluated are established and the structure of the analysis is defined.
(b) **Identify risks.** Identify what, why and how things can arise as the basis for further analysis.
(c) **Analyse risks.** Determine the existing controls and analyse risks in terms of likelihood and consequence in context of these controls. The analysis should consider:
    (i) how likely is an event to happen; and
    (ii) what are the potential consequences and their magnitude.
    Combine these elements to produce an estimated level of risk.
(d) **Evaluate and prioritize risks.** Compare estimated levels of risk against the pre-established criteria. Risks are then ranked to identify management priorities. If the levels of risk established are low, then risks may fall into an acceptable category and treatment may not be required.
(e) **Treat risks.** Accept and monitor low priority risks. For other risks develop and implement a specific risk management plan which includes consideration of funding.
(f) **Monitor and review.** Monitor and review the performance of the risk management system and changes which might affect it.

The entire process is iterative (refer to Figure B.2). For each stage of the process, adequate records should be kept sufficiently to satisfy independent audit.

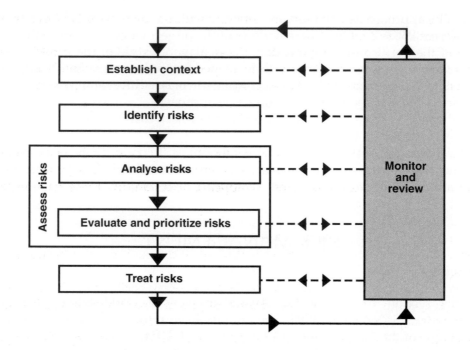

Figure B.2 The iterative risk management process

Managing risk is a diverse process undertaken by the project team and can include inputs from other parts of the organization. The process occurs within the organization's strategic, business and project context.

Establishing the context

Risks that could affect the project must be identified and evaluated during the early phases of the project, and contingency plans developed either to avoid the risks or to mitigate their impact. It is easier to influence cost and make changes during the earlier phases of the project than in later phases.

The strategic context

Chapter 4 developed the concept of the Wrappers™ model, comprising the Strategic Wrapper, the Business Wrapper and the Project Wrapper. This model sets out the portfolio of projects in the context of the organization's business objectives.

The Strategic Wrapper defines the relationship between the organization and its environment, identifying the organization's strengths, weaknesses, opportunities and threats (SWOT). The context includes social, technical, economic and environmental issues, political/public perceptions, and operational and legal aspects of the organization's functions (STEEPOL).

The executive level of the organization owns the Strategic Wrapper, and is accountable for setting the overall risk approach of the performing organization. This forms the parameters and guidelines for business and project-related risk management.

The business context

Before undertaking a risk analysis, it is necessary to understand the business context of the organization and its capabilities, as well as the business objectives, goals and strategies that are contained in the Business Wrapper. Understanding these relationships is important for the following reasons:

● Risk management takes place within the Business Wrapper.
● Business objectives must be achieved through the enabling deliverables from the portfolio of projects.
● Upper management is accountable for the business-focused risks. Project sponsors and managers are responsible for integrating them into the project risk structure, and managing them jointly with the project process risks.
● The organizational policy and goals assist in defining the criteria by which a project risk is acceptable, and provides a basis for risk options and treatment.

The project context

The project context is contained within the Project Wrapper. The purpose, objectives, strategies, scope, stakeholder analysis and communication strategy, and key assumptions are all essential inputs to the risk management process. These elements are described in Chapter 5 under the section 'Strategic and business planning', which discusses project proposal and business case contents, and in Chapter 8, The project definition phase.

The project sponsor owns the Project Wrapper. The project manager and team members manage this level and are consequently responsible for the project risk management. The ODPM process developed in Part III highlights the important stages where a specific risk analysis is required as well as reinforcing the need for continual review, monitoring and control of risks across the life cycle.

Determining the scope and boundaries of an application of the risk management process involves:

● recognizing and incorporating the influences from an organization's environmental scan for influence and adjustment to strategies;
● developing the project proposal and business case (Chapter 5, p 94, section Strategic and business planning'), as these capture the business interface of the project;
● defining the project as set out in the project definition phase (Chapter 8);

- scanning the sources of generic risk areas in the organization and business sector – organizations that value project learning as a key strategy to improving performance and reducing risk develop databases of risk sources that project participants can access;
- identifying any studies needed and their scope, objectives and the resources required;
- defining the extent and comprehensiveness of risk management activities to be carried out, considering the importance of the project on business outcomes and stakeholder interests.

Also to be considered in the application of risk are:

- the roles and responsibilities of the various parts of the organization contributing to managing the risk;
- interfaces between the project and other functions in the performing organization, as well as the relationship with external organizations working on the project.

Risk evaluation criteria

Risk evaluation is done against a set of criteria that enables risks to be compared and evaluated on a similar basis. Therefore, quantitative evaluation involves comparison of a quantitative level of risk against quantitative criteria. For example, if one criterion is that cost overruns exceed 10 per cent of total budget, then the financial manager must be alerted when this situation arises and a recovery plan developed by the team. Both the sponsor and financial manager must approve the plan. The same approach is valid for qualitative criteria. (See below under 'Types of analysis', p 289, for more detail.)

The performing organization's risk guide is an important input to the development of risk evaluation criteria by the project team. Decisions as to what criteria are appropriate should carefully consider the STEEPOL elements given above and their relevance to the project context. Stakeholder perception and the performing organization's policies, goals and objectives, as contained in the Business Wrapper, are essential factors to consider when developing the criteria.

Criteria are further influenced by the specific and unique aspects of a project, which distinguish it from other organization initiatives. The project management process and business results will form part of the risk evaluation analysis and be measured against their stated objectives.

Risk identification

This process involves identifying the risks that need to be managed. Comprehensive identification using a well-structured systematic process is essential, as risks that are not identified at the early stages of projects could result in major implementation problems downstream. The identification should include all risks, whether they are under the control of the performing organization or not. The following steps indicate a method of risk identification.

Develop a structure

This involves breaking down the project into a logical framework for identification and analysis. The proposal and business case described in Chapter 5 and the project definition phase of the ODPM process explained in Chapter 8 together provide a sound basis for the development of such a framework. The DBS, milestone objective chart and milestone responsibility chart are ideal breakdown tools.

List potential risks (what can happen)

The result of this step is a comprehensive list of events that could affect each element in the structure referred to above. These events are then considered in more detail to determine what can happen. The generic risk areas referred to under the heading 'The project context' above are an important input to this step.

- Sources of generic risk and areas of impact provide a framework for risk identification and analysis.
- Sources of risk include human behaviour and natural events, as well as the STEEPOL elements already identified.

Areas of impact include costs, people, stakeholders, performance, resource base, timing and schedule of activities, environment, intangibles and organizational behaviour.

Scenarios and causes (how and why things can happen)

After listing possible events, the causes and scenarios must be considered – how and why each event could occur. It is important at this point that the significant causes are well understood and documented.

Tools and techniques

Management tools and techniques used to identify risks include brainstorming, issues generation, purpose, scope and objectives analysis, deliverables breakdown structures, milestone objective charts, checklists, judgements based on experience and records, flow analysis, systems analysis and scenario analysis.

The approach used depends on the nature of the project and the types of risk being analysed. A risk event in a 'high risk' project that has the potential for serious impact on an organization will require a comprehensive and detailed application of tools and techniques, while a 'low risk' project would require a lighter approach.

Risk analysis

Risk is analysed by estimating the likelihood of the event occurring and the consequences or impact of the event if it does occur, within the context of the project criteria and control measures. The aims of the analysis are to prioritize the risks – separating the minor, acceptable risks from the major risks – and to provide data to assist in the evaluation and treatment of risks.

Initial and detailed analysis

An integral part of the proposal and business case development is the development of an initial risk analysis. The result is that low risk events are excluded from detailed analysis. These should be documented to demonstrate the completeness of analysis and be available for review as the project progresses along the life cycle.

Determine existing controls

It is important to identify and understand the organization's management and technical systems and procedures for controlling risk. The project should consider the interface with and integration of these controls into the management of the project.

Likelihood and consequences (impacts)

Next, the likelihood of events occurring and the magnitude of their impacts are evaluated in the context of the organization and project controls. Likelihood and impacts are combined in a matrix that results in a level of risk, often referred to as the 'severity level' (see 'Types of analysis' below).

This analysis uses judgements and assumptions based on information. To minimize the effect of any subjective bias, the best available information sources and techniques should be used when analysing likelihood and impacts. Such sources include:

● relevant experience;
● historic records;
● industry practices;
● published literature;
● marketing research;
● specialist and expert judgements;
● experiments and prototypes;
● economic models.

Some of the techniques include:

● structured interviews with subject matter experts;
● individual assessments using questionnaires;
● computer and other modelling;

- influence diagrams;
- decision tree analysis;
- probability analysis.

For the purposes of recording and analysis downstream in the life cycle, the confidence placed on the estimates of the level of risk should be included in the analysis. The confidence is indicated qualitatively – such as high, medium or low confidence in the estimates of risk being considered. The project participants and functional managers have input into the level of risk assessment.

Types of analysis

Depending on the needs of the project and the information available, risk analysis can be undertaken to various degrees of refinement. Analysis may be qualitative, semi-quantitative, quantitative, or a combination of the three. Most business projects of a small to medium size can survive with qualitative and some semi-quantitative analysis. Complex business projects and large engineering projects require quantitative and some qualitative analysis.

In practice, as the project progressively elaborates, the first analysis is mostly qualitative, and gives a general indication of the level of risk (at the proposal and business case stage). Later, during the project definition phase, it may be necessary to undertake more specific quantitative analysis.

The types of analysis are described in detail in AS/NZS 4360:1995. A brief overview is quoted here, followed by guidelines for application in a project context.

(a) **Qualitative analysis.** Qualitative analysis uses word form or descriptive scales to describe the likelihood of each event arising and its consequences. These scales can be adapted or adjusted to suit the circumstances and different descriptions may be used for different risks.
Qualitative analysis is used:
(i) as an initial activity to identify risks which require more detailed analysis;
(ii) where the level of risk does not justify the time and effort required for a fuller analysis; or
(iii) where the numerical data are inadequate for a quantitative analysis.

A tool that can be used to assist in the qualitative analysis of risk is the project risk analysis matrix shown in Table B.2. This matrix can be used to assess the likelihood of the risk occurring and the consequences/impacts of the risk. The result of this analysis is the severity level, expressed in a qualitative manner. This enables an initial prioritization of risks.

In the matrix:

H = High risk; detailed analysis and management planning required at upper management levels.

S = Significant risk; sponsor/upper management input required, project manager coordinates.

M = Moderate risk; project and functional management responsibility.

L = Low risk; project manager and team responsibility.

Table B.2   Risk analysis matrix

Consequence/impact

Likelihood of occurrence		Major	High	Moderate	Low
	Almost certain	H	H	S	M
	Likely	H	S	S	M
	Moderate	S	M	M	L
	Unlikely	L	L	L	L

The severity level does not determine whether a risk should be managed – all risks must be addressed and managed and have contingency plans and strategies devised. The severity level simply indicates the intensity of management required.

(b) **Semi-quantitative analysis.** In semi-quantitative analysis, qualitative scales such as those described above are given values. The number allocated to each description does not have to bear an accurate relationship to the actual magnitude of likelihood or consequence. The numbers can be combined by any one of a range of formulae provided that the system used for prioritization matches the system chosen for assigning numbers and combining them. The objective is to produce a more detailed prioritization than is usually achieved in the qualitative analysis, not to suggest any realistic values for risk such as is attempted in quantitative analysis. (AS/NZS 4360:1995).

The combination of levels of consequence/impact and likelihood of occurrence can be expressed numerically, in a range such as 1 to 64, where 1 is extremely high and 16 is very low. The number is referred to as the severity level (Table B.3).

Table B.3   Severity level matrix

Consequence/impact

Likelihood of occurrence		Major (8)	High (6)	Moderate (4)	Low (2)
	Almost certain (8)	H (64)	H (48)	S (32)	M (16)
	Likely (6)	H (48)	S (36)	S (24)	M (12)
	Moderate (4)	S (32)	M (24)	M (16)	L (8)
	Unlikely (2)	L (16)	L (12)	L (8)	L (4)

As a further improvement to both the qualitative and semi-quantitative analysis, the likelihood of an event can be broken down into two further elements: exposure and probability.

Exposure relates to how often a source of risk could arise, and probability is the chance that when the risk does arise, certain consequences will follow. This refinement can be built into the above matrix by first analysing the likelihood of occurrence in terms of frequency of risk source arising (high, medium, low) and the probability that consequences will follow (high, medium, low). The result will be nine combinations for the likelihood of occurrence that will need to be integrated into the matrix. For more detail, readers are referred to Australian/New Zealand Standard® AS/NZS 4360:1995:

(c) **Quantitative analysis.** Quantitative analysis uses numerical values (rather than descriptive scales used in qualitative and semi-quantitative analysis) for both likelihood and consequences using data from a variety of sources [such as those referred to under 'Likelihood and consequences' above]. The quality of the analysis depends on the accuracy and completeness of the numerical values used.

Likelihood is usually expressed as either:
(i) a probability;
(ii) a frequency; or
(iii) a combination of exposure and probability (AS/NZS 4360:1995).

Quantitative analysis can be used in a wide range of risk analyses – financial risk ratios, risks in the health sector, fatality risk calculations on roads, and simulation results. Complex and large projects may require modelling to simulate the final product and outcome, as precedents or historic data do not exist. Modelling can be complex and expensive, and careful consideration must be given to the performance criteria, design and construction and value of the analysis before committing the required resources.

Sensitivity analysis

Sensitivity analysis is a technique used to assess the variability of quantitative factors subject to different scenarios. For example, the return on investment (ROI) resulting from implementing a project is based on assumptions relating to certain costs, market conditions, competitors, project costs and timings, and production volumes and costs. Considering the assumptions as factors and varying them individually or in combination and then observing the effect on the ROI would typically be a sensitivity analysis.

Sensitivity analysis can be required: 1) when the estimates made in the quantitative analysis are too imprecise to test the effect of changes in assumptions and data; 2) to test the sensitivity of the model to changes in numeric values as various scenarios are analysed.

Risk evaluation

Risk evaluation compares the risks derived from the analysis process with previously established risk criteria. This enables the prioritization of the list of risks and assists with deciding whether the risk can be accepted and treated. An example of such a list is shown in Table B.4.

Table B.4 Example of project risk register

Project report no:						Date:		
Current rank	Prior rank	RISK **What can happen? How it can happen?**	Occurrence AC L M U	Impact Maj Hi Mo L		Severity level	Existing controls	
1		Union injunction/consultation on redundancy provisions; risk introduction of legal proceedings	Likely – new to organization L	Major – to change programme Maj		H (48)	Poor	
2		Achieving and retaining sector and external stakeholder confidence	Likely – currently not good L	Major – affects senior management credibility Maj		H (48)	Good	
3		Service delivery drop during implementation of restructuring	Moderate – operations are aware M	Major – public at risk Maj		S (32)	Average	
4		Management of this project inadequate	Moderate – project new to organization M	Major – performance will be poor Maj		S (32)	Average	
5		Responsibility for the strategy and design component not clear	Moderate – organization has experience M	High – project will falter Hi		S (32)	Average	
6		Priority that project has in the organization, the sector and with other stakeholders is not clear	Likely – priorities new to organization L	Moderate – difficult to manage project Mo		S (24)	Poor	
7		Completion of the change strategy is delayed	Unlikely – history shows late sometimes U	High – unfocused change Hi		L (16)	Good	

The comparison should be carried out on a consistent basis. So qualitative evaluation involves comparing a qualitative level of risk against qualitative criteria, and similarly for a quantitative evaluation. Decisions should take account of the wider context of the risk and include consideration of the ability of external parties to carry the risk. As a guiding principle, the organization most able to carry the risk should be responsible for that risk.

The project objectives and potential opportunity that could result from accepting the risk should be considered. If risks do not fall in the low or acceptable category they should be treated using one or more of the options set out in the next section.

Risk treatment

Risk treatment involves identifying the range of options for treating risk, assessing those options, preparing risk treatment plans and implementing them.

Identifying options for risk treatment

Once risks have been identified they may be treated by using one or more options. Treatment options can be classified into the following general groups.

Avoidance

This means avoiding the activity or factor that causes the risk without having a detrimental effect on the project scope, organization, cost, time and quality. Avoiding a risk could require changes to scope, planning, technique, design and so on.

Organizations and people that are naturally risk averse may introduce new risks or increase the importance of other risks by trying to avoid a particular risk. Risk aversion can result in:

- avoiding making decisions to resolve major issues;
- selecting treatment options that are low risk and thereby increasing downstream ownership and operational risks; for example if achieving stakeholder agreement on the project plan is avoided because it would be too difficult or slow, the consequent risk to ownership and effective operationalizing is high;
- not making critical choices or avoiding the resolution of key issues, which results in confusion for the project team and the loss of authority for those who should be responsible for making these decisions;
- failure to treat the risk, resulting in a fire-fighting culture that eventually becomes a way of doing business. Those who continually put out fires are often created heroes – but in some cases they are the arsonists!

Acceptance

Acceptance and retention are often confused. Acceptance is a clear decision that the risk should be accepted by the organization and form part of the treatment process.

Abatement

This generally describes the combination of reducing the possible impact and the probability of occurrence to diminish the severity of loss should the risk occur.

Reducing the likelihood of risk events occurring can be achieved through actions such as organization audit and compliance processes, formal project health checks, and reviews of specifications, analysis/design and implementation, project management, portfolio management, quality assurance, training, supervision, testing and research and development. An example could be changes in procurement procedures to ensure that materials arrive on time.

Reducing the impact of the risk events is more focused on mitigation and containment of the consequences. This can include contingency planning, contractual conditions and arrangements, disaster recovery plans, minimizing the exposure to the sources of risk, portfolio planning, stakeholder relations and design features. Examples are standby equipment, additional personnel, increasing time and cost, and accepting a lower level of quality.

Transfer

This involves shifting the risk burden from one party to another by contractual or other means such as partnerships and joint ventures. Insuring against the risk is a means of transferring risk.

It is important to appreciate that transferring risk to other parties will reduce the risk to the organization, but not necessarily the overall risk to stakeholders. Therefore, transferring risk may introduce different risks to the organization.

Retention

Risks can be retained by default, for example if there has been a failure to identify a risk, or a risk has emerged during the project process and the organization must retain it.

Assessing risk treatment options (risk reduction measures)

Treatment options should be assessed considering the extent of risk reduction and the extent of benefits or opportunities created. Options should be considered individually and in combination with others, with the aim of reducing the overall level of risk.

Selecting the most appropriate option or combination involves balancing the total cost of implementation against the benefits derived. As a rule the cost of managing risks should be commensurate with the benefits obtained.

It is clear that an option should be implemented if large risk reduction can be obtained at a relatively low cost. In other cases, the options for risk reduction may be uneconomic, and considered judgements need to be made. Special care should be taken when considering rare but severe risks, which may warrant risk reduction measures that are not justifiable on strictly economic grounds. For example, the survival of an organization following a major earthquake could not be constrained by cost factors.

In some situations the risk level may be high but considerable opportunities could result from taking the risk, for example bidding low to enter a market or introducing new technology. Risk assessment in this scenario needs to consider the costs of risk treatment and the rectifying of potential consequences versus the opportunities afforded by taking the risk.

It is also important to consider how risk is perceived by affected stakeholders, as well as the most appropriate ways to communicate to those stakeholders.

Preparing the risk treatment plan

The plan should document how the chosen risk treatment option will be implemented. It will need to identify:

- the selected option;
- responsibilities for managing implementation;
- a time schedule for implementation;
- the expected outcome of the treatment;
- financial implications;
- performance measures;
- the review process.

The risk plan is usually developed during the project definition phase as described in Chapter 8. Table B.5 shows a typical risk plan.

The key events, or milestones, in the risk treatment plan should be integrated into the overall project planning and specifically with the deliverables breakdown structure. These milestones can then be monitored against the overall project performance as well as the risk implementation plan.

Implementing the plan

Responsibility for implementing the risk treatment should be allocated to those best able to control the risk. The successful implementation of a risk management plan relies on an effective management system that specifies the treatment chosen, assigns responsibilities and accountabilities for actions and monitors them against set criteria.

Table B.5 Project risk treatment and plan

Project report no: Date:

Current rank	Prior rank	RISK What can happen How it can happen	Occurrence AC L M U	Impact Maj Hi Mo L	Severity level	Preferred risk treatment option	Management responsibility	Timetable for implementation	How will risk and treatment options be monitored
1		Union injunction/ consultation on provisions; risk introduction of legal proceedings	Likely – new to organization L	Major – to change programme Maj	H (48)	Direction to team on what planning and design work can go ahead; must follow good practice industrial strategy.			
2		Achieving and retaining retaining sector and external stakeholder confidence	Likely – currently not good L	Major – affects senior management credibility Maj	H (48)	Sponsor to develop overall strategy and objectives for each area. The achievement responsibility lies with planning and communications functional managers.			
3		Service delivery drop during implementation of restructuring	Moderate – operations are aware M	Major – public at risk Maj	S (32)	Operations sub-project to plan for risk. Develop and monitor indicators and adjust navigation plan			
4		Management of this project inadequate	Moderate – project new to organization M	Major – performance will be poor Maj	S (32)	Ensure sound project planning and management agreed with stakeholders. External health check and advice.			
5		Responsibility for the strategy and design component not clear	Moderate – organization has experience M	High – project will falter Hi	S (32)	Planning and development to agree responsibility for this area and communicate to organization and team.			
6		Priority that project has in the organization, the sector and with other stakeholders is not clear	Likely – priorities new to organization L	Moderate – difficult to manage project Mo	S (24)	Mandate from CEO (sponsor) regarding the high priority of project. Direction required on how organization's resourcing/budgets will be affected.			
7		Completion of the change strategy is delayed	Unlikely – history shows late sometimes U	High – unfocused change Hi	L (16)	Build on planning of xx.xx.xx; process development by Strategy Group and Change Strategy development by Change Strategists.			

Monitoring and review

It is important to monitor the effectiveness of the risk treatment plan and its activities, and the management system set up to control implementation.

Risks are generally not static. Ongoing review is essential to ensure that the plan remains relevant and manageable. Factors that affect the likelihood and impacts of a risk may change, resulting in the need to reconsider the appropriateness and cost of the treatment option. It is essential to regularly review the risk management process as an integral part of the project management process.

COST MANAGEMENT

Costing concepts

In order to understand the concepts of cost estimating and budgeting, we must first define what 'costs' mean in the context of a project.

Costs are usually defined by accountants as 'resources sacrificed or foregone to achieve a specific objective'. This definition has relevance on a project, where resources such as equipment, materials, human resources and services are consumed in order to achieve the desired objectives (the project and the deliverables). This discussion covers the concepts of cost, cost estimating and budgeting as applied to projects.

The following three types of cost influence the costing of a project:

- **Fixed costs.** These are costs that are incurred at a specific point in time. In this category would be costs such as the establishment of the project accommodation, the purchase of specialized testing equipment and the purchase of computer equipment or software. Fixed costs are typically one-time costs.
- **Quantity-related costs.** These costs are incurred in proportion to the amount of work produced. Material and direct human resource costs to produce the project's products or outcomes are in this category. These costs will increase if the amount of work increases and will decrease if the amount of work decreases.
- **Time-related costs.** Costs that are incurred by the provision of resources and services such as supervision, management, hire of equipment and rental of accommodation on a regular basis (daily, monthly, weekly) over the duration of the project.

To guide decisions, managers want to know the cost of something. This may be a product, a group of products, a service rendered, a human resource hour, a cubic metre of concrete, a kilometre of highway, or any other activity or thing related to the project. This 'something' is called a cost objective (or cost object) and is defined as any element for which a separate measurement of costs is desired. Costing is the process of determining the cost of doing or obtaining that 'something'. Cost accumulation is the collection of the cost data in an organized way through a cost collection system.

Why is costing needed? For a number of reasons, the most important of which are:

- for monitoring the performance of a project against budget;
- for controlling the expenditures and income of a project;
- for decision making (cost, time, quality, scope trade-offs);
- as a basis for claims;
- to assist in trade-off decisions between increased costs and the payment of penalties;
- to assist in preparing estimates for future projects.

It is important to understand the influence that different types of costs have on project costing. There is always a trade-off between the elements of scope, quality, cost and time. Fixed costs are normally impervious to changes in scope, quality and time. Quantity-related costs and time-related costs are not. If the scope of the project changes, quantities may change, which will cause a change to all costs related to quantity. In turn, if the element of time changes due to acceleration or schedule overruns, the time-related costs will change. Poor quality could mean rework, which in turn could increase time or quantities causing associated costs to change. Proper classification and recording of the cost elements assists the project manager to determine the impact of time, scope and quality changes on cost and assists in the determination of claims and trade-offs between penalties and increases in production.

Costs are monitored against cost budgets. The following description defines a cost budget from a project perspective:

> The cost budget is a quantitative expression of a plan of action and an aid to coordination, monitoring and control. It quantifies the expectations regarding project revenue, cost and time baselines and is the culmination of a series of decisions resulting from a careful evaluation of the project's scope, estimates and time-plan.

Note that the definition above refers to time. The interaction between time and cost is explored later. Cost does not only refer to money. Items such as the quantity of resources used and the quantity of work units produced should also be estimated, budgeted, monitored and recorded wherever applicable.

Estimates and budgets

It is important to establish the difference between the terms 'estimate' and 'budget'. These terms are often used in the same context, but they do differ. An **estimate** is done in order to determine what the project may cost and is normally based on some form of specification such as a bill of materials or a bill of quantities, or it may be prepared from a work specification such as a WBS or DBS. The term estimate tends to be used during the early phases of the project life cycle.

A **budget** on the other hand is normally used during the execution phase of the project life cycle and sets the quantity and money objectives for a particular item of work, outcome or resource within a project. A budget is a statement of the base against which the project will be controlled. It is usually prepared from an estimate but is more detailed.

Estimates and budgets are also used for different purposes. Estimates are used to take feasibility decisions and to choose between alternatives. Budgets are used to monitor, control and evaluate progress and efficiency.

Although budgets on a project may change as circumstances change, there is usually only one budget against which monitoring takes place. In contrast, estimating is a continuous process. It starts when the initial project concept is formulated and is expanded as more accurate and detailed plans are developed, leading eventually to the project budget. Each phase in the planning process is accompanied by a particular type of estimate based on the information available at that time. Below is a brief description of four recognized types of estimates. The percentages stated indicate the likely over- and under-budget difference:

- **Order-of-magnitude estimate.** This is made without any detailed data and may have an accuracy of approximately 35%. It is normally prepared during the early phases of the project and is based on past experience, scale factors or capacity estimates.
- **Approximate estimate (or top-down estimate).** This is also made without any detailed data and may have an accuracy of approximately 15%. It is prorated from previous projects similar in scope and capacity (and may also be called estimating by analogy, rule of thumb) or from an indexed cost of similar activities adjusted for capacity and technology.
- **Elemental cost estimate.** This is done from more detailed data and may have an accuracy of approximately 10%. Since more detail is available, the estimate can be broken into elements, with each then estimated using a similar process as for the approximate estimate.
- **Definitive estimate (or detailed estimate).** This is prepared from well-defined data, bills of materials or quantities (including vendor quotes), reasonably complete specifications, plans, unit prices and estimates to complete. Since this estimate is done in detail, it usually has an accuracy of approximately 5%. The final operating budgets are prepared from this estimate.

Estimating on a project does not stop once the final baseline budgets are set. As part of the monitoring process, the project team will continuously estimate the amount of money still required to complete the project. This estimate is known as the estimate to complete. Adding this to the moneys already committed, an estimate at completion is obtained. These figures allow forward funding to be planned and allow action to prevent budget overruns, such as replanning production rate changes or changes in work methods.

Using the WBS for estimating

It is rare for estimates and budgets to be expressed as one global figure for the entire project. They are usually broken down into smaller elements to allow for easier management.

The concept of breaking down a project into manageable components is discussed in the section describing the work breakdown structure (WBS) at the start of this appendix (p 279).

Once the WBS has been developed and the codes assigned, it is possible to attach cost estimate information to each code. Basically this consists of determining the elements of cost (resources) such as equipment, human resources, materials, subcontractors and overheads that may be attached to each component in the WBS. In many industries, these elements are referred to as 'allowables'. This term means exactly what it says. They are what is 'allowed' to be expended (quantity and money) on resources to carry out a specific task.

Each component of the lowest level of the WBS is then evaluated and the use of each resource or 'allowable' to perform that task is estimated. These resources then form the lowest level of the WBS. They are added to the code list but rarely to the WBS diagram.

The estimates calculated will be both quantitative and monetary. Certain resources such as one-time payments or fees may not have quantities attached. Once estimates are attached to each code in the WBS, they can be collated to determine the estimated costs for each component of each level of the WBS and ultimately for the project.

Certain estimates are based on production rate assumptions. In this case, the assumptions should be kept for performance measures or objectives during the project implementation phase.

The cost breakdown structure (CBS)

The section above describes the basic process of developing the budgets or estimates. In practice, however, other factors must also be taken into consideration, such as the complexity of specific tasks, wastage and risks such as weather or lack of scope information. These factors must be carefully considered and provided for in the budget, possibly by increasing quantities, unit rates, or lump sum amounts. There will, of course, always be cases where it will not be possible to determine a reasonable cost estimate. In such situations, a figure might be set that is deliberately higher than the best estimate. This safety factor (or 'sludge' factor as it is sometimes called) is the project's cost contingency and a method for compensating for incomplete data or risk. Over-estimating is acceptable provided the estimate is not unreasonably high, and it is not applied too often. Remember that it is better to be conservative (higher) rather than optimistic (lower) if there is uncertainty.

There is the danger, however, that when the project is executed, extra provisions may be assumed to be available for consumption even if the situation for which they were allowed does not occur. For this reason, it is common practice to lump such provisions together under contingency codes, which are then allocated to operating budgets when a situation arises that requires more resources.

Budgeting does not only involve costs. When projects are done for the purpose of earning revenue, that revenue must be budgeted for either in total or preferably against the WBS elements. This is done in a similar manner to estimating costs, except that the question is 'What will we earn from doing this piece of work?' rather than 'What will it cost to do this work?'

The addition of the above budget elements expands the WBS by adding items that are not necessarily related to work. When this is done the resultant structure or code list becomes the cost breakdown structure (CBS) and the allocated codes are cost codes. The code list in Table B.6 shows the additions to the WBS example used in the discussion on the WBS at the start of this appendix. The additional cost codes are highlighted.

Table B.6 Costs codes added to the WBS

1. Project ABC	Factory	
1.1 Pickling Plant		
1.1.1 Buildings		
1.1.1.1 Structure		
1.1.1.1.1	Civils	
1.1.1.1.2	Excavate	
	1.1.1.1.2.1	Equipment
	1.1.1.1.2.2	Materials
	1.1.1.1.2.3	Human resources
	1.1.1.1.2.4	Subcontractors
	1.1.1.1.2.5	**Overheads**
	1.1.1.1.2.6	**Contingencies**
	1.1.1.1.2.7	**Revenue**
1.1.1.1.3	Steel fixing	
	1.1.1.1.3.1	Equipment
	1.1.1.1.3.2	Materials
	1.1.1.1.3.3.	Human resources
	1.1.1.1.3.4.	Subcontractors
	1.1.1.1.3.5	**Overheads**
	1.1.1.1.3.6	**Contingencies**
	1.1.1.1.3.7	**Revenue**

Table B.6 shows overheads, contingencies and revenue at the same level for each element of the CBS. This is not a rule. Many CBSs show these at higher levels. Where they are placed will depend on how easy they are to calculate and allocate to. For example, if revenue cannot be calculated at level 5 but only at level 3, then the CBS shown in Table B.7 may be more practical.

Using budgets

When creating the budgets, it is important to keep in mind that they are the cost/revenue targets or objectives for the project against which progress and performance will be monitored. As such, these budgets need to be able to be identified in a way that will allow actual numbers to be allocated against them. If this cannot happen, their purpose becomes obscure and can lead to misinterpretation. Codes should also be kept to a minimum. Having too many codes makes it difficult to decide against which one a

Table B.7 Alternative cost coding

1.	Project ABC Factory

1. Project ABC Factory
   1.1 Pickling Pant
       1.1.1 Buildings
             1.1.1.1 Structure
                     1.1.1.1.1 Civils
                     1.1.1.1.2 Excavate
                                1.1.1.1.2.1 Equipment
                                1.1.1.1.2.2 Materials
                                1.1.1.1.2.3 Human resources
                                1.1.1.1.2.4 Subcontractors
                                1.1.1.1.2.5 Overheads
                                1.1.1.1.2.6 Contingencies
       **1.1.9 Pickling
               plant
               revenue**

specific cost must be allocated. This leads to the 'dartboard' syndrome – where it would be easier to arrange the codes on a dartboard and throw a dart to select one!

Table B.8 shows a simple estimating table for part of a CBS. Note that it shows a column labelled Profit/Loss. This is a calculation of the revenue less the total costs and is useful in projects done for profit where it then becomes an objective.

The time factor

As projects are carried out over a period of time, it is obvious that costs are expended and revenue earned over that same period. The budgeting model above gives the numbers in lump sums, as they should be at the end of the project. On some simple projects of short duration, this is normally all that is required. On larger projects of long duration that involve large quantities of resources (and therefore money), the time factor has to be taken into consideration. This is done by spreading the calculated budgets over the time it will take to perform the tasks to which they relate. The time could be obtained from milestone charts, Gantt charts and critical path networks developed for the project.

There are different methods for spreading the budgets or estimates over time. Which method is used depends on the detail of data available and the required level of accuracy of the estimate or budget. A combination of methods can be used on a single project. The more common spreading methods are explained here:

- **Straight line.** The budgeted amount is divided by the number of time periods to which it relates and an equal amount is then allocated to each period.
- **Percentage profile.** A profile is built that indicates that, for example, 60 per cent of the budget occurs in the first five periods, 10 per cent over the next three, and 30 per

Table B.8   Cost estimate table

		Equipment	Human resources	Material	Sub-contractors	Total cost	Revenue	Profit/Loss
1.1	Pickling plant							
1.1.1	Buildings							
1.1.1.1	Structure							
1.1.1.1.1	Civils	34,000	29,000	14,000		77,000	86,000	9,000
1.1.1.1.2	Excavate	44,000	29,500			73,500	94,000	20,500
1.1.1.1.3	Steel fixing	2,500	1,800	16,980	1,800	39,280	42,000	2,720
1.1.1.1.4	Shuttering		30,000	40,620		70,620	100,000	29,380
1.1.1.1.5	Concreting	10,600	5,000	78,000		93,600	110,000	16,400
1.1.1.1.6	Steelwork			129,000	159,000	288,000	310,000	22,000
1.1.1.1	Total structure	91,100	95,300	278,600	177,000	642,000	742,000	100,000

cent over the remaining four. The budgeted amounts are split according to the percentages and 'straight-lined' within the corresponding split periods.

● **Start/end.** A percentage of the budget is taken in the first period and the rest in the last period. No budget is allocated to the intermediate periods. Alternatively, all the budget can be taken in the first or last period.

● **Detailed.** Each period is examined and a budget is prepared specifically for that period. Once the period budgets have been calculated, it is possible to determine the cash flow of costs expended and revenue earned spread over the duration of the project. Table B.9 shows a time breakdown for the budgeted total costs shown in Table B.8.

Project cash flow

Aggregating each period's budgets results in the cash flow for the project, which can be expressed as a graph. These graphs are also known as 'S-curves' due to their distinctive shape. Figure B.3 shows a typical cash flow graph.

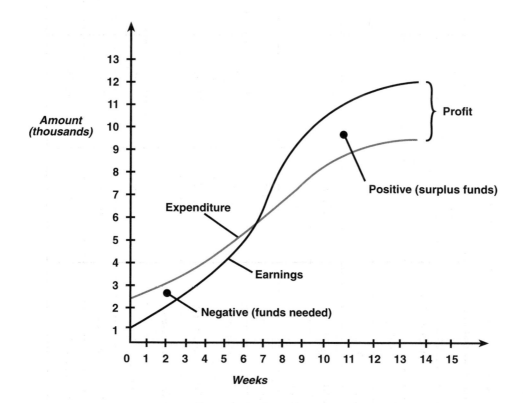

Figure B.3 Typical cash flow graph or 'S'-curve

Table B.9   Example of a cash flow schedule

		Period 1	Period 2	Period 3	Period 5	Total
1.1	Pickling plant					
1.1.1	Buildings					
1.1.1.1	Structure					
1.1.1.1.1	Civils	77,000				77,000
1.1.1.1.2	Excavate	9,375	27,375	30,375	6,375	73,500
1.1.1.1.3	Steel fixing	820	18,820	17,820	1,820	39,280
1.1.1.1.4	Shuttering	10,000	20,000	30,000	10,620	70,620
1.1.1.1.5	Concreting	13,000	33,800	36,400	10,400	93,600
1.1.1.1.6	Steelwork			138,000	150,000	288,000
Total structure cost		110,195	99,995	252,595	179,215	642,000
1.1.11.9	Revenue	109,500	108,250	268,250	256,000	742,000
Surplus/Shortfall		−695	8,255	15,655	76,785	100,000

Why are cash flow schedules and graphs needed? As well as acting as objectives for specific periods, the cash flow schedules and graphs can be used to determine the funding requirements of the project.

Subtracting the costs from the revenue gives an indication of surpluses and shortfalls. If there is a shortfall, funding must be obtained, and in the case of a surplus, funds are available to be used to offset shortfalls or for investment. Where funding is a problem, the sequence of work packages can be rescheduled within the project timeframe so that the costs and revenues are 'smoothed' over time. In Figure B.3, the project will need funding until approximately week 8, after which it funds itself and produces funds.

It is important to note that a project does not generate profits until the final accounting is done – a project only delivers a profit at the end. During the project, any surplus funds remain the property of the project until it finishes. The reason is that the surplus could be a reflection of contingencies not taken which could still be required in the future. This is often a source of conflict between the project and the financial department.

The above discussion assumes that the project is being done for profit.

Inflation and escalation

For long-duration projects, it is important to consider the effect of escalation and inflation. Existing standards, such as the cost of living indices, inflation rates and escalation indices for various materials and services, can be used to adjust any estimates and budgets. This compensates for the effects of escalation and inflation in a realistic manner.

It is usual to negotiate the method of calculating escalation with the client. Quotations and estimates are always expressed in current terms and the differences due to escalation are calculated as the project progresses or at the end.

Costing versus accounting

A question often raised is that since financial accounting systems always exist in an organization, why are project costing systems required? Financial accounting by definition deals with financial issues (money) and occurs against the fiscal calendar of the organization. Project cost accounting deals with more than just money. Resource and material consumption as well as production rates are costed, monitored and controlled in both quantitative and monetary terms. These are monitored against the project's time schedule, which does not necessarily relate to the organization's fiscal calendar. The fiscal accounts are coded according to the dictates of balance sheets, income statements and so on. The CBS codes relate to the work to be done and are different from the fiscal codes.

A further difference relates to timing. Broadly speaking, in accounting, a cost occurs when payment is made and revenue when payment is banked. Normally, payment occurs some time after an invoice has been received, which in turn is presented some time after the delivery of the material or service. This time delay in cost reporting diminishes its usefulness in project management.

To be able to react to budget overruns early, project teams require more immediate cost information than that produced by the accounting process. To overcome this time delay it is usual to cost a project on timesheets, purchase orders issued, or on delivery of materials or services. This means that project costs at any point in time tend to be higher then those recorded in the accounting system. This concept is known as 'commitment costing' in that the cost is considered to occur when a commitment is made to spend the money (purchase orders and delivery of services) and not on actual payment (invoices and payrolls). Remember that the only control over money is the control over money not yet spent. The sooner we are aware of how much has been spent and how much we have left, the faster we can take action.

There is often conflict between the project and the finance department over the responsibility for costing activities. It is vital to resolve this early in the project and distinguish the differences between the functions of the finance department and those of the project cost engineer. Cost engineer is a role rather than a position. On construction projects, for example, this role is filled by the quantity surveyor. On other projects, a costing specialist in the finance department could do it. On small projects it could typically be the responsibility of the project manager.

The finance department is responsible for the organization's fiscal accounts and accounting procedures. In other words, they are responsible for ensuring that the organization's funds are used in a correct and auditable way, and for their allocated purpose. In short, the finance department controls the chequebook.

The cost engineer, on the other hand, monitors and controls costs and quantities on a project to ensure that the project achieves its objectives within the baseline cost budgets. The cost engineer also ensures that the budgets are applied in a cost-effective manner. The cost engineer does not sign any cheques. Any funding required by the project is always channelled through the finance department. In this manner they act as a control on the money transactions of the project and can advise on matters of a financial nature.

A finance manager should be one of the project manager's and cost engineer's closest allies. The finance manager should assist in the financial aspects of setting up project tasks and can assist in the interpretation of cost variances. Any questions the finance manager may have about the financial implications of a prospective change must be satisfied before the change is approved.

ESTIMATING TIME

Throughout the planning process, activity time (duration) must be estimated. This can be quite straightforward if the same or similar activities have been done before. Alternatively, the activities may not be within the previous experience of the project team, even if the project itself is similar to past endeavours.

Both familiar and new activities must be estimated. Estimating activity duration can be done in the following ways:

- Similar or sufficiently familiar activities can be estimated from previous experience. Care is still needed though, as the unfamiliar part of an activity can be underestimated, leading to overruns.
- New or unfamiliar activity duration is usually determined by the following method:
  - Determine what has to be done to achieve the activity. Convert the 'what' into a measurable work content, such as number of units, person-hours.
  - Consider the production rate of people, teams, machines, etc. Divide the work content by the expected production rate to get an indication of the estimated time.
  - Make adjustments for the learning curve effect, time off from work, machine breakdowns, productivity skills levels and material availability.

There will, of course, always be cases where it will not be possible to determine a reasonable time. In such situations, a duration might be set which is deliberately higher than the best estimate. This safety factor is the estimator's contingency and a method for compensating for incomplete data or for risk. Overestimating is acceptable provided the estimate is not unreasonably high and it is not applied too often. Remember that it is better to be conservative (higher) rather than optimistic (lower) if there is uncertainty.

Estimating activity time in a highly speculative or uncertain environment requires acknowledging that certain events will happen but their exact duration is not known. Consequently there is the possibility of a large variation between estimates and actual times for these activities. Time estimation in this situation can be based on a formula that accounts for variations and yields a weighted average as follows:

$$\text{Expected activity completion time (E)} = \frac{o + 4m + p}{6}$$

In this formula:

o = Most optimistic time
m = Most likely time
p = Most pessimistic time

The most optimistic time is the 'shortest' possible time to complete the activity. In this situation, all inputs to the activity are available at the earliest possible time, the work is correctly resourced and progresses as anticipated.

The most pessimistic time is the 'longest' possible time to complete the activity. This relates to a situation where all inputs to the activity are available late, the work is under-resourced and progresses sporadically.

The most likely time is the time that the activity would take if it were repeated many times and observed and recorded. Owing to the nature of project activities the most likely time tends to be closer to the most pessimistic time.

For example, estimating the activity duration for developing user requirements on a software project could have a most optimistic time of four weeks, a most pessimistic time of eight weeks, with a most likely time of seven weeks. Using the formula above, the estimated activity completion time would be calculated as follows:

Expected activity completion time $= \dfrac{4 + (4 \times 7) + 8}{6} = 6.66$ weeks

This approach is also used extensively with the PERT method, which is a variation of the critical path analysis method discussed later.

GANTT CHART

What is a Gantt chart?

One of the oldest methods of presenting time schedule information is the Gantt chart, developed around 1917 by Henry Gantt. A Gantt chart is one of the most convenient, most commonly used, easy-to-grasp presentations of project activities.

It is a two-dimensional graphical representation of the activities that make up the project. The vertical axis lists the project activities, one per line, while the horizontal axis indicates time. Once the scheduled start and completion dates for every activity have been determined, the Gantt chart can be constructed. Figure B.4 shows a typical Gantt chart as planned and Figure B.5 shows the same chart progressed.

An added value of the Gantt chart is that the activities are time-scaled, which provides a perspective not possible with other project charts such as network diagrams. A time-scaled network diagram can be developed which allows progress to be indicated similar to a Gantt chart. Networks are described in the next section, 'Critical path analysis'.

The Gantt chart is a particularly effective and easy-to-read method of indicating the actual current status of activities compared to the planned progress. As a result, the Gantt chart can be helpful in expediting, sequencing and reallocating resources to activities, as well as keeping track of progress. In addition, the charts can contain a number of specialized symbols to designate or highlight items of special concern to the situation being charted.

Advantages and disadvantages of the Gantt

The Gantt has the following general advantages over other planning tools such as network diagrams:

- Although they contain a great deal of information, they are easily understood.
- While they require frequent updating (as does any scheduling/control tool), they are easy to maintain.
- They provide a clear, simple picture of the state of the project.
- They are easy to construct and are not based on any mathematical model.
- The Gantt may be constructed without a critical path analysis (CPA) being needed. They can, however, also graphically represent the output of a CPA.

Figure B.4   Gantt chart planned

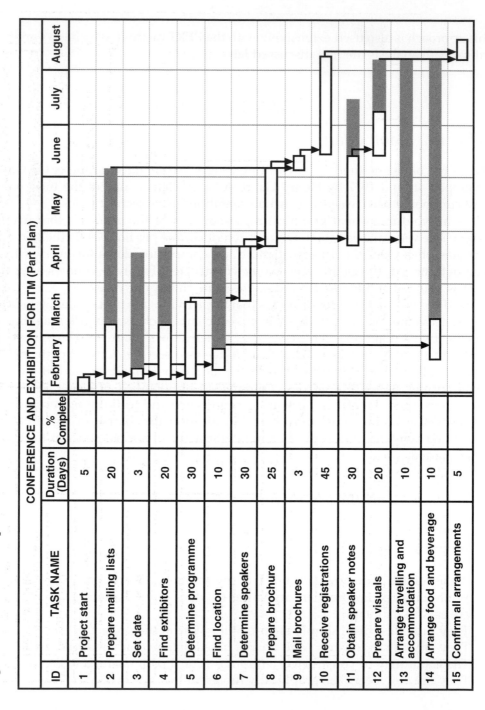

Figure B.5 Progressed Gantt chart

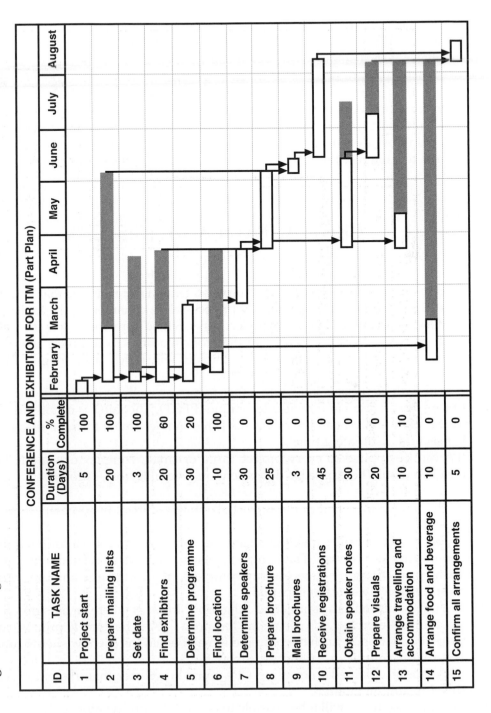

ID	TASK NAME	Duration (Days)	% Complete	February	March	April	May	June	July	August
1	Project start	5	100							
2	Prepare mailing lists	20	100							
3	Set date	3	100							
4	Find exhibitors	20	60							
5	Determine programme	30	20							
6	Find location	10	100							
7	Determine speakers	30	0							
8	Prepare brochure	25	0							
9	Mail brochures	3	0							
10	Receive registrations	45	0							
11	Obtain speaker notes	30	0							
12	Prepare visuals	20	0							
13	Arrange travelling and accommodation	10	10							
14	Arrange food and beverage	10	0							
15	Confirm all arrangements	5	0							

CONFERENCE AND EXHIBITION FOR ITM (Part Plan)

A close relationship exists between Gantt charts and CPA networks (PERT or CPM). Generally Gantt charts are derived from CPA networks by plotting the activity from its calculated earliest time for the length of its duration. If an activity has float, then this can be shown as a differently patterned bar at the back of the plotted activity bar.

The major disadvantage of the Gantt chart is that the relationships or dependencies between activities are not as explicit as in CPA networks. Unless connecting lines are drawn on the Gantt chart, it is not possible to determine the links between activities. Modern computer packages, however, can now show these connecting lines if required.

The Gantt chart has survived for more than 80 years. Considering that in 1917 Henry Gantt could not have visualized the proliferation of sophisticated project management tools and techniques, the Gantt chart continues to prove its usefulness beyond any doubt!

CRITICAL PATH ANALYSIS (CPA)

Introduction

What is critical path analysis (CPA)? Simply stated, it is a technique that determines the shortest time it will take to complete a project, while considering the logical flow and dependencies between the various project tasks. Stated conversely, it is the longest path through a project, which indicates all the work required to complete the project, and therefore determines the earliest time a project will finish. This longest path is also known as the critical path.

Critical path analysis is known by other names as well – critical path method (CPM) and project evaluation and review technique (PERT). The latter is a statistical approach to critical path analysis and involves the three-time estimate formula discussed in the earlier section 'Estimating time'.

CPA can be applied to every project, large or small, complex or simple. When and where CPA should be applied is dependent on several factors, as follows:

● Is the time component of the project absolutely critical to success – that is, is time fixed?
● Is the project complex, involving many organizations and disciplines requiring close monitoring and control? This complexity is not necessarily related to the project size.
● Is the project large (not necessarily complex), requiring large amounts of resources over a relatively short time period?
● Is a CPA required as a contractual obligation? In cases where an outside contractor is executing the project, the client may require a CPA to be done at proposal and/or at project initiation. A further requirement may be that the client wishes to monitor and control the contractor's progress using CPA.
● The benefit obtained from using CPA must be greater than the effort required to develop and maintain it.
● If CPA is not used, will it be possible to control the project efficiently?

- If the impact of a delay on a portion of the project or the complete project cannot be evaluated, what will the consequences be? Can this be evaluated without CPA?

This discussion is an introduction to CPA and in no way attempts to be a comprehensive handling of the topic. Readers needing a more in-depth discussion of the subject could check more detailed reference works, such as those by Moder, Phillips and Davis[64], Meredith and Mantel[60], Nicholas[67], Badiru[7], Ahuja[1], Lewis[53] and Lockyer[57].

CPA definitions

The terminology of critical path analysis can make it seem somewhat mysterious. The following definitions are essential to an understanding of CPA. The terms and definitions given are those for the precedence networking method, which is the most commonly used CPA method.

Activity

An activity is a specific task or set of tasks that is required to be executed to achieve the project. Activities consume resources and take time to complete. The time an activity takes is referred to as its duration. In a precedence network diagram, an activity is normally shown as a rectangle containing a description of the activity and its duration. It is the basic element of a precedence network diagram.

```
Activity A
6 days
```

Milestone

A milestone indicates a culmination of a series of activities and events. Milestones are route markers along the road to project completion. A milestone normally has a date attached to it, by which time the milestone must have been reached. Milestone dates are sometimes referred to as 'plug' dates.

Dependency links or logic links

Activities are connected together to form a network. In the precedence network diagram the dependency links or logic links between activities are indicated by lines.

Finish-to-start

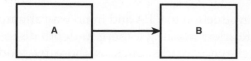

The arrowhead on the line indicates the direction of flow and thus the precedence. Activity A is the predecessor to activity B. Activity B is A's successor. The logical link shown here is called a 'finish-to-start' link, as it connects the finish of activity A to the start of activity B. This means that activity B cannot start until activity A has ended.

There are other logic links, as shown in the next two diagrams.

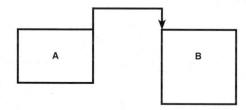

A start-to-start link shows that activities A and B can start at the same time.

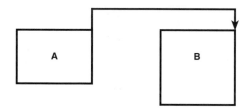

This link indicates that activity B cannot finish until activity A finishes.

A 'start-to-finish' link also exists, but although it is logically correct, it is never used and is rarely catered for in computer packages.

For the rest of this section, the examples use the 'finish-to-start' logic link.

Lead and lag

The dependency or logic links can themselves have a duration, which is called a lead or a lag depending on whether it is positive or negative. A lag is positive and indicates the number of time periods that must pass before the succeeding event can start. For example, a lag of +5 placed on a finish-to-start link means that activity B can start five time units after activity A has ended.

A lead is negative and indicates the number of time periods that a succeeding event can start before the end of its predecessor. For example, a lead of –5 placed on a finish-to-start link indicates that activity B can start five time units before activity A ends.

Activity sequencing

Activity sequencing entails arranging activities in sequence connected by logical links. This is often referred to as the technological sequence. Certain activities may be done in parallel while others may be done in series.

An activity sequence list showing immediate activity predecessors and durations is often used in CPA network development. An example of a sequencing table is shown in Table B.10.

Table B.10 Activity sequencing table

Activity description	Immediate predecessor	Duration (weeks)
Start	–	0
A	Start	16
B	Start	20
C	Start	30
D	B	15
E	B	10
G	D	3
H	D	16
J	A	15
K	J, G, E	12
Finish	K, H, C	0

The activity description column usually contains a short description of the activity. For simplicity of discussion, symbols have been used here. Immediate predecessor refers to the activities that have input to the activity under consideration, and creates the network logic. The duration is the expected activity completion time. This can be a one-time estimate or result from the three-time estimate discussed in the earlier section 'Estimating time' (p 307).

Network diagram

The visual representation of all the activities defining the project and the relationships between them is called a network diagram. Networks are usually drawn from left to right. Networks are logic diagrams that do not reflect activity durations in a graphic manner in the way of a Gantt chart. Networks are usually drawn from data in an activity sequence table. A large part of the so-called complexity of critical path analysis lies in the actual drawing and layout of the network diagram.

Figure B.6 shows the network diagram derived from the activity sequence table given above.

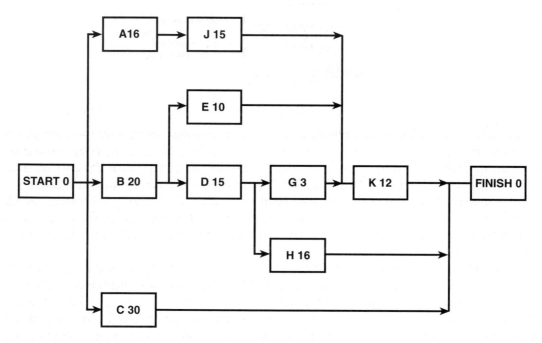

Figure B.6   Network diagram

Network path

This is a series of connected activities creating a path through a network. There are usually a number of paths running through a network.

Critical path

The critical path is the path of activities in a network which, if delayed, will delay the completion of the project. It is the sequence of critical activities that connects the project's start activity to its finish activity. The sum total of the activity durations along the critical path will give the duration of the project.

Calculating the critical path duration

The network described in the activity sequencing table above and shown as the network diagram will be used to illustrate the network calculations. The network calculations will result in a number of values being determined for each activity. All the values need to be recorded on the diagram or in a table. If recorded in the network diagram, the values are attached to the activity as follows.

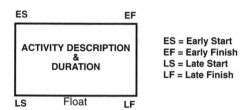

The early start time (ES) for an activity is the earliest time that an activity can start given that all its predecessor activities have been completed. The ES of an activity having no predecessor is always set to 0. The early finish time (EF) of an activity is the earliest time that an activity can be completed. It is equal to its ES time plus its estimated duration.

The ES time of an activity that has one predecessor is the EF of the predecessor. The ES time of an activity that has two or more predecessors is the greatest of the EF of all its predecessors. To calculate these times, work forward through the network – performing a forward pass.

The late start (LS) time and late finish time (LF) of an activity are the latest times at which an activity can start (LS) or be completed (LF) without affecting the project duration. The LS of an activity is equal to its LF minus its estimated duration. The LF of an activity that has only one successor is the LS of the successor. The LF of an activity having two or more successors is the least of the LS of all its successors. To calculate these times, work backwards through the network – performing a backward pass.

The forward pass

A forward pass is performed as follows:

1. Set the ES of the first activity in the network to 0 and its EF equal to the activity duration.
2. Then for each other activity in the network calculate its ES as the greatest of the EF of all its predecessor activities. Calculate each activity's EF as its ES plus its duration.

After performing the forward pass, the network now looks as shown in Figure B.7 (refer to the legend above).

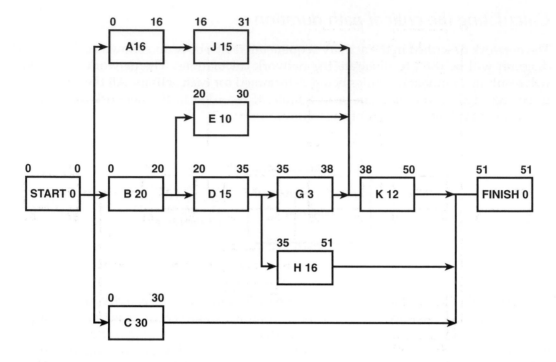

Figure B.7 The forward pass

The backward pass

The backward pass is performed as follows:

1. First set the LF of the last activity on the network to the EF of that activity. Calculate its LS as its LF minus the activity's duration.
2. Then for each other activity in the network calculate its LF as the least of the LS of all the activities for which it is the predecessor. Calculate each activity's LS as its LF minus its duration.

After performing the backward pass, the network now looks as shown in Figure B.8 (refer to the legend above).

The resulting network diagram indicates the various paths through the project network logic, the relationship between the various activities and paths through the network, and provides information on time duration – all of which are necessary to determine the critical path.

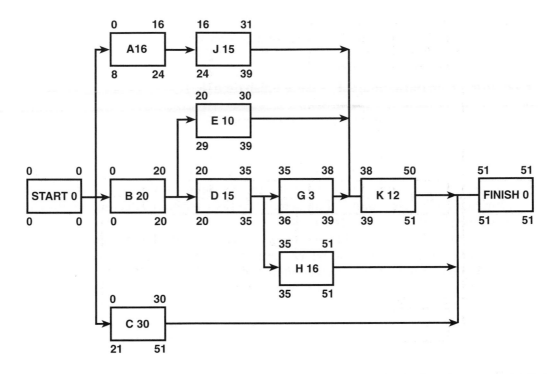

Figure B.8 The backward pass

The critical path and float

As discussed earlier, the critical path is that path of activities that, if delayed, will cause the project to be delayed. Put differently, it is those activities that have no leeway or margin for error – there is no difference between the EF and LF (or the ES and LS). The difference between the times is called the activities' float. Therefore the critical path for the purposes of this book is based on zero float.

This book focuses on two types of float: total float and free float. The most commonly used is total float and this is discussed first. The third type of float is independent float, and is not often used.

Total float

The forward and backward pass calculations yielded the ES, LS, EF and LF. Referring to the calculated network above, if activity J is converted to a bar chart (as in Figure B.9), it clearly shows that this activity may start at the beginning of week 16 or it may be delayed until the beginning of week 24 without increasing the total project duration.

Knowledge of this flexibility or 'float' is valuable in many ways. The total amount an activity may move without affecting the total project time is called total float and is calculated as:

Total float = Late finish time (LF) – Early finish time (EF)
or
Total float = Late start time (LS) – Early start time (ES)

Free float

While total float does not affect the total project time, it may delay the start of succeeding activities. The ability of an activity to float without affecting a subsequent activity is given by the activity's free float.

As free float involves succeeding activities it cannot be calculated from the four start and finish times of the activity. Reference must be made to all immediate successors since it is the float in these that is to be unaffected.

Consider the following sequence of activities.

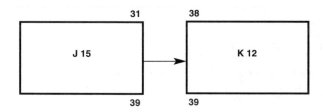

If the total float in activity J of eight weeks is used up, it will finish at week 39. This will prevent activity K from starting at its earliest start time of week 38, as it will be pushed along by one week, thus diminishing its float by one week. Activity J may only float to week 38 without affecting activity K, and therefore its free float is only seven weeks:

Free float = Early start time (ES) of the successor – Early finish time (EF) of the predecessor

Figure B.9 is activity J viewed in a Gantt chart form. Table B.11 shows the final critical path and float analysis table.

The critical path is determined by connecting all the activities with the least float (in this case the 'zero float' convention has been used, as it is the most common in industry). In the above network the critical path is START – B – D – H – FINISH. The project can be completed in 51 weeks. The complete calculated network diagram is shown in Figure B.10 with the critical path highlighted.

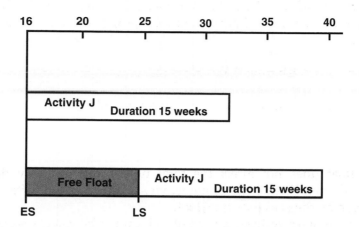

Figure B.9 Activity J Gantt chart

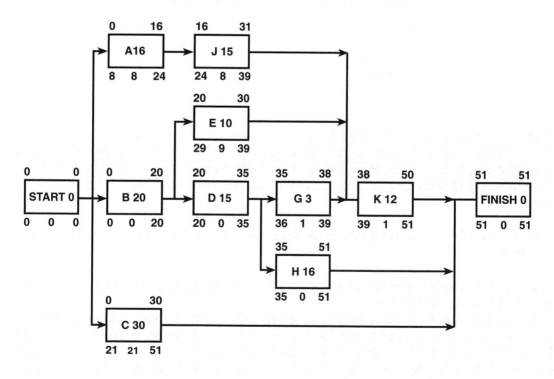

Figure B.10 Complete network diagram

Table B.11 Final critical path and float analysis table

| Activity | | Start times | | Finish times | | Float | |
Description	Duration	Early	Late	Early	Late	Total	Free
A	16	0	8	16	24	8	0
B	20	0	0	20	20	0	0
C	30	0	21	30	51	21	21
J	15	16	24	31	39	8	7
D	15	20	20	35	35	0	0
E	10	20	29	30	39	9	8
G	3	35	36	38	39	1	0
H	16	35	35	51	51	0	0
K	12	38	39	50	51	1	1

It was stated earlier that the critical path is determined by connecting those activities with the least float and not the activities with zero float. Consider if the project only needs to be completed at the latest by week 55. On the backward pass, instead of making the LF of the final activity equal to its EF, the LF is set to 55. Calculating the backward pass now yields a float of 4 weeks on those activities that previously had a float of 0. By the same token, if the latest the project can complete is by week 50, then the activities with zero float will now have a float of –1. The critical path therefore is made up of those activities with the least float.

The near critical path

The near critical path is the path through the network that contains the least total float. It is the path which, if the least float is used up, will also become critical. If more than the least float is consumed, the near critical path will become the critical path from that point onwards. The implications are that a critical path can jump around quite rapidly when projects experience delays and changes to scope.

In most cases the near critical path contains part of the critical path and a part of the network that links to it. The near critical path in Figure B.10 is through activities G and K both having a total float of 1 unit of time. Should G and K be delayed by 1 unit of time, there will be two critical paths, namely, Start B D H Finish and Start B D G K Finish. Should G and K be delayed by more that 2 units of time, the near critical path will become the new critical path and the existing critical path will become the near critical path. This needs to be verified at all project scope changes.

Users of time and resource software packages should have a fundamental understanding of CPA and the practical implications are when using the software. Many inexperienced users often hit the critical path analysis button without understanding the underlying theory and principles, yet manage on the attractive Gantt charts (in triplicate colour) showing critical paths!

The use of critical path analysis

Remember that the CPA is modelling the future to enable better management decisions. CPA is a tool that both the project manager and the project team members will use throughout the life of the project. For the project manager, it is a tool for planning, implementation and control. For the project team, it is a tool to manage their own work and to brief new team members and organizations on the project and its status.

Specifically, the use of CPA enables the project manager and team to:

● show the interdependencies between all project activities so the project can be viewed in its entirety;
● determine the shortest project duration or longest path through the network for a specific combination of resources and time;
● manage both the total and free float to the advantage of the project;

- manage by exception, by concentrating on the critical path while keeping an eye on the 'near' critical paths;
- establish the time baseline for monitoring and control once the project is implemented;
- evaluate the impact of delays and variations on the critical path, and on the project network as a whole;
- carry out cost/time trade-off analyses when considering the impact of acceleration or variation to the project;
- execute resource scheduling in a scientific manner (float determines which activities have first demand on activities);
- litigate contractual claims, as CPA is widely recognized as a sound scientific basis for analysing the impact of events on a project (initially drawn critical paths as well as after-the-fact critical path networks have been admitted in courts of law);
- simulate the project execution process on computer, by comparing how the planned and actual progress and events unfolded.

A Gantt chart is readily produced from the information contained in a calculated network diagram. The Gantt chart is a user-friendly representation of the network diagram, and serves as an important communication tool for project participants and stakeholders.

Appendix C – Reasons for failure and guidelines for success

Introduction

This chapter supplements the text, by considering the factors that influence project success and failure. Underlying the discussion of success and failure are performance criteria measures, and their impact on stakeholder perception. This appendix ends with a list of guidelines that will assist practitioners in enhancing project success.

PROJECT-RELATED PROBLEMS

> In the quest for success, failure is the constant companion.
>
> Dennis Comninos and Enzo Frigenti

To discover how to achieve success, we must better understand the reasons for failure.

Project-related problems form a sound basis for understanding the concepts of success and failure. It is therefore useful to have a brief overview of project-related problems and understand their impact on outcomes. In the past decade, a considerable amount of research has been undertaken in the area of project problems. In this section the authors review some of the findings in relation to project success and failure.

From a stakeholder perception, far too many projects fail or are not as successful as they should be. These perceptions are supported by a number of studies, as discussed by

Wells[95] in an informative and interesting summary. The review of approximately 8,400 IT projects concluded that:

- about one-third of the projects were outright failures and were or would be cancelled before completion;
- 50 per cent were 'in recovery', but would overrun their initial cost estimates by up to 200 per cent; and
- only 16 per cent were accomplished on time, within budget and according to specifications.

(Gopal Kapur (1997) 'IT project management can succeed!' *Managing Office Technology*, **42**, 22).

The Standish Group (reported in Pinto and Millet[70a]) offers a further bleak picture of the current state of IT project implementation, stating that of approximately 175,000 projects costing more that $250 billion each year, 52.7 per cent will overrun their initial cost estimates by 189 per cent. Most of these projects are delivered with only 74 per cent of the original functionality. The Standish Group concluded that the average success rate of business-critical application development projects is a minuscule 9 per cent!

These figures demonstrate that some problems do exist in IT projects.

J G Shanks, in the article 'Inflating or deflating projects depends on the Big Four' (*Data Management*, **23** (8), 18–21), states that 'over the years various studies have analyzed and debated the ever increasing phenomenon of project failure', and goes further to develop the 'Big Four' reasons for project failure:

- inadequate project definition;
- lack of general information;
- poor scheduling and allocation of resources;
- losing control of the project.

It is interesting to note that the majority of these reasons for project failure are directly attributable to project management.

Michael William Hughes gives a more general description of project failure in 'Why projects fail: the effects of ignoring the obvious' (*Industrial Engineering*, April 1986: 14–18). Hughes argues that 'most project failures occur because basic and obvious principles of management are ignored, not because of failure in a complex (technical) area. Networks and schedules are supposed to help manage the project, but they sometimes become the project, resulting in an inappropriate focus for the project management system.'

This argument reinforces the authors' view that project failure has more to do with project management than technical competence. It also makes an important point that applying some project management tools and techniques can tend to become the project rather than assisting the project participants. The authors have observed this concerning trend growing, and question the value that an excessive focus on tools and techniques brings to business projects. There are many reasons for this trend – a few of the more important ones include:

- project managers who lack business management experience;
- project managers using heavyweight methodologies and approaches to projects that require flexibility and simple methods;
- the proliferation of software packages that focus attention on time and resource management, resulting in project managers giving prominence to these as the key tools for managing projects.

Experienced business-focused project participants soon see gaps in this management approach, which misdirects effort and measures only a few important areas of the project process.

John Saunders, in the article 'Bad project management remains a problem' (*Computing Canada*, 22 December 1997: 1–2, 4), says about project failure, 'it is interesting that almost everyone agrees that poor planning is still the major problem'. Again, this is a fundamental project management responsibility. Saunders also refers to a KPMG survey that concluded that the major causes of project failure were:

- bad planning;
- a weak business case; and
- a lack of senior management involvement.

It is interesting to note that the first point is directly under the control of the project manager, while the second and third points are partly the responsibility of the project manager and partly that of upper management.

Deborah Kezsbom notes that frequently reported problems on projects are: 1) schedule slippage; 2) goal or priority definition. Kezsbom examined the connection between such problems and the conflict engendered by improperly designed and managed, cross-functional, multi-discipline project teams. Conflict, and the associated dysfunctional communications, can lead to schedule slippage, work stoppage, or outright sabotage.

In a study of 285 managers, Kezsbom discovered that the number one conflict issue centred on goal or priority definition ('Bringing order to chaos: pinpointing sources of conflict in the nineties' *Cost Engineering*, **34** (11), November 1992: 9–16). This is an upper management and project management responsibility which, if not agreed and supported by upper management and the project participants, will lead to project failure.

Although his paper was not specifically written for project management, John Tudel suggests in 'Learning faster than your competitors' (*Upside*, September 1996) that the most imposing barrier corporations face is their inability to learn quickly. An associated tendency is toward the mindless, rote processes and other management measures that lead to fear and blocked learning. Projects are no different in that often complex processes are applied and less than effective measures are dogmatically pursued, adding little value to the organization.

Jean Posson points to business failures as centred on management weakness, financial weakness and strategic weakness. Management weakness includes technical incompetence, lack of interpersonal skills and lack of general management or business experience. ('Corporate failure: the lessons to be learned' *Credit Management*, April 1996: 32–34). Although not directly applicable to projects, it is interesting to note the inclusion of technical incompetence as a contributing factor to business failure. In projects that require new technologies to perform, it is not difficult to appreciate how critical this component is to project success.

Reviewing the above summary of Wells[95], the statement Nicholas[67] makes appears most appropriate: 'Experienced project managers will tell you that failure or success of a project has something to do with its management'. Nicholas concludes from a survey of project management literature over the past 20 years, across the construction, research and development, data processing and product development industries, that 'project failure and success do depend on project management – a great deal, in fact'.

PERCEPTIONS OF FAILURE AND SUCCESS

Obeng, in *The Project Leader's Secret Handbook – All Change!*[68], states: 'Project success is and can only be defined by the stakeholders'. Assuming this statement is correct, it is evident that the concepts of success and failure are, at times, elusive and difficult to define. It raises questions about which stakeholders are the most important, which perceptions are the most critical, and what factors influence perception. As each stakeholder has different priorities and preferences, the project manager and sponsor have a challenging task in meeting expectations. Some stakeholders are concerned with the more tangible and fixed aspects of the change resulting from the project, whereas others are interested in the more intangible and transient aspects of change. Irrespective of which combination of soft and hard criteria represents an optimum balance, success and failure can be measured by whether the project has met the expectations of stakeholders, according to their standards and criteria.

Soft criteria

There are numerous soft criteria that influence project perceptions. The following soft criteria are drawn from those that Obeng[68] lists as featuring regularly in stakeholders' measures of success:

- *Empathy*: Stakeholders need to feel and see that the project team is sensitive to their point of view (sincerity).
- *Reliability*: Stakeholders need to know that the project team will do whatever they say they will do.
- *Error-freeness*: Stakeholders are often heavily reliant on the results the project delivers. Errors – large or small – can upset stakeholders, especially those who are new to a project environment.

- *Honesty*: Stakeholders believe that the project team is honest if they do what they say they will do ('walk the talk'), but as importantly, they will feel comfortable if they do not have to watch their backs. The project team also demonstrates honesty by explaining the process, so stakeholders will not experience surprises that could put them in a difficult position later on.
- *Fun*: Most people enjoy a relaxed atmosphere and a laugh from time to time to relieve tension and create a sense that 'there is life after the project'.
- *Appearance*: Most stakeholders value professional presentations when communicating progress, status, messages and reports. This extends to personal appearance, as no stakeholder will feel comfortable entrusting so much to a team that appears scruffy and unprofessional.
- *Politics*: Stakeholders usually do not want to be involved with project-related politics. Clear roles, responsibilities and reporting relationships are essential. Covert positions and self-bestowed importance can become problematic for stakeholders.

The above soft criteria generally apply to all projects. Knowing which criteria are important to key stakeholders is invaluable when considering perceptions of success. Finding out what the stakeholder likes or dislikes, what values are important to them and what they perceive to be professional work standards will be most helpful to the project team.

Hard criteria

The hard, tangible criteria are easier to define and form part of a project's performance measures.

From the perspective that a project creates change, the criteria for success can be found in answering the question, 'Why is this change being carried out?' (Obeng[68]). From a classic project point of view, the hard criteria cover the measures such as time, cost, specifications and scope. Knowing why the change is being carried out, together with a clear understanding of what benefits will flow from the project, assists the team in defining performance measures that are broader than these standard ones. Understanding the hard criteria enables the project team to develop a set of credible measures that focus the team and engender trust among the important stakeholders.

It is the project team's responsibility to ensure that all participants have a clear understanding of the hard criteria that will determine the project's success. Stakeholders need to agree to this set of criteria. The project manager and sponsor are responsible for ensuring that reporting against the criteria is carried out regularly during the life of the project.

Chapter 2 discussed the interrelationship between four basic objectives of scope, time, cost and performance, and the unique manner in which they relate:

- time is the time schedule;
- cost is the project budget;
- performance encompasses the specifications of the project deliverables (also referred to as quality, although quality applies to all dimensions of project management);

- scope is the sum of the deliverables (products and services) to be developed through the project process.

This interrelationship is repeated here in Figure C.1.

Scope is bound by the constraints of time, cost and performance. Often a project's time, cost and performance are determined before definition of the scope, resulting in the scope being limited to the surface area of the triangle.

Figure C.1 The project criteria triangle

Sponsors and project managers have an obligation to determine which of the four criteria are negotiable in the view of key stakeholders. A key stakeholder should not fix all four criteria and expect the project team to deliver. This will lead to stakeholder expectations that cannot be met and to the perception of project failure, when in fact it could not have been delivered successfully in the first place.

The criteria illustrated in Figure C.1 are 'traded off' against each other throughout a project, particularly at times of important change or decision making. One criteria cannot be altered without impact on the others.

Over the life cycle of a project, the criteria priorities will alter, meaning that stakeholder agreement will not necessarily be fixed in the early stages. Market conditions may change, competitor products force a change in strategy, or the intended solution becomes less attractive and a change in direction is required to continue the project. As the project unfolds, changing criteria priorities usually creates lively debate amongst project participants and stakeholders. The project team must stay close to the stakeholder perceptions of what is important to achieve a successful result. Trying to accommodate all of them is a challenge.

As discussed in Chapter 2, beware of fixing the classic hard criteria of time and cost at an early stage of project development. Stakeholders will always remember the numeric values of time and cost and invariably forget the conditions attached to these two criteria, leading to performance perception that is both unjustified and damaging to project team morale. In certain project environments, early fixing of time and cost is virtually always the norm, for example in fixed-price, turnkey and ad-measure contracts. These projects are usually in developed mature industries, with established risk management capability.

PERFORMANCE CRITERIA MEASURES

It is easy to lose ourselves in efficiency, to treat that efficiency as an end in itself and not a means to other ends.

Charles Handy, British academic, business consultant and author,
The Age of Paradox (1994)

Chapter 3 described project success as being perceived and measured in terms of business results (effectiveness), supported by the project process (efficiency). An efficient process is necessary but insufficient to ensure success.

It is a known fact in business that most attention is paid to the things that get measured. The same is true for projects. Therefore, a project must align with organization strategy, identify its own strategies, develop critical success factors (the things that must go right), undertake risk analyses and establish performance measures that are results-focused. It is then the role of the sponsor and project manager to focus efforts on those crucial areas of success, manage them with vigour and enthusiasm, and ensure that a robust, organized and simple project process is in support.

From then on, monitoring, measuring and taking corrective action are needed to ensure that the critical areas are achieved and project results delivered. Project measures that merely evaluate project management efficiency and not business results will misdirect upper management, the sponsor, the project core team and stakeholders. The project team must ensure that the correct performance measures are developed and continually monitored during the life of the project.

The project team must guard against developing performance measures that they cannot deliver on. A project manager and team may make the mistake of agreeing with stakeholders on a performance measure that can only be achieved once the project products have been handed over to operations. This type of performance measure leads to problems in that stakeholders will perceive that the project has not been fully delivered, as the business benefits are not yet achieved, while the team will believe they performed well because they handed over the project products. Team frustration may also ensue, as project completion is difficult to determine. There is often no team celebration of project achievements and completion.

Upper management and stakeholders must understand that the project team is responsible for the four basic project process criteria, but not the achievement of the business benefits flowing from the fully operationalized product or service. However, effectiveness measures can be put in place for the handover of project products; for example, how well the products were integrated into the business, what level of end-user acceptance existed during transfer, and what impact there was on the organization's ability to deliver services. These are effectiveness criteria that have an important impact on stakeholder perception of success and failure.

Thus the challenge is for the project team to develop a balanced set of performance criteria that measure the critical business needs of key stakeholders and the efficiency of the project process. Experienced project managers will tend to focus on the major stakeholder criteria first, as this reflects the uniqueness of the project, and then on the more familiar project process criteria.

GUIDELINES TO ENHANCE SUCCESS

Fools you are to say you learn by your experience. I prefer to profit by others' mistakes and avoid the price of my own.
Otto von Bismarck-Schönhausen (1815–98), Prusso-German Statesman, first Chancellor of the German Empire

The following section provides some good practice guidelines that will draw together the ideas and discussions of earlier chapters. They are intended to guide the reader in developing a broader and deeper understanding of the project–business interface. These guidelines are not intended to be an exhaustive analysis, but rather a summary of the important factors the authors have found to contribute to project success.

The guidelines

The guidelines are grouped into five aspects of projects and project management.

The context of projects

1. The three pillars upon which project change is constructed are mandate, purpose and capability. Ensure that the mandate from stakeholders is sound, project purpose is clear and agreed by both project participants and key stakeholders, and capability is available, before embarking on project change.
2. View projects in the context of organizational strategy, business benefits and a project management approach and process – as illustrated in the Wrappers™ model (Chapter 4).
3. Always develop a specific project life cycle around the products that the project delivers. Then integrate this life cycle with the project process phases.
4. Accept that the four project types require different management approaches, as well as a different mix of tools and techniques.
5. Be careful not to make the project management process more important than the project itself.

Project manager and team

1. Build a project team by focusing on one individual at a time.
2. Empower the team with strong project leadership from both the sponsor and project manager.
3. Cultivate vigorous debate among core team members, and resolute commitment once agreement is reached.
4. Agree on who will make key decisions, to avoid impasses on important issues later on.
5. A keystone to success is the 'contract' between upper management, the sponsor and the project manager. Build this keystone into your project approach.
6. Integrate horizontally by developing a strong focus on the vertical functions delivering to the project. Engage functional managers, as they mostly own the resources.
7. Measure project results as well as functional contribution. This will enhance the level of functional contribution, as what gets measured gets done.
8. Three characteristics always present in the behaviour and attitudes of leaders and members of high performing teams are time, feeling and focus. Ensure these are present in the project core team.
9. Remove impediments for the project team and ensure the celebration of success.

Stakeholders

1. Use broader business-focused project measures, in harmony with project process measures. This results in a stronger stakeholder focus.
2. Success criteria must consider both soft and hard stakeholder criteria.
3. Project success is defined by stakeholders, and therefore determined by their perceptions. Ensure that their definition of success is built into the plans.
4. Understand that the four basic project management objectives of scope, time, cost and performance can be traded off. The challenge is to know which of these are more important to the key stakeholders.
5. *A Guide to the Project Management Body of Knowledge*[73] lists the nine project management areas of *integration, scope, time, cost, quality, human resources, communication, risk* and *procurement management*. The tenth, and arguably the most important, is *stakeholder management*. Manage it well.

Developing project management in the organization

1. Build an organization environment that supports project management by:
   - obtaining upper management support;
   - setting up a Project Management Initiative Group;
   - developing management's ability to manage projects;
   - making project management a key management competency;
   - developing project learning in the organization.

2. Visualize projects in organizations as a portfolio of programmes and projects, thus ensuring that the business benefits are linked to the project results.
3. Develop proposals and business cases for each project, to ensure that value is created for the business.
4. Ensure that operational areas, which will operate the project products developed, have ownership of the project processes and products.
5. Make learning as important as the producing of services and products.

Programme management

1. Ensure that the complexity and extent of the programme is not underestimated.
2. Obtain access to critical information and internal communication channels.
3. Devote considerable effort to integrating the deliverables from the projects forming the programme.
4. Strong programme sponsorship and management is critical to a successful programme.
5. Contain any requirements creep, as it can destroy a programme, slowly but surely.
6. An effective implementation strategy, owned by operations, is vital to best practice programme management.
7. A programme must be viewed as the creation of a new business group, or of new services in an existing group.

Glossary

accountability Being answerable for the satisfactory completion of specified objectives.

activity An element of work performed during the course of a project. An activity normally has an expected duration, an expected cost, and expected resource requirements.

actual cost of work performed (ACWP) Total costs incurred (direct and indirect) in accomplishing work during a given time period. See also *earned value.*

actual finish date (AF) The point in time that work actually ended on an activity. (Note: in some application areas, the activity is considered 'finished' when work is 'substantially complete'.)

authority The power to make final decisions that others are compelled to follow. With authority goes accountability and responsibility.

backward pass The calculation of late finish dates and late start dates for the uncompleted portions of all network activities. Determined by working backwards through the network logic from the project's end date. The end date may be calculated in a *forward pass* or may be set by the customer or sponsor. See also *network analysis.*

bar chart A graphic display of schedule-related information. In the typical bar chart, activities or other project elements are listed down the left side of the chart, dates are shown across the top, and activity durations are shown as date-placed horizontal bars. Also called a Gantt chart.

baseline The original plan (for a project, a work package, or an activity) plus or minus approved changes. Usually used with a modifier (such as cost baseline, schedule baseline, performance measurement baseline).

budget at completion (BAC)   The estimated total cost of the project when done.

budgeted cost of work performed (BCWP)   The sum of the approved cost estimates (including any overhead allocation) for activities (or portions of activities) completed during a given period (usually project-to-date). See also *earned value*.

budgeted cost of work scheduled (BCWS)   The sum of the approved cost estimates (including any overhead allocation) for activities (or portions of activities) scheduled to be performed during a given period (usually project-to-date). See also *earned value*.

chart of accounts   Any numbering system used to monitor project costs by category (such as labour, supplies, materials). The project chart of accounts is usually based on the corporate chart of accounts of the primary performing organization.

charter   See *project charter*.

communications planning   Determining the information and communication needs of the project stakeholders.

contingencies   See *reserve*.

contract   A mutually binding agreement that obligates the seller to provide the specified product and obligates the buyer to pay for it. Contracts generally fall into one of three broad categories:

- Fixed price or lump sum contract – involves a fixed total price for a well-defined product. Fixed price contracts may also include incentives for meeting or exceeding selected project objectives, such as schedule targets.
- Cost reimbursable contract – involves payment (reimbursement) to the contractor for actual costs. Costs are usually classified as direct costs (costs incurred directly by the project, such as wages for members of the project team) or indirect costs (costs allocated to the project by the performing organization as a cost of doing business, such as salaries for corporate executives). Indirect costs are usually calculated as a percentage of direct costs. Cost reimbursable contracts often include incentives for meeting or exceeding selected project objectives such as schedule targets or total cost.
- Unit price contract – the contractor is paid a pre-set amount per unit of service (such as $70 per hour for professional services, or $1.08 per cubic metre of earth removed) and the total value of the contract is a function of the quantities needed to complete the work.

control   The process of comparing actual performance with planned performance, analysing variances, evaluating possible alternatives, and taking appropriate corrective action as needed.

core project team   The members of the *project team* who are directly involved in project management activities and who will remain with the project from definition stage to close-out. See also *project management team*.

corrective action   Changes made to bring expected future performance of the project into line with the plan.

cost management   A subset of project management that includes the processes required to ensure that the project is completed within the approved budget. It consists of *resource planning*, cost estimating, cost budgeting and cost control.

cost performance index (CPI) The ratio of budgeted costs to actual costs (BCWP/ACWP). CPI is often used to predict the magnitude of a possible cost overrun using the following formula: original cost estimate/CPI = projected cost at completion. See also *earned value*.

cost plus fixed fee (CPFF) A type of *contract* where the buyer reimburses the seller for the seller's allowable costs (as defined by the contract) plus a fixed amount of profit (fee).

cost plus incentive fee (CPIF) A type of *contract* where the buyer reimburses the seller for the seller's allowable costs (as defined by the contract), and the seller earns its profit if it meets defined performance criteria.

cost variance (CV) Any difference between the estimated cost of an activity and the actual cost of that activity. In *earned value*, BCWP less ACWP.

critical activity Any activity on a *critical path*. Most commonly determined by using the *critical path method*. Although some activities are 'critical' in the dictionary sense without being on the critical path, this meaning is seldom used in the project context.

critical decision point In every project there are points at which critical decisions are required that have a major bearing on the project results. These are referred to as Critical Decision Points (CDPs), and typically are major go/no-go decisions.

CDPs often appear at the end of project life cycle phases. This may occur for example in research projects, where results are progressively achieved.

CDPs also occur prior to committing large amounts of resource on projects, for example where no value is obtained until the project is completed.

critical path In a *project network diagram*, the series of activities that determines the earliest completion of the project. The critical path will generally change from time to time as activities are completed ahead of or behind schedule. Although normally calculated for the entire project, the critical path can also be determined for a milestone or sub-project. The critical path is usually defined as those activities with float less than or equal to a specified value, often zero. See *critical path method*.

critical path analysis (CPA) See *critical path method*.

critical path method (CPM) A *network analysis* technique used to predict project duration by analysing which sequence of activities (which *network path*) has the least amount of scheduling flexibility (the least amount of *float*). Early dates are calculated by means of a *backward pass* starting from a specified completion date (usually the calculated project *early finish date*).

deliverable Any measurable, tangible, verifiable outcome, result, or item that must be produced to complete a project or part of a project. Often used more narrowly in reference to an external deliverable, which is a deliverable that is subject to approval by the project sponsor or customer.

deliverables breakdown structure (DBS) A grouping of the deliverables that a project must deliver. Each descending level represents an increasingly detailed definition of a project's deliverables.

dependency See *logical relationship*.

duration The number of work periods (not including holidays or other non-working periods) required to complete an activity or other project element. Usually expressed as workdays or workweeks. Sometimes incorrectly equated with elapsed time. See also *effort*.

early finish time (EF) In the *critical path method*, the earliest possible point in time at which the uncompleted portions of an activity (or the project) can finish based on the *network logic* and any schedule constraints. Early finish dates can change as the project progresses and changes are made to the project plan.

early start time (ES) In the *critical path method*, the earliest possible point in time at which the uncompleted portions of an activity (or the project) can start, based on the *network logic* and any schedule constraints. Early start dates can change as the project progresses and changes are made to the project plan.

earned value (EV) (1) A method for measuring project performance. It compares the amount of work that was planned with what was actually accomplished to determine if cost and schedule performance is as planned. See also *actual cost of work performed, budgeted cost of work performed, budgeted cost of work scheduled, cost performance index, cost variance, schedule performance index and schedule variance*.
(2) The *budgeted cost of work performed* for an activity or group of activities.

effort The number of labour units required to complete an activity or other project element. Usually expressed as staff-hours, staff-days or staff-weeks. Should not be confused with **duration**.

estimate An assessment of the likely quantitative result. Usually applied to project costs and durations and should always include some indication of accuracy (such as + *x* per cent). Usually used with a modifier (for example, preliminary, conceptual, feasibility). Some application areas have specific modifiers that imply particular accuracy ranges (order-of-magnitude estimate, budget estimate and definitive estimate in engineering and construction projects).

estimate at completion (EAC) The expected total cost of an activity, a group of activities, or the project when the defined scope of work has been completed. Most techniques for forecasting EAC include some adjustment of the original cost estimate based on project performance to date. Often shown as EAC = actuals-to-date + ETC. See also *earned value* and *estimate to complete*.

estimate to complete (ETC) The expected additional cost needed to complete an activity, a group of activities, or the project. Most techniques for forecasting ETC include some adjustment to the original estimate based on project performance to date. See also *earned value* and *estimate at completion*.

exception report A document that includes only major variations from the plan (rather than all variations).

fast tracking Compressing the project schedule by overlapping activities that would normally be done in sequence, such as design and construction. Sometimes confused with concurrent engineering.

finish-to-finish (FF)   See *logical relationship*.

finish-to-start (FS)   See *logical relationship*.

firm fixed price (FFP)   A type of *contract* where the buyer pays the seller a set amount (as defined by the contract) regardless of the seller's costs.

fixed price incentive fee (FPIF)   A type of *contract* where the buyer pays the seller a set amount (as defined by the contract), and the seller can earn an additional amount if it meets defined performance criteria.

float   The amount of time that an activity may be delayed from its early start without delaying the project finish date. Float is a mathematical calculation and can change as the project progresses and changes are made to the project plan. Also called slack, total float and path float. See also *free float*.

forecast final cost   See *estimate at completion*.

forward pass   The calculation of the early start and early finish dates for the uncompleted portions of all network activities. See also *network analysis* and *backward pass*.

free float   The amount of time an activity can be delayed without delaying the *early start time* of any immediately following activities. See also *float*.

functional manager   A manager responsible for activities in a specialized department or function (such as engineering, manufacturing, marketing).

Gantt chart   *See* bar chart.

human resource management   A subset of project management that includes the processes required to make the most effective use of the people involved with the project. It consists of organizational planning, staff acquisition and team development.

integrated cost/schedule reporting   See *earned value*.

integration management   A subset of project management that includes the processes required to ensure that the various elements of the project are properly coordinated. It consists of project plan development, project plan execution, and overall change control.

lag   A modification of a *logical relationship* that causes a delay of the successor task. For example, in a *finish-to-start* dependency with a 10-day lag, the successor activity can start 10 days after the predecessor has finished. See also *lead*.

late finish time (LF)   In the *critical path method*, the latest possible point in time that an activity may be completed without delaying a specified milestone (usually the project finish date).

late start time (LS)   In the *critical path method*, the latest possible point in time that an activity may begin without delaying a specified milestone (usually the project finish date).

lead   A modification of a *logical relationship* that allows an acceleration of the successor task. For example, in a *finish-to-start* dependency with a 10-day lead, the successor activity can start 10 days before the predecessor has finished. See also *lag*.

levelling   See *resource levelling*.

line manager   (1) The manager of any group that actually makes a product or performs a service.
(2)   A *functional manager*.
link   See *logical relationship*.
logical relationship   The relationship between two activities in a *network diagram*. Refer to Appendix B (section on critical path analysis).
loop   A *network path* that passes the same *node* twice. Loops cannot be analysed using traditional *network analysis* techniques such as *CPM* and *PERT*.

management reserves   A separately planned quantity used to allow for future situations that are impossible to predict (sometimes called 'unknown unknowns'). Management reserves may involve cost or time. Management reserves are intended to reduce the risk of missing cost or schedule objectives. Use of management reserves requires a change to the project's cost baseline.
master schedule   A summary-level schedule that identifies the major activities and key milestones.
matrix organization   Any organizational structure in which the project manager shares responsibility with the functional managers for assigning priorities and for directing the work of individuals assigned to the project.
milestone   A significant event in the project, usually completion of a major deliverable.
milestone objective chart (MOC)   The graphical representation of *milestone* events and their logical dependencies, descriptions and timing.
milestone responsibility matrix (MRM)   A matrix indicating the entities responsible for each *milestone* event on an *MOC*.
mitigation   Taking steps to lessen risk by lowering the probability of a risk event's occurrence or reducing its effect should it occur.
monitoring   The capture, analysis and reporting of project performance, usually as compared to plan.

network   See *project network diagram*.
network analysis   The process of identifying early and late start and finish dates for the uncompleted portions of project activities. See also *critical path method* and *programme evaluation and review technique*.
network diagram   See *project network diagram*.
network logic   The collection of activity dependencies that make up a *project network diagram*.
network path   Any continuous series of connected activities in a *project network diagram*.
node   One of the defining points of a network; a junction point joined to some or all of the other dependency lines. See *precedence diagramming method*.

order of magnitude estimate (OME)   See *estimate*.
organizational breakdown structure (OBS)   A depiction of the project organization arranged so as to relate *work packages* to organizational units.

path   See *network path*.

percent complete (PC)   An estimate, expressed as a percentage, of the amount of work that has been completed on an activity or group of activities.

performing organization   The enterprise whose employees are most directly involved in doing the work of the project.

phase   See *project phase*.

plan   See *project plan*.

PMBOK® Guide   See *Project Management Body of Knowledge*.

precedence diagramming method   A network diagramming technique in which activities are represented by boxes (or nodes). Activities are linked by precedence relationships to show the sequence in which the activities are to be performed.

predecessor activity   In the *precedence diagramming method*, the 'from' activity.

procurement planning   Determining what to procure and when.

programme   A group of related projects managed in a coordinated way. Programmes usually include an element of ongoing activity.

programme evaluation and review technique (PERT)   An event-oriented *network analysis* technique used to estimate project duration when there is a high degree of uncertainty with the individual activity duration estimates. PERT applies the *critical path method* to a weighted average duration estimate.

project   A temporary endeavour undertaken to create a unique product or service.

project charter   A document issued by senior management that provides the project manager with the authority to apply organizational resources to project activities.

project life cycle   A collection of generally sequential *project phases* whose names and number are determined by the control needs of the organization(s) involved in the project.

project management (PM)   The application of knowledge, skills, tools and techniques to project activities in order to meet or exceed stakeholder needs and expectations from a project.

Project Management Body of Knowledge (PMBOK®)   The sum of knowledge within the profession of project management. As with other professions such as law, medicine and accounting, the body of knowledge rests with the practitioners and academics who apply and advance it. The PMBOK includes proven traditional practices that are widely applied as well as innovative and advanced ones, which have seen more limited use. The PMBOK® Guide is a publication of the Project Management Institute that provides a guide to the knowledge areas.

project management team (PMT)   The members of the project team who are directly involved in project management activities. On some smaller projects, the project management team may include virtually all of the *project team* members. See also *core project team*.

project network diagram   Any schematic display of the logical relationships of project activities. Always drawn from left to right to reflect project chronology. Often incorrectly referred to as a 'PERT chart'.

project phase   A collection of logically related project activities, usually culminating in the completion of a major *deliverable*.

project plan   A formal, approved document used to guide both project execution and project control. The primary uses of the project plan are to document planning assumptions and decisions, to facilitate communication among stakeholders, and to document approved scope, cost and schedule baselines. A project plan may be summarized or detailed.

project schedule   The planned dates for performing activities and the planned dates for meeting milestones.

project team   The people who report either directly or indirectly to the project manager.

quality assurance (QA)   (1)   The process of evaluating overall project performance on a regular basis to provide confidence that the project will satisfy the relevant quality standards.
(2)   The organizational unit that is assigned responsibility for quality assurance.

quality control (QC)   (1)   The process of monitoring specific project results to determine if they comply with relevant quality standards and identifying ways to eliminate causes of unsatisfactory performance.
(2)   The organizational unit that is assigned responsibility for quality control.

quality planning   Identifying which quality standards are relevant to the project and determining how to satisfy them.

remaining duration   The time needed to complete an activity.

request for information (RFI)   A document used to obtain information from prospective sellers of products or services.

request for proposal (RFP)   A type of bid document used to solicit proposals from prospective sellers of products or services. In some application areas it may have a narrower or more specific meaning.

request for quotation (RFQ)   Generally, this term is equivalent to *request for proposal*. However, in some application areas it may have a narrower or more specific meaning.

reserve   A provision in the project plan to mitigate cost and/or schedule risk. Often used with a modifier (such as management reserve, contingency reserve) to provide further detail on what types of risk are meant to be mitigated.

resource levelling   Any form of *network analysis* in which scheduling decisions (start and finish dates) are driven by resource management concerns (such as limited resource availability or difficult-to-manage changes in resource levels).

resource planning   Determining what resources (people, equipment and materials) are needed in what quantities to perform project activities.

responsibility   An obligation that results from a person's formal role in an organization to perform assigned tasks effectively.

responsibility assignment matrix (RAM)   A structure that relates the project organization structure to the *work breakdown structure* to ensure that each element of the project's scope of work is assigned to a responsible individual.

retention   A portion of a contract payment that is held until contract completion in order to ensure full performance of the contract terms.

risk event A discrete occurrence that may affect the project for better or worse.
risk identification Determining which risk events are likely to affect the project.
risk quantification Evaluating the probability of risk event occurrence and effect.
risk response Responding to changes in risk over the course of the project.

schedule See *project schedule*.
schedule performance index (SPI) The ratio of work performed to work scheduled. (BCWP/BCWS). See *earned value*.
schedule variance (SV) (1) Any difference between the scheduled completion of an activity and the actual completion of that activity.
(2) In earned value, BCWP less BCWS.
scheduled finish time The point in time at which work was scheduled to finish on an activity. The scheduled finish date is normally between the *early finish time* and the *late finish time*.
scheduled start time The point in time at which work was scheduled to start on an activity. The scheduled start date is normally between the *early start time* and the *late start time*.
scope The sum of the deliverables (products and services) to be developed through the project process.
scope change Any change to the project scope. A scope change almost always requires an adjustment to the project cost or schedule.
scope definition Breaking down the major deliverables into smaller, more manageable components to provide better control.
scope planning Developing a written scope statement that includes the project justification, the major *deliverables* and the project objectives.
scope verification Ensuring that all identified project *deliverables* have been completed satisfactorily.
S-curve Graphic display of cumulative costs, labour hours or other quantities plotted against time. The name derives from the S-like shape of the curve (flatter at the beginning and end, steeper in the middle) produced on a project that starts slowly, accelerates and then tails off.
slack Term used in *PERT* for *float*.
stakeholder Individuals and organizations that are involved in or may be affected by project activities.
start-to-finish (SF) See *logical relationship*.
start-to-start (SS) See *logical relationship*.
statement of work (SOW) A narrative description of products or services to be supplied under contract.
sub-network A subdivision of a *project network diagram* usually representing some form of sub-project.
successor activity In the *precedence diagramming method*, the 'to' activity.

target completion date (TC) An imposed date which constrains or otherwise modifies the network analysis.

team   See *project management team* and *project team*.

time remaining   See *remaining duration*.

total float   See *float*.

total quality management (TQM)   A common approach to implementing a quality improvement programme within an organization.

work breakdown structure (WBS)   A deliverable-oriented grouping of project elements that organizes and defines the total scope of the project. Each descending level represents an increasingly detailed definition of a project component. Project components may be products or services.

work item   See *Activity*.

work package   A deliverable at the lowest level of the *work breakdown structure*. A work package may be divided into activities.

Bibliography

1. Ahuja, H N (1984) *Project Management – Techniques in Planning and Controlling Construction Projects*, John Wiley & Sons, New York
2. Andersen, E S, Grude, K V and Haug, T (1988) *Goal Directed Project Management* (with Turner, J R); (1998) *Goal Directed Project Management*, 2nd edn, Kogan Page/Coopers & Lybrand, London
3. Armstrong M (1990) *How to be an Even Better Manager*, 3rd edn, Kogan Page, London
4. Association of Project Managers (APM) (March 1996) *Body of Knowledge*, Version 3, Association of Project Managers, High Wycombe
5. Augustine, N R (1989) *Managing Projects and Programs,* Harvard Business School Press, Boston, Massachusetts
6. Australian Institute of Project Management (AIPM) (1996) *National Competency Standards for Project Management*
7. Badiru, A B (1991) *Project Management Tools for Engineering and Management Professionals*, Industrial Engineering and Management Press, Institute of Industrial Engineers, Norcross, Georgia
8. Baker, S and Baker, K (1998) *The Complete Idiot's Guide™ to Project Management*, Alpha Books, Macmillan General Reference, New York
9. Barrie, D S and Paulson, J R (1978) *Professional Construction Management*, McGraw-Hill, New York
10. Block, T R and Frame, J D (1998) *The Project Office*, Crisp Publications, Merlo Park, California
11. Burke, R (1992) *Project Management – Planning and Control*, 2nd edn, Management Press

12.   Cabanis, J (November 1998) Outsourced, dejobbed, downsized, projectized? (interview with William Bridges, author of *Jobshift*), PM Network, 12 (11)

13.   Cabanis, J (September 1998) Passion beats planning, limiting scope is stupid, women rule... (interview with Tom Peters), *PM Network*, **12** (9)

14.   Chapman, C and Ward, S (1997) *Project Risk Management – Processes, Techniques and Insights*, John Wiley & Sons, New York

15.   Cleland, D I *et al* (Ed) (1998) *Project Management Casebook*, Project Management Institute, Newton Square, Pennsylvania

16.   Cleland, D I and King, W R (Ed) (1988) *Project Management Handbook*, Van Nostrand Reinhold, New York

17.   Clough, R H and Sears, G A (1979) *Construction Project Management*, 2nd edn, John Wiley & Sons, New York

18.   Dando-Collins, S (1998) *The Penguin Book of Business Wisdom*, Penguin Books, London

19.   Darnall, R W (1996) *The World's Greatest Project*, Project Management Institute, Newtown Square, Pennsylvania

20.   De Young-Currey, J and Knutson, J (December 1998) Want better project estimates? Let's get to work!, *PM Network*, **12** (12)

21.   Dinsmore, P C (December 1998) A journey through never-never land – from business planning to project implementation, *PM Network*, **12** (12)

22.   Dinsmore, P C (October 1998) Converging on enterprise project management, *PM Network*, **12** (10)

23.   Dinsmore, P C (February 1999) Tips for executives: looking astute in the third millennium, *PM Network*, **13** (2)

24.   Dryden, G and Vos, J (1997) *The Learning Revolution* (rev edn), The Learning Web Ltd, Auckland, New Zealand

25.   Duncan, R (January 1999) The project manager, *PM Network*, **13** (1)

26.   Fayol, H (1949) *General and Industrial Management*, Pitman, London

27.   Fern, E J (January 1999) Time-to-market project management, *PM Network*, **13** (1)

28.   Fleming, J M (November 1998) Meet the project manager: the newest entrepreneur, *PM Network*, **12** (11)

29.   Fleming, Q W and Koppelman, J M (1996) *Earned Value Project Management*, Project Management Institute, Newtown Square, Pennsylvania

30.   Frame, J D (1994) *The New Project Management*, Jossey-Bass, San Francisco

31.   Garrehy, P (1999) Project managers need real-time data – and a couple of ERP modules of their own, *PM Network*, February, **13** (2)

32.   Goldratt, E M (1997) *Critical Chain*, The North River Press Publishing Corporation, Great Barrington, Massachusetts

33.   Goldratt, E M and Cox, J (1997) *The Goal* (2nd rev edn), National Productivity Institute, Cape Town, Republic of South Africa

34.   Graham, R J and Englund, R L (1997) *Creating an Environment for Successful Projects*, Jossey-Bass, San Francisco

35.   Hallows, J E (1998) Managing for benefits in information technology projects, *PM Network*, December, **12** (12)

36. Hallows, J E (1998) The fourth dimension – justifying information technology projects, *PM Network* November, **12** (11)
37. Harris, F and McCaffer, R (1983) *Modern Construction Management* (2nd edn), Granada, London
38. Harrison, F L (1985) *Advanced Project Management* (2nd edn), Gower Publishing Company
39. Haynes, M E (1996) *Project Management – From Idea to Implementation* (rev edn), Crisp Publications, Merlo Park, California
40. Hunter, D, Bailey, A and Taylor B (1994) *The Art of Facilitation*, Tandem Press, Auckland, New Zealand
41. Ibbs, C W and Young-Hoon Kwak (1997) *The Benefits of Project Management*, Project Management Institute: Educational Foundation
42. IPMA (International Project Management Association) (1989) *Proceedings of the 13th International Expert Seminar*, Internet IPMA
43. Joint Standards Australia/Standards New Zealand Committee OB/7 (1995) *AS/NZS 4360:1995 Australian/New Zealand Standard ® – Risk Management*, Joint Standards Australia/Standards New Zealand
44. Kamp, D (1997) *Sharpen Your Team's Skills in People Skills*, McGraw-Hill, New York
45. Kaplan, R S and Norton D P (1996) *The Balanced Scorecard*, Harvard Business School Press Boston, Massachusetts
46. Kerzner, H (1992) *Project Management – A Systems Approach to Planning, Scheduling and Controlling* (4th edn), Van Nostrand Reinhold, New York
47. Kezsbom, D S, Schilling, D L and Edward K A (1989) *Dynamic Project Management*, John Wiley & Sons, New York
48. Kimmons, R L and Loweree, J H (ed) (1989) *Project Management – A Reference for Professionals*, Marcel Dekker Inc, New York
49. Knutson, J (1999) From making sense to making cents: measuring project management ROI – Part 1, *PM Network*, January, 13 (1); *PM Network*, February, **13** (2)
50. Knutson, J (1998) The project office: an evolutionary implementation plan, *PM Network*, September, 12 (9)
51. Larson, C E and LaFasto, F M J (1989) *Teamwork – What must go right/What can go wrong*, Sage Publications Inc, Thousand Oaks, California
52. Lewis, J P (1997) *Fundamentals of Project Management*, Amacom, American Management Association, New York
53. Lewis, J P (1998) *Mastering Project Management*, McGraw-Hill, New York
54. Lewis, J P (1995) *Project Planning, Scheduling & Control*, Irwin Professional Publishing, Chicago
55. Lewis, J P (1997) *Team-based Project Management*, Amacom, American Management Association, New York
56. Lock, D (1993) *Project Management* (5th edn), Gower, Aldershot
57. Lockyer, K (1984) *Critical Path Analysis and other Project Network Techniques* (4th edn), Pitman, London

58. Lord, A M (1993) 'Implementing strategy through project management', Long Range Planning, February, 26 (1)

59. Martin, P K and Tate, K (1998) Kick off the smart way, *PM Network*, October, **12** (10)

60. Meredith, J R and Mantel, S J (1995) *Project Management – A Managerial Approach* (3rd edn), John Wiley & Sons, New York

61. Mian, S A and Xiaoyi Dai, C (1999) Decision-making over the project life cycle: an analytical hierarchy approach, *Project Management Journal*, March, **30** (1)

62. Michael, N and Burton, C (1991) *Basic Project Management*, Reed Books, Auckland, New Zealand

63. Milosevic, D Z (1999) Echoes of the silent language of project management, *Project Management Journal*, March, **30** (1)

64. Moder, J J, Phillips, C R and Davis, E W (1983) *Project Management with CPM, PERT and Precedence Diagramming* (3rd edn), Van Nostrand Reinhold, New York

65. Neale, R H and Neale, D E (1989) *Construction Planning*, Thomas Telford Ltd, London

66. New Zealand Y2K Readiness Commission (December 1998) *Managing the Year 2000 – a structured approach for small and medium businesses*, New Zealand Y2K Readiness Commission

67. Nicholas, J M (1990) *Managing Business & Engineering Projects – Concepts and Implementation*, Prentice Hall, Englewood Cliffs, New Jersey

68. Obeng, E (1994) *The Project Leader's Secret Handbook – All Change!*, Pitman, London

69. O'Neil, J (1999) Short-staffed? Maximise scarce resources with knowledge resource planning, *PM Network*, February, **13** (2)

69a. Peters, T (1999) *Reinventing Work: or Fifty Ways to transform every 'Task' into a Project That Matters*, Alfred A. Knopf, Inc., New York

70. Pinto, J K (1996) *Power & Politics in Project Management*, Project Management Institute

70a. Pinto, J K and Millet, I (1999) *Successful Information System Implementation: The Human Side* (2nd edn), Project Management Institute, Newtown Square, Pennsylvania

71. Pitagorsky, G (1998) Building a communications infrastructure, *PM Network*, August, **12** (8)

72. Pither, R and Duncan, R (1998) ISO 10006: A risky business, *PM Network*, October, **12** (10)

73. PMI Standards Committee (1996) *A Guide to the Project Management Body of Knowledge*, Project Management Institute, Newtown Square, Pennsylvania

74. Prashing, B (1996) *Diversity is our Strength – The Learning Revolution in Action*, Profile Books, Auckland, New Zealand

75. Project Management Institute (1998) 1997 PMI Annual report – a time of transition, *PM Network*, August, **12** (8)

76. Quirke, B (1995) *Communicating Change*, McGraw-Hill, Maidenhead

77. Raz, T and Globerson, S (1998) Effective sizing and content definition of work packages, *Project Management Journal*, December, **29** (4)

78. Reis, G (1982) *Project Management Demystified* (1st edn), E & F N Spon, London

79. Senge, P M (1990) *The Fifth Discipline*, Random House, Milsons Point, NSW

80. Smith, M (1998) Service and outsourcing: a growing project management trend, *PM Network*, October, **12** (10)

81. Smith, S (ed) (1997) *Make Things Happen! Readymade Tools for Project Management*, Quest Toolbox Series, Kogan Page, London

82. Stewart, T A (1995) The corporate jungle spans a new species: the project manager, *Fortune*, 10 July, **132** (1)

83. Telaro, D (1999) The next generation project manager, *PM Network*, January, **13** (1)

84. Terpstra, V (1998) *Building a Project Management Organisation*, MBA Project Management Paper, Massey University, New Zealand

85. The Price Waterhouse Change Integration® Team (1996) *The Paradox Principles*, Irwin Professional Publishing, Chicago

86. Thoms, P and Pinto, J K (1999) Project leadership: a question of timing (Paper of the Year), *Project Management Journal*, March, **30** (1)

87. Toney, F and Powers, R (1997) *Best Practices of Project Management Groups in Large Functional Organizations*, Project Management Institute Research Report

88. Turner, R J (1995) *The Commercial Project Manager*, McGraw-Hill, New York

89. Turner, R J (1999) *The Handbook of Project-based Management* (2nd edn); (1993) The *Handbook of Project-based Management*, McGraw-Hill, New York

90. Turner, R J (ed), Grude K V and Thurloway, L (1996) *The Project Manager as Change Agent*, McGraw-Hill, New York

91. Turner, S G, Utley, D R and Westbrook J D (1998) Project managers and functional managers: case study of job satisfaction in a matrix organisation, *Project Management Journal*, September, **29** (3)

92. von Clausewitz, K (1852) *On War*, Harmondsworth, Penguin (translation published 1968)

93. Weaver, R G and Farrell J D (1997) *Managers as Facilitators*, Berrett-Koehler Publishers, San Francisco

94. Weiss, J W and Wysocki, R K (1992) *5-Phase Project Management – A Practical Planning and Implementation Guide*, Addison-Wesley

95. Wells, W G Jr (1998) From the Editor (editorial on project success and failure), *Project Management Journal*, December, **29** (4)

96. Wheelwright, S C and Clark K B (1992) Creating plans to focus product development, *Harvard Business Review*, March/April, **70** (2)

97. Williams, L (1998) Evaluating project management software: an excerpt from the Project Management Software Survey, *PM Network*, December, **12** (12)

98. Wilson, J M *et al* (1994) *Leadership Trapeze: Strategies for Leadership in Team-Based Organisations*, Jossey-Bass, San Francisco

Index

NB: page numbers in italic indicate figures or tables